AFTER RWANDA

After Rwanda

The Coordination of United Nations Humanitarian Assistance

Edited by

Jim Whitman

Leader, United Nations Project
Global Security Programme
University of Cambridge

and

David Pocock

Group Captain, Royal Air Force
Seconded to the Global Security Programme
University of Cambridge

First published in Great Britain 1996 by
MACMILLAN PRESS LTD
Houndmills, Basingstoke, Hampshire RG21 6XS
and London
Companies and representatives
throughout the world

A catalogue record for this book is available
from the British Library.

ISBN 0–333–64588–X hardcover
ISBN 0–333–65852–3 paperback

 First published in the United States of America 1996 by
ST. MARTIN'S PRESS, INC.,
Scholarly and Reference Division,
175 Fifth Avenue,
New York, N.Y. 10010

ISBN 0–312–15956–0

Library of Congress Cataloging-in-Publication Data
After Rwanda : the coordination of United Nations humanitarian
assistance / edited by Jim Whitman and David Pocock.
p.   cm.
Includes bibliographical references and index.
ISBN 0–312–15956–0
1. International relief.   2. Humanitarianism.   3. United Nations–
–Armed Forces.   I. Whitman, Jim.   II. Pocock, David.
HV553.A39   1996
361.2'6—dc20
96–11322
CIP

Selection and editorial matter © Jim Whitman and David Pocock 1996
Chapter 12 © Sir Michael Rose 1996, Chapters 1-11 and 13–18 and Afterword
© Macmillan Press Ltd 1996

10   9   8   7   6   5   4   3   2   1
05   04   03   02   01   00   99   98   97   96

Printed in Great Britain by
Ipswich Book Co Ltd, Ipswich, Suffolk

For all humanitarian workers, especially those in
the field

Contents

Preface and Acknowledgements

This book is a product of a research programme on the coordination of UN humanitarian assistance funded by the W. Alton Jones Foundation of Charlottesville, Virginia. We thank them for their generous support and for making the entire project possible.

Many of these chapters were written by practitioners while holding demanding appointments in the field or at headquarters; for this reason, we are especially grateful for their contributions.

The book has its origins in a conference held at the Royal College of Defence Studies (RCDS) on 1–2 June 1994, 'Coordinating UN Peace Support Operations: A Practitioners' Conference'. The event hinged on the creative spark and administrative efficiency of Commander Ian Bartholomew (then seconded from the Royal Navy to the Global Security Programme). We are grateful to Air Marshal Sir Timothy Garden, the Commandant, for his initiative in having made the RCDS available for the occasion, and for the enthusiastic support given by his staff who made extraordinary administrative demands seem routine. Additional funding for the conference was provided by the Ploughshares Fund of San Francisco.

Our colleagues within the Global Security Programme, and the Faculty of Social and Political Science of which it is a part, have been constant in their support and helpful guidance. Also, we are extremely grateful to the many UN staff, in New York, Geneva and the field, who have been so helpful to us in our wider researches.

JIM WHITMAN
DAVID POCOCK

Glossary

ACBAR	Agency Coordinating Body for Afghan Relief
AEW	Airborne Early Warning
ASEAN	Association of South East Asian Nations
AWACS	Airborne Warning and Control System
BAOR	The British Army of the Rhine
BBGNU	Broad Based Government of National Unity (Rwanda)
C3I	Command, Control, Communications and Intelligence
CAFOD	Catholic Fund for Overseas Development
CAP	Consolidated Appeals Process (UN)
CARE	Cooperative of American Relief Everywhere
CCFADM	Commission for the Formation of the Mozambican Defence Force
CENE	Comissão Executiva Nacional de Emergencia (Mozambique)
CERF	Central Emergency Revolving Fund (UN)
CFC	Cease Fire Commission (Mozambique)
CGDK	Coalition Government of Democratic Kampuchea
CIDA	Canadian International Development Agency
CIS	Commonwealth of Independent States
CJTF	Combined Joint Task Force
CMAC	Cambodian Mine Action Centre
CNN	Cable News Network
CORE	Commission for Reintegration of the Demobilized Soldiers (Mozambique)
CRDA	Christian Relief and Development Agency
CRR	Consolidated Rwanda Report
CSC	Supervision and Monitoring Commission (Mozambique)
CSCE	Conference on Security and Disarmament in Europe
DART	Disaster Assistance Response Team (USA)
DHA	Department of Humanitarian Affairs (UN)
DPA	Department of Political Affairs (UN)
DPI	Department of Public Information (UN)
DPKO	Department of Peacekeeping Operations (UN)
ECOSOC	Economic and Social Council of the United Nations
ECOWAS	Economic Community of West African States
EP5	Expanded Permanent Five
FAO	Food and Agriculture Organisation

FUNCINPEC	Front Uni National pour une Cambodge Indépendent, Neutre, Pacifique et Coopératif
FYROM	Former Yugoslav Republic of Macedonia
HPZ	Humanitarian Protection Zone (Rwanda)
HRFOR	Human Rights Field Operation in Rwanda
HRS	(Baidoa) Humanitarian Relief Sector
IASC	Inter-Agency Standing Committee
ICHRDD	International Centre for Human Rights and Democratic Development
ICRC	International Commission of the Red Cross
ICVA	International Council of Voluntary Associations
IDP	Internally-Displaced Person
IFRCS	International Federation of Red Cross and Red Crescent Societies
IHL	International Humanitarian Law
IISS	International Institute for Strategic Studies
IMF	International Monetary Fund
IOC	Integrated Operations Centre (Rwanda)
IOM	International Organization for Migration
IRC	International Rescue Committee
KPNLF	Khmer Peoples' National Liberation Front
LNF	Lebanese NGO Forum
LPA	(USAID Bureau for) Legislative and Public Affairs
MCDA	Military and Civil Disasters Assistance
MINIREISO	Minister/Ministry of Rehabiliation and Social Integration (Rwanda)
MOVCOM	Movement Control Unit
MPLA	Popular Movement for the Liberation of Angola
MSC	Military Staff Committee (UN)
NACC	North Atlantic Cooperation Council
NATO	North Atlantic Treaty Organisation
NGHA	Non-Governmental Humanitarian Agency
NGO	Non-Governmental Organisation
NORAD	Norwegian Agency for Development Corporation
OAS	Organisation of American States
OAU	Organisation for African Unity
ODA	Overseas Development Agency (UK)
OFDA	US Office of Foreign Disaster Assistance
ONUC	Opération des Nations Unies au Congo
ONUMOZ	United Nations Peacekeeping Operations in Mozambique

ORC	Open Relief Centre (Rwanda)
OSCE	Organisation for Security and Cooperation in Europe
PDK	Party of Democratic Kampuchea (Khmer Rouge)
PfP	Partnership for Peace
PVO	Private Voluntary Organisation (US)
RCDS	Royal College of Defence Studies
RENAMO	Resistençia Nacional Mozambicana
RGF	Rwandan Government Forces
RIC	Rwanda Information Center
RPA	Rwandese Patriotic Army
RPF	Rwanda Patriotic Front
SCR	Security Council Resolution
SoC	State of Cambodia
SRPA	Special Relief Programme to Combat the Effects of Drought in Angola
SRSG	Special Representative of the Secretary-General
UCAH	Humanitarian Assistance Coordination Unit (Angola)
UN	United Nations
UNAMIR	United Nations Assistance Mission for Rwanda
UNAVEM	United Nations Angola Verification Mission
UNCHR	Office of the High Commissioner for Human Rights
UNCIVPOL	United Nations Civilian Police
UNDP	United Nations Development Programme
UNDRO	Office of the United Nations Disaster Relief Coordinator
UNEP	United Nations Environment Programme
UNESCO	United Nations Educational, Scientific and Cultural Organisation
UNFICYP	United Nations Peacekeeping Force in Cyprus
UNHCR	United Nations High Commissioner for Refugees
UNICEF	United Nations Children Fund
UNIFIL	United Nations Interim Force in the Lebanon
UNITA	National Union for the Total Independence of Angola
UNITAF	Unified Task Force (US)
UNMIH	United Nations Mission in Haiti
UNMO	United Nations Military Observer
UNOHAC	United Nations Office for the Coordination of Humanitarian Assistance
UNOMUR	United Nation Observer Mission in Uganda/Rwanda
UNOSOM	United Nations Operations in Somalia
UNPROFOR	United Nations Protection Force
UNREO	United Nations Rwanda Emergency Office

UNSCERO	United Nations Special Coordinator for Emergency Relief
UNTAC	United Nations Transitional Authority in Cambodia
UNTAG	United Nations Transition Assistance Group (Namibia)
UNTSO	United Nations Truce Supervision Organisation
USAID	United States Agency for International Development
WEU	Western European Union
WFP	World Food Programme
WHO	World Health Organisation

Notes on the Contributors

Aldo Romano Ajello trained as a lawyer and thereafter pursued careers as a journalist and an international civil servant. He served as a Senator in Rome before being elected to the European Parliament in 1976. Mr Ajello was a member of the Italian Parliament (1979–83) before joining UNDP where he became Assistant Administrator and Director of the Bureau for Special Activities. On 13 October 1992, he was appointed SRSG for Mozambique where his efforts culminated in 1994 with the declaration of that country's 'free and fair' elections.

Dame Margaret J. Anstee spent several years working for the UK Foreign Office before embarking on a 40-year career with the UN, which included postings to Latin America and Africa. From 1987 to 1992, she was Under-Secretary-General and Director-General, UN Office at Vienna and Head of the Centre for Social Development and Humanitarian Affairs. During the period March 1992–June 1993, Dame Margaret was Under-Secretary-General, SRSG for Angola and Chief, UNAVEM II. She currently works as an independent consultant and adviser to the Government of Bolivia.

Jon Bennett was Executive Director of ACBAR in Pakistan/Afghanistan during 1990–2, then Director of ICVA's NGO Coordination Programme from 1992 to 1994. Prior to this, he spent 10 years working in the Horn of Africa for a number of NGOs, including Oxfam (where he was Regional Representative in South Sudan, and earlier in Tigray, Ethiopia), CAFOD and ACORD. He is now a Research Associate at the Refugee Studies Programme at Oxford University, and is an independent consultant.

Major-General Roméo A. Dallaire enrolled in the Canadian Army in 1964 and has held various command, staff and training appointments in Canada and Germany. Promoted to the rank of brigadier-general in July 1989, he assumed command of the Collège Militaire Royal de St-Jean. After studying at the British Higher Command and Staff Course at Camberley, he was appointed Commander 5e Groupe-Brigade Mécanisé du Canada at Valcartier in 1991. In July 1993, he took command of the UN Observer Mission – Uganda and Rwanda (UNOMUR) and the UN Assistance Mission for Rwanda (UNAMIR). Since September 1994, General Dallaire has been the Deputy Land Force Commander at St-Hubert.

Dr Juergen Dedring joined the UN Department of Political and Security Council Affairs in 1975 as a political affairs officer. In 1987, he transferred to the Office for Research and the Collection of Information as a senior political affairs officer. In March 1992, he joined the newly-created DHA, where he is responsible for policy planning and evaluation, especially early warning, mass exoduses and various political matters. Dr Dedring has served on visiting Missions to Zambia, Lesotho, Iraq, Peru and Haiti.

Lieutenant Colonel Bruno Doppler is a member of the Swiss Army. In addition to regimental and staff duty, Colonel Doppler has served as the ICRC delegate in Pakistan and South America (1972–5), the Programme Director of Enfants du Monde (1976–81), a member of the ICRC personnel department (1981–2), and then for seven years as ICRC delegate to the Armed Forces. From 1990 to 1994, he was in charge of the ICRC Law of War field courses. Currently, he is Head of the ICRC's Dissemination to the Armed Forces Division.

William J. Garvelink is the Deputy Director of the Office of US Foreign Disaster Assistance (OFDA), the disaster response branch of the US Agency for International Development (USAID). As Deputy Director of OFDA, Mr Garvelink formulates policy and strategy for US Government humanitarian assistance in disaster-stricken regions. Prior to his assignment to OFDA in 1988, Mr Garvelink served for two years as Deputy Director of the Office of African Refugee Affairs in the Bureau for Refugee Programs, US Department of State. From 1979 to 1986, he worked for USAID in La Paz, Bolivia as a Program Officer, and in the Bureau of Policy and Planning Coordination. He spent two years as a staff member of the House Foreign Affairs Committee, Sub-Committee on International Organisations.

Larry Hollingworth, CBE was commissioned into the British Army in 1961. After retiring as a lieutenant colonel, he served with the UNHCR in Sudan, Ethiopia and Kenya prior to becoming the Head of Civil Affairs for UNPROFOR. He has most recently worked in the Caucasus with the refugees from Chechnya.

Dr Randolph C. Kent, author of *Anatomy of Disaster Relief: The International Network in Action*, was head of the National Disaster Prevention and Preparedness Unit of the UN Emergency Prevention and Preparedness Group in Ethiopia from 1988 to 1990 before becoming Chief of the UN Emergency Unit in the Sudan (1990–1). At the end of 1991, he became deputy to the Coordinator of the UN Special Emergency Programme for the Horn of Africa (1991–2) until, with the creation of the UN DHA, he was appointed Coordinator for the Inter-Agency Support Unit of the Inter-Agency-Standing Committee. Since the end of October 1994, Dr Kent has been UN Humanitarian Coordinator in Rwanda.

David Lightburn retired from the Canadian Armed Forces as a colonel in 1987 after 30 years service. He joined the NATO International Staff in October 1987 and currently works in the Defence Planning and Policy Division as the principal staff officer for the development of Alliance peacekeeping policy and concepts, the development of practical measures of cooperation between NATO and its Cooperation Partners, and the monitoring of the implications for NATO defence planning of Allies' and Alliance involvement in peacekeeping.

David Pocock is a Group Captain in the Royal Air Force, and is currently seconded to the Global Security Programme at the University of Cambridge.

General Sir David Ramsbotham was commissioned into The Rifle Brigade in 1958 and served in Borneo, Belfast, and BAOR. In 1974–6, he commanded the 2nd Battalion Royal Greenjackets followed by a number of staff and command appointments including Commander, 3 Armoured Division (1984–7) and Commander, UK Field Army and Inspector-General Territorial Army (1987–90). He served as Adjutant-General from 1990 to 1993 before retiring from the Army. General Ramsbotham has been a consultant to the Ministry of Defence on improving the management of the United Kingdom's contribution to UN peacekeeping operations, and to the Under-Secretary-General for Peacekeeping Operations on improving command and control of UN peacekeeping operations. He is presently a consultant with Defence Systems Ltd which provides security, management and logistics services to the UN, UN Agencies and NGOs.

Lieutenant-General Sir Michael Rose was commissioned into the Coldstream Guards in 1964 and served in Aden, Germany and Northern Ireland. After attending the Army Staff College, Camberley in 1973, he was appointed Brigade Major of 16 Parachute Brigade and subsequently commanded G Squadron 22 Special Air Service Regiment, with which he saw active service in the Falkland Islands. After attendance at the RCDS, and then commanding the School of Infantry, he was appointed Director Special Forces and, in 1989, General Officer Commanding North East District and 2nd Infantry Division. After commanding the UK Field Army, in January

1994 General Rose was appointed Commander, UN Bosnia-Herzegovina Command. He now holds the appointment of Adjutant General.

Peter Shiras is currently the Director of Government Relations and Public Outreach for InterAction, a coalition of 160 US-based relief and development organisations, based in Washington DC. Prior to joining InterAction, he worked for Catholic Relief Services for 13 years in a variety of capacities, including Director of Public Policy (1993–4), Senior Director for the Africa Region (1990–3) and Country Representative for Kenya, Sudan and Uganda (1987–90).

Lieutenant-General John M. Sanderson graduated into the Royal Australian Engineers from the Royal Military College Duntroon in 1961. He saw active service in East Malaysia in 1966 and in Vietnam in 1970–1 when he commanded the 17th Construction Squadron. Other appointments have included command of the 1st Field Engineer Regiment (1979–80) and the 1st Brigade (1987–88), instructing at the British Army Staff College Camberley (1976–8), attending the US Army War College (1985–6) and, as Assistant Chief of the Defence Force (Policy), conducting a review which resulted in the reform of the higher Australian Defence Force organisation and processes. From November 1991–March 1992, General Sanderson was attached to the UN to complete the detailed planning for UNTAC and he then commanded UNTAC's Military Component from March 1992–October 1993. Currently the Commander Joint Forces Australia, he has been nominated as the next Chief of the Australian General Staff.

Dr Shashi Tharoor has worked for the UN since 1978, including three and a half years in charge of the UNHCR office in Singapore during the 'boat people' crisis. At present, he is Special Assistant to the Under-Secretary-General for Peacekeeping Operations. In this capacity, he deals with a range of peacekeeping issues around the world and leads the team responsible for UN peacekeeping operations in the former Yugoslavia.

Cedric Thornberry joined the UN in 1978 and became involved in the internationally-supervised settlement of the Namibia question, and was also in charge of the operational planning for its non-military side. During UNTAG, he was the Director of the Office of the SRSG responsible for coordination and the Mission's day-to-day political operation. Mr Thornberry also served as Senior Political and Legal Adviser to UNFICYP and to UNTSO, and was Director of Administration and Management of the UN for four years. He was appointed Director of UNPROFOR Civil Affairs at the beginning of the Mission in February 1992, and shortly afterwards became Assistant-Secretary-General when he was made Deputy Chief of Mission. Until the appointment of an SRSG, he was in charge of UNPROFOR's political, civil, legal and police activities. He remained Head of UNPROFOR's Civil Affairs until early 1994.

Professor Mark Walsh earned his bachelor's degree from the US Military Academy at West Point and Masters degrees from the University of Illinois and Boston University. After an army career which included service in the Dominican Republic, Brazil, Vietnam, Belgium and Germany as well as with UNTSO in Israel and Lebanon, and holding the George C. Marshall Chair of Military Studies at US Army War College, he retired with the rank of colonel. Professor Walsh served as the Zone Director with UNOSOM from April to October 1993. At present, he is a member of staff at the US Army War College Peacekeeping Institute.

Dr Jim Whitman is the leader of the Global Security Programme's UN Project at the University of Cambridge.

Neill Wright, while still a serving officer in the British Army, was seconded to UNHCR during August 1992–February 1993 as an advisor to the Special Envoy for Former Yugoslavia and as a Military Liaison Officer. In March 1993 he left the Army to join the UNHCR, becoming the Chief of Operations and Deputy Chief of Mission for Bosnia and Herzegovina until November 1993. He is presently the Special Advisor (Military/Logistics) at the UNHCR Headquarters in Geneva. He coordinated the humanitarian airlift into and within the Rwanda and Burundi emergency areas.

Introduction

This is a volume of practitioner perspectives on the coordination of complex UN humanitarian assistance operations involving the specialised Agencies, NGOs and military forces. The phrase 'UN humanitarian assistance' is not intended to suggest that NGOs cannot work independently of – and indeed, sometimes in the absence of – the UN; nor that the UN has the prerogative in humanitarian assistance, either in principle or in the field. Since our concern is with the larger and more devastating humanitarian emergencies which are now so frequently militarised, the deployment of military forces by the UN (the only body capable of authorising intervention) is often essential to begin, restore or augment humanitarian relief in stricken areas.

To the extent that the international community expresses a certain resolve in such instances, the humanitarian relief floodgates can open and the practical possibilities burgeon even in the absence of clearly defined or shared objectives. Thus, the first coordination need is what might be termed cultural: until quite recently, the majority of military–civil field encounters took place within the context of peacekeeping operations, where liaison was the order of the day. But in volatile or high-risk areas, troops supporting the humanitarian mission and their NGO counterparts have had to initiate more formal relations, both in the field and at the level of headquarters. To their great credit, the relevant UN Agencies, some NGOs and the military establishments of several countries were quick to recognise this need and have been instrumental in bridging these two quite different worlds. Understanding is not identical with coordination – or even unstrained cooperation – but is now recognised as an essential element in the professional approach of both communities.

Coordination of the UN system itself, usually under the rubric of 'reform', has long been with us. But unlike calls for a reduction of bureaucracy, the changes necessitated by major humanitarian emergencies combine elements of headquarters re-organisation, intra-Agency lines of authority and relations with other actors.

The NGO community can seem dispiritingly diverse – a great strength in terms of adaptability, but hardly an aid to regularising and formalising relations with other organisations. However, the largest and best-established NGOs evince a professionalism to match any organisation, and their efforts to form themselves into more clearly discernible communities, and to establish norms, work to the benefit of all.

The diversity of the organisations participating in humanitarian relief and the burdens and obstacles with which they are obliged to cope are well reflected in the chapters which follow. Because we sought to include as many perspectives as possible in this volume, it was not our aim to find consensus but rather to disseminate the views of practitioners. For all of their differences, and their considerable institutional experience, the contributors to this book do share a telling emphasis on the importance of individuals: the 'chemistry' worked by key figures; the need for a measure of autonomy and delegation without second-guessing; better, more frequent inter-community training; and the need continually to refresh headquarters staff with people of recent field experience.

The larger conclusions are tempered by a recognition that much though we strive to learn from experience, to communicate more effectively and to improve our institutional and practical capacities, the largest and worst humanitarian emergencies can only be anticipated in outline. Whether this represents a failure of the imagination or a wish to avoid contemplating the depths of inhumane behaviour, is immaterial. But it is certain that our individual and institutional response to these tragedies will always require a measure of improvisation. The contributors to this volume have endeavoured to further the now-widespread discussion of humanitarian assistance in an effort to make everyone's work more effective.

This book was conceived in the week that hundreds of thousands of men, women and children fled the genocide in Rwanda. The title is intended less as a temporal marker than in the hope that should we again fail to prevent such a disaster, we might still alleviate it more swiftly and comprehensively after the fact.

Part I
Political Overview

1 The Political Limits of Humanitarian Assistance
Jim Whitman

Let us assume that the principal fixtures and dynamics of the UN and its member states, and the main currents of international relations, remain essentially unchanged but that unprecedented levels of cooperation and coordination for the provision of humanitarian assistance combine in a widening virtuous circle. How much could we then accomplish through the betterment of our operational capabilities? After improvements to the timeliness, efficiency and possibly even the scope of our activities, what would still remain on any humanitarian agenda? We know that the most appalling humanitarian disasters can engender a combination of hard-headed practicality and heart-felt goodwill capable of cutting through entrenched interests, institutional inertia and all manner of otherwise insurmountable obstacles, but has a recurrence of these catastrophes been rendered any less likely as a result?

This is not a heartening line of speculation to place beside the bravery and dedication required to save lives in difficult and often dangerous circumstances. But it is all the more pertinent because the three communities of actors involved – national militaries deployed on the authority of the UN, the specialised Agencies and the NGOs – have indeed achieved novel and more effective means of combining their resources and efforts for the provision of humanitarian assistance. But they do so within a context which is contracting in political and resource terms, even as the emergencies increase in number, severity and complexity. The prospects are such as to confound even utopian expectations.

'FRAMING' EMERGENCIES

It was necessity rather than foresight which initiated the reconceptualisation of peace support operations as they edged ever further from 'classic' peacekeeping after 1988.[1] A re-reckoning of UN–civil–military relations has followed, as large-scale humanitarian emergency compounded by war or civil unrest and the increasing involvement of a wide range of NGOs made some degree of cooperation essential, much though 'coordination' remained anathema to many. However, while the delineation of legal and organisational preconditions and the refinement of UN, military and NGO operational matters continue apace,[2] the encompassing political milieu is largely accepted as a 'given'.

Of course, those most immediately involved in responding to humanitarian emergencies cannot be expected to concern themselves with larger issues, at least to the extent that they do not immediately impact on the crises to hand. But away from the field of operations, Zygmunt Bauman's observation that 'all social organisation, whether purposeful or totalizing . . . consists in subjecting the conduct of its units to either instrumental or procedural criteria of evaluation'[3] is much reinforced by the nature of the work and the expectations of those who support it, in moral as well as practical terms. An often undifferentiated insistence on 'effectiveness' and an expectation of 'success' work to keep attention focused on the ground and away from the political horizon, even as other disasters, impending or sidelined, loom over the work.

Moreover, in the kinds of militarised humanitarian emergencies which now appear to be the norm, perceived national interests are not only central to peace support operations, but are formative of the character and duration of the response – however much NGOs assert their operational independence. In such situations, NGOs and the specialised Agencies do not have the capacity to re-open airports or sea ports, mount enormous logistical operations, establish comprehensive communications systems or provide physical security. In the worst crises, it is the commitment by governments of their militaries, particularly those of the larger and better-equipped powers, that makes possible a Security Council resolution – and the subsequent arrival or return of the majority of civilian organisations. The UN can commit to a humanitarian peace support operation only through the agency of its member states and this is in turn contingent upon such factors as existing military commitments and the readiness of military forces, domestic political considerations and perceived national interest. Despite the popular perception of the UN that it operates an international community 'ambulance service', the true situation is quite different: the governments of the UN's member states take into account the full range of national considerations in respect of humanitarian peace support operations as they do in any other deployment of their troops abroad, so a range of political calculations – by no means limited to humanitarian concerns – is a precondition for the operational matters that subsequently become the focus of attention.

The character and pervasiveness of national and international media are also hugely formative. Broadcast media in particular rely heavily on framing stories and presenting them in relatively simple narrative terms, which does much to render a complex and intractable situation apparently amenable to 'emergency action' and 'success'. There are further pressures on all of the external actors involved: securing public attention and a sizable portion of a shrinking resource pool; generating good publicity; and being seen as caring and quick to respond. The focus shifts from the disaster, its causes – and its victims – to the intervening parties and their techniques. Something is seen to be done – and the problem soon fades from the domestic political arena.

It is therefore a curious if unsurprising phenomenon that even as the principal organisational participants and contributors to UN humanitarian assistance operations consider the coherence of their approach, not least through their relationships with one another, the surrounding political medium through which they all act is rarely engaged. Reinforced by the urgency and intensity of the tasks – now almost continuous – the effect is that even first-order planning and discussion are all too easily abstracted from the main political currents of the wider world. The humanitarian emergencies to which the 'international community' responds are constructs as well as palpable human tragedies – at least as notable for what they exclude as what they address. Randolph Kent has described a similar 'framing' of natural disasters:

> The propensity to separate disaster phenomena from normal life distorts some of the most fundamental aspects of disasters. By regarding disasters as discrete occurrences, the observer evades basic causation. One ignores the fact that disasters are an integral part of environmental abuse and economic and social exploitation, and instead hides in the assumption that disasters, 'by definition', are 'separate', 'uncertain' and 'unprecedented'. The truth more often than not is the opposite. Disasters are the consequence of the way humanity lives its 'normal life'. Disaster agents do not foster vulnerability, but the ways in which human beings organise their social and economic lives do.[4]

When, after a generation of slaughter and destruction, does a situation become an emergency? Why, even after the genocide of as many as a million people was the UN Secretary-General unable to find a nation willing to commit its Forces to Rwanda – while at the same time preparations were in hand to counter the threat to international peace and security posed by Haiti? How is it that governments are able to export weapons to repressive and even genocidal regimes, yet also commit their troops to the protection of the suffering innocent? Rhetorical as these questions may be, they nevertheless place the humanitarian crises, together with the nations and communities of actors who seek to address them, in the same harsh light. Where is the international community and what is its business when it is not performing good works? It will not serve to paraphrase Norbert Wiener, that the international community is 'not stuff that abides, but patterns that perpetuate themselves', except to the extent that the most enduring patterns run counter to the dictates of humane decency and purposes with which the majority of people associate the phrase.

Until 1990, it was possible to view the UN as another arena for the ongoing drama of the Cold War; now it is said to operate in the 'post-Cold War world' – a depiction indisputable in temporal terms, but a rather convenient way of deflecting responsibility for the world's crises away from the actions and omissions of the UN's more powerful member states and on to a more nebulous 'new world disorder' – as though many of the world's worst humanitarian disasters were not linked directly to the larger facts and mechanisms of international life which those states determine or dominate. Something similar is at work in the recent spate of articles concerning the vast stretches of land and peoples engulfed in chaotic and degraded circumstances, which are ascribed to a variety of indigenous deficiencies, or descend into 'heart of darkness' fear and loathing.[5] Likewise, there is a good deal of interest in the mechanism by which some situations are suddenly brought to prominence and politically activated – usually subsumed under the simple label, 'CNN factor'; what receives less speculation but which is of equal interest is what it is that keeps situations of this kind away from widespread attention and concern. There is much talk of early warning, but given the numbers of unattended, large-scale, politically-driven human tragedies still extant, the frequent recourse to calls for a better-developed early warning capacity is rather suggestive of a form of denial. No one could claim that events in Rwanda came as a complete surprise; the same might come to apply to Burundi.

The crisis in funding of humanitarian relief which has been mounting for some time cannot be forestalled indefinitely: demand is increasing, and at an ever-faster rate.[6] If our emergency capacity reaches breaking point, will the 'frame' be shrunk by way of terminology: 'prioritisation', 'triage',[7] 'reducing expectations'? How much failure can be accommodated, and with what consequences, for the UN, for the nascent international community and for the victims? Whether or not nations and regions can effectively be 'written off' might be a question of whether denial in its various forms can be sustained. However, diminishing that possibility is an essential part of the work of the NGOs and Agencies. Individuals and groups animated by the ideals of humanitarianism and justice, even those which have emergency relief as their raison d'etre, can hardly be expected to relish dealing with symptoms – and the best of them do not. The impressive range of their specialist remits carry across the bounds of emergencies by focusing attention on causes and aftermaths.

Although NGOs are not the *deus ex machina* of the international system, there is some hope that through their collective strength, they can be both agent and agency in penetrating some of the concentrations of power and some of the rigidities of the present constellation of forces:

> NGOs have emerged as prime movers on a broad range of global issues, framing agendas, mobilizing constituencies toward targeted results, and monitoring compliance . . . International regimes protecting human rights and the environment would arguably amount to nothing without initial and continuing NGO pressure, presaging a next wave of less developed but emerging norms that recognise other non-national interests and groupings.[8]

The pursuit of their individual agendas as part of a larger, cooperative relief effort has created difficulties within some UN operations, and between some NGOs themselves, but is essential if the inclusive nature of the humanitarian obligation is to find expression beyond the operational and the functional within the context of emergency action. What serves as the conscience in particular operations also acts to draw attention outside of the 'frame' – ensuring that we cannot escape the knowledge that humanitarian peace support operations are what we do when we fail.

The danger is that as increasing energy and resources are devoted to coping, the NGOs and Agencies are less able to give attention to reform, prevention and development. Caught up in the unending succession of crises, they lend tacit, albeit reluctant, credence to the framing of emergencies. But their presence, popular standing, and principled commitment serve to some degree to subvert the 'packaging' of emergencies, and without their continuous goading and the publicity they generate, humanitarian peace support operations would become, at best, the tangible expression of our charitable impulses with a UN gloss; and at worst a form of triage, with the national interests of the powerful as the principal determinant. There can be little doubt that our reluctance to make of the UN something more than an agency of last resort and a sanctioning authority is rooted in a reluctance to initiate corresponding changes at the national level.

MILITARY RISK AND POLITICAL COMMITMENT

In the kinds of UN humanitarian initiative under discussion, the interests of participating nations combine powerfully with the importance and relatively high profile of military deployments, and the moral gravity of the work, to concentrate attention and analyses away from the larger political arena – and indeed, even medium- to long-term political ends in the field of operations itself. It was Clausewitz who asserted that 'War has its own language but not its own logic'. By this, we may take him to mean the 'language' of military means and the 'logic' of political ends. Can it also be said of UN humanitarian peace support operations that they have their own language but not their own logic? Is the supporting political machinery clear, consistent, unified; what Clausewitz himself would recognise as a 'logic'? No amount of improvement in the 'language' of peace support operations without a corresponding improvement in their 'logic' will move us much beyond the belated, the marginal and the short-term. The point here is not the requirement for improved civil–military coordination in the field, but for the coordination of political objectives consistent with humanitarian purposes beyond the palliative. The obstacles are formidable.

First, the increasing frequency of calls upon the larger military powers to commit troops to a variety of peace support operations comes at an important historical juncture. Not only are these militaries contracting very quickly,[9] but public willingness to accept the death or injury of soldiers continues to diminish. Expressed differently, the political risks of any military commitment are increasing. The ratio of risk to commitment might be particularly high where the national interest as popularly understood is not thought to be under threat. Our political leaders are therefore often on uncertain ground in peace support operations. 'Sending in the troops' can be regarded as a government's highest expression of political commitment; but all too frequently in humanitarian peace support operations, the deployment of military forces is in some measure a substitute for commitment. 'Exit strategies' in this context are not about tactical and operational prudence but about political caution. And framed emergencies delimit both responsibility and action. For all of the apparent resolve in the dispatch of troops, we are seeing an increasing trend toward short-term, fixed deployments, with little in the way of political commitment at the temporal borders.

Second, the intervention of UN-sanctioned military forces into a militarised or highly unstable humanitarian emergency – so often the necessary prelude to the re-commencement of humanitarian assistance – requires a Security Council resolution, but the form of the resolution and the disposition of the contributing country or countries arise together. In combination with the often belated recourse to military means, this can have a number of unfortunate consequences, most importantly: unintegrated military and civil–humanitarian functions; political goals which are ill-defined, unelaborated or conveniently ambiguous; and Security Council resolutions with 'lead nation' configurations and 'all necessary means' remits. The last was the case with the resolutions authorising the two-month French intervention in Rwanda and the proposed US intervention in Haiti.[10] Such arrangements further underscore the fact that the UN is without the means to exercise political control over every military operation it mandates, thus undermining its perceived legitimacy.[11]

Third, as a general retrenchment in overseas aid and development assistance continues, it is reasonable to expect this to be reflected in the calculations which inform government deliberations as to when and to what extent to commit troops to humanitarian peace support operations. We may expect that nations willing to dedicate troops for this purpose will be increasingly less likely to be concerned with long-term viability than short-term threat, the cessation of the worst of the violence and containment. There is nothing to exclude genuine humanitarian impulses from an agenda headed by more determinedly self-interested motives; nevertheless, the Clinton Administration's principal policy statement on multilateral peace operations is suggestive of the direction of the tide:

> It is not US policy to seek to expand the number of UN peace operations or US involvement in such operations. Instead, this policy . . . aims to ensure that our use of peacekeeping is *selective* and more *effective*.[12]

But what shall be the criteria for effectiveness – and who shall determine them? Although all parties to a UN operation subscribe (at least nominally) to the political ends delineated in the relevant Security Council resolution, what if the nation supplying all or most of the military force is able to employ 'all necessary means'? It is certain that a nation or nations so empowered will have an explicit 'exit strategy', but what provision can be made for delay or failure? Are we ever likely to see the phrase 'all necessary means' employed in respect of resources rather than military licence? Is the attention given to 'end states', prudent as it might be in military–operational terms, part of the same impulse to 'frame' emergencies?

Such questions do not always apply; in many cases, the presence of national militaries is essential, but not dominant because the security situation is not volatile, so the initiative lies principally with the NGOs and the specialised Agencies. Furthermore, a gratifying majority of military personnel employed on such missions believe that there is no finer soldiering than assisting the helpless and protecting the innocent. And criteria of effectiveness is not a common denominator even amongst the NGO community.[13] But the tension between emergency needs and the difficulty of defining – and attracting support for – long-term political goals remains a central problem, exacerbated by the growing reluctance of developed nations to avert crises structurally or to deal with them in a timely fashion, particularly in areas of the world peripheral to their perceived interests. Within governments, a predictable sequence can act as a negative feedback loop, with the failure of a UN Mission or collapse of a militarily-engendered 'peace' reflected back as justified prudence and then expressed in policy-making as a reluctance to commit on any but the most narrowly-conceived terms. With substantial cutbacks in foreign aid and development assistance, together with the contraction of military forces currently under way, it is possible in many of the larger military powers that public anguish over the next humanitarian disaster will meet with a high-profile military response, but operationally constrained and of short, fixed duration. A variety of domestic constraints clustered principally around the prospect of bodybags and a 'fear of entanglement' will draw the frame around humanitarian emergencies ever tighter. With the UN and its Agencies also starved of funds, and the larger NGOs unable to stretch their personnel and resources, we might yet find that 'triage' is indistinguishable from catastrophic failure.[14]

THE TRANSITION TO RECONSTRUCTION AND DEVELOPMENT

When does a humanitarian emergency end and the politics of development begin? Whether an emergency is 'humanitarian' or 'political' might be in the eye of the donor; as might be the determination of whether an emergency is simply another 'situation' of the type to which we have become accustomed. The humanitarianism practised by states, no less than the emergencies themselves, can be framed – activated by the consequences of the world's structural inequalities, which otherwise remain largely unchallenged. This illustrates clearly the tentativeness of government-mediated humanitarianism, the segmentation of commitment and the politically embedded nature of professed impartiality.[15]

At the operational level, the transition from war or strife to 'peace' can be uneven or difficult to discern on the ground in some situations, so even with abundant goodwill and an uncommon level of commitment, it might still be difficult to specify a precise mechanism or time for a transition to post-emergency tasks – whether demobilisation, democratic elections or repairing infrastructure. On the other hand, SCR 940 which authorised the invasion of Haiti by 6000 troops also approved the establishment of an 'advance team of UNMIH of not more than 60 personnel' which was to monitor the operations of the force and 'to assess requirements and to prepare for the deployment of UNMIH upon completion of the mission of the multinational force'. Whatever was at work in the crafting of this device, one is reminded of the conference plenary at which a military doctrine writer said: 'We have no difficulty sharing the field with NGOs. We'll go in, decapitate the bad guys and then hand the mission over.'

The initiation of an emergency response which is both adequate to immediate needs yet also sufficiently flexible to meet subsequent developments can hardly be guaranteed even with abundant coordination and commitment. Humanitarian emergencies are not static and rarely distinct in terms of location, so the management of transitions will never be simple. Even as the Rwandan refugee crisis was culminating, the victorious RPF found itself as the government of a country but without the means to govern: quite aside from the dislocation of genocide and exodus, the majority of public and commercial buildings had been damaged or looted; there was no viable currency and key elements of the infrastructure were functioning intermittently at best. Against the pull of the humanitarian emergency in the refugee camps which commanded the attention of much of the outside world, the SRSG was soon concerned to secure funds and assistance to begin the work of 'pump priming'. Yet an SRSG has no authority over the specialised Agencies, nor indeed over the wishes of donors – who sometimes expect to see a degree of sophistication in development proposals which are wholly inapplicable to war-ravaged countries. The Rwandan experience is notable for a further, complicating factor: following a reported massacre of Hutu refugees, the European Union withdrew pledges of assistance of £41.5 million for the reconstruction of the country's infrastructure.[16] The dilemmas posed by human rights violations for donors and field workers alike are an additional challenge when managing any humanitarian initiative on this scale. It is unlikely that this instance will prove to have been an anomaly.

If only on a popular level, it is not difficult to understand the preoccupation with the immediate, operational aspects of humanitarian disaster response: urgency, genuine moral weight, newsworthiness, public support and, frequently, the deployment of soldiers are an arresting combination. Much less appealing to our moral and imaginative energies are the resettlement of refugees, mine clearance, infrastructural programmes, demobilisation and demilitarisation. And what is true at the level of popular perception is no less true of donors. The following is noteworthy for its suggestion that those immediately concerned with maintaining the momentum of an humanitarian assistance operation must frame the depiction of their activities to match the prevailing political ethos of the donors:

Relief aid is 'easy' money, development aid is not: this reinforces the tendency to dress up interventions as being pure relief, rather than dressing them down as appropriate to longer-term development as well. Aid money for rehabilitation and recovery is often hardest of all to access, despite the fact that this may ease the transition from relief to development. In countries no longer eligible for development aid, doing any rehabilitation work at all becomes almost impossible.[17]

Implicit in the notion of transition is not only a level of coordination as yet achieved but intermittently, but of shared purpose which extends beyond the remits of individual actors. The difficulty here is not so much that most organisations would sooner maximise cooperation rather than submit to direction, but that there is no single locus for the determination of ends on the 'grand strategic' level. Despite the UN's inclusiveness, its legitimacy, the size and expertise of its specialised Agencies, and its authority to sanction intervention, the objectives and the motive force of participating organisations are self-generated and self-directed. This does not inhibit all inter-agency cooperation and coordination; indeed, it necessitates it – to a degree. A swarm can be as effective as a hive, but the question of how common purpose is communicated and the work divided in such an organisational form is for our purposes less a matter of fascination than continual striving.

The larger challenge facing the UN and NGOs is to find approaches to the complex of political issues which comprise rebuilding war-torn societies. Our tentative use of terminology in this context – nation-building, sustainable development, civil society – is currently useful more for its suggestive possibilities than its conceptual clarity. The present, rather narrow scope for the quality and duration of political commitment that would almost certainly be required for concerted long-term programmes is not encouraging; nor is it clear that any applicable generic lessons can be learned from the experiences in countries as diverse as Cambodia, Lebanon and the former Yugoslavia. But however much these differ, the point is not a search for a template but to uncover and consider themes and issues which recur – class, ethnicity, gender, patterns of land ownership, social organisation and sources of power, representation and democracy, notions of standing and of justice and many others – which may also impact on rehabilitation, reconstruction and development. Moreover, the very determination to take account of the intellectual foundations of humanitarian activity will strengthen and deepen the political commitment. It behoves us to maintain an appropriate humility about the provision of humanitarian assistance: the history of development assistance is littered with the unhappy consequences of our ignorance. Repairing war-damaged infrastructures might be straightforward, at least on a practical level; presuming to restore civil society in a devastated country is quite another matter. However, in conducting the work of humanitarian assistance, even modest indicators of progress or success also work on the larger political environment. It is both the burden and the privilege of humanitarian assistance that the prized abstractions, human rights and justice, find such ready, practical expression.

BEYOND COPING?

The UN's ability to alleviate the suffering of populations will never exceed the demand. The UN itself, together with the NGOs, specialised Agencies and national militaries with which it shares the work, are as much a part of the international system as the structures and dynamics which produce and support large-scale poverty, repression, war and state collapse. One need not believe either that the persistence of UN humanitarian assistance is the tangible expression of an international community or that what sustains the work is little more than conscience money. There is a felt need on the part of millions which has found all manner of institutional expression and, in the field, common cause if not shared ideology. Consider the business of organising a democratic election in Cambodia in the wake of its recent history; of delivering aid in the midst of the Bosnian civil war; or bringing an accord between the warring parties in Angola while dealing with the 3 million people in need of food and other emergency assistance – and wonder that so much is still accomplished, and with so comparatively little. *That* we cope and how well we accomplish the tasks is subject to the selflessness, common sense, imagination and goodwill of those doing the work; how much coping they will have to do and how long the strains can persist or conditions continue to deteriorate is a political question which can only partly be addressed in the field.

Notes

1. See Boutros Boutros-Ghali, *An Agenda for Peace 1995* (2nd edition) (New York: United Nations, 1995); John Mackinlay and Jarat Chopra, 'Second

Generation Multinational Operations', *The Washington Quarterly* (Summer 1992) pp. 113–31.

2.   The following are indicative: UN Economic and Social Council, 'Final Report on the In-depth Evaluation of Peacekeeping Operations: Start-up Phase' (E/AC. 51/1995/2); Task Force on Ethical and Legal Issues in Humanitarian Assistance, 'The Mohonk Criteria for Humanitarian Assistance in Complex Emergencies' (World Conference on Religion and Peace, February 1994); Amnesty International, 'Peacekeeping and Human Rights' (IOR 40/01/94); UK Army Field Manual, Vol. 5: Operations Other Than War, Part 2, 'Wider Peacekeeping' (D/HQDT/18/34/30).

3.   Zygmunt Bauman, *Modernity and the Holocaust* (Cambridge: Polity Press, 1991) p. 213 (italics omitted).

4.   Randolph C. Kent, *Anatomy of Disaster Relief: The International Network in Action* (London: Pinter Publishers, 1987) p. 4.

5.   See for example, Robert D. Kaplan, 'The Coming Anarchy', *Atlantic Monthly* (February 1994) pp. 44–76.

6.   The 1993 UNHCR Report, *The State of the World's Refugees* (London: Penguin, 1993) said of the situation, 'There is no daylight between crises; crisis has become the norm' (p. 96); see also David Keen, *Refugees: Rationing the Right to Life* (London: Zed Books, 1992). More recently, the executive director of the World Food Programme said that her Agency was 'operating hand-to-mouth' and that 'Usually we can borrow from somewhere by putting one pot on the back burner while another is boiling, but now all our pots are boiling', *The Guardian* (27 April 1995).

7.   See Thomas G. Weiss, 'Triage: Humanitarian Interventions for a New Era', *World Policy Journal*, Vol. XI, No. 1 (Spring 1994) pp. 1–10.

8.   Peter J. Spiro, 'New Global Communities: Nongovernmental Organisations in International Decision-Making Institutions', *The Washington Quarterly*, Vol. 18, No. 1 (Winter 1995) pp. 45–6.

9.   See for example, *UK Statement on the Defence Estimates 1995*, Cm2800 (London: HMSO); United States General Accounting Office, *Peace Operations: Heavy Use of Key Capabilities May Affect Response to Regional Conflicts* (Washington, DC: GAO/NSIAD-95-51).

10. S/RES/929 (22 June 1994) and S/RES/940 (31 July 1994) respectively.

11. See Jim Whitman and Ian Bartholomew, 'Collective Control of UN Peace Support Operations: A Policy Proposal', *Security Dialogue*, Vol. 25, No. 1 (March 1994) pp. 77–92.

12. 'The Clinton Administration's Policy on Reforming Multilateral Peace Operations', Department of State Publication 10161 p. 3 (italics in original). Note, too, 'our use of' rather than 'our participation in'.

13. In April 1995 ICVA Zagreb listed some 200 NGOs of every origin, size and orientation then operating in the former Yugoslavia. ICVA Zagreb, 'ICVA Zagreb Directory: List of NGOs, UN and European Family Organisations operating in the countries of the former Yugoslavia' (April 1995).

14. 'By the end of this decade, some 300 million people – half Africa's population – could be living below subsistence levels, with potentially disastrous consequences for democracy and stability. It is hard to imagine that the rest of the world would escape the consequences.' Kevin Watkins, 'A Continent Driven to Economic Suicide', *The Guardian* (20 July 1994).

15. Jon Bennett has argued that 'The growth in humanitarian relief lies at the very centre of policies reflecting a profound change in North–South relations: relief, as a policy model, is a form of disengagement from the South'. *Meeting Needs: NGO Coordination in Practice* (London: Earthscan, 1995) p. xiv.
16. 'EU Halts Aid for Rwanda', *The Guardian* (27 April 1995).
17. Margaret Buchanan-Smith and Simon Maxwell, 'Linking Relief and Development: An Introduction and Overview', *IDS Bulletin*, Vol. 25, No. 4 (October 1994) p. 3.

Part II
UN Perspectives

2 The Future of Peacekeeping
Shashi Tharoor

Early in 1995, *The New York Times* turned its magisterial gaze upon the future of UN peacekeeping, an activity that had come in for considerable criticism in the American media over the preceding two years. 'Rethinking and retrenchment are in order . . . There should be a shift back toward more limited objectives like policing cease fires', it declared. 'UN peacekeeping does what it can do very well. It makes no sense to continue eroding its credibility by asking it to do what it cannot.'[1] This somewhat startling advocacy of a return to traditional verities gave pause to many of us who had been engaged in the practice of peacekeeping during its recent tumultuous history. Was *The New York Times* right, and if so, were we to contemplate a future of retreating headlong into the past?

At one level, there is something oddly comforting about the thought of seeking safety in well-worn practices; resting on old laurels is a good deal easier than wresting new ones. Yes, 'traditional peacekeeping' is something the UN has done well and continues to know how to do. Our least problematic operations are always those where the parties agree to end their conflicts and only need our help to keep their word, where the risks are low, the tasks assigned to the peacekeepers are those that are basic bread-and-butter skills for any army in the world, and the shoestring resources available to the UN are adequate for the job at hand. In these situations, the UN can bring a wealth of experience and precedent to bear in the successful conduct of such peacekeeping operations. Many of us in this business would like nothing more than to say: 'Give us the buffer zones in Cyprus or Kuwait, the elections in Cambodia or Mozambique, the package deals in Namibia or El Salvador, and we'll deliver you an effective, efficient success story, on time and under budget.' All professionals – and UN peacekeepers are no exception – are always happy to be asked to do what they can do best.

Sadly, however, this attractive formula has one thing wrong with it: it's a good answer, but only to part of the question. Traditional peacekeeping is all very well if the only crises confronting the UN are those which are ripe for the peacekeeping treatment. But classical, consensual peacekeeping does not respond fully to the nature of the world we live in and the challenges the new world disorder poses to the international community.[2] If the nature of UN peacekeeping has acquired a certain elasticity in recent years, it is precisely because circumstances have led the world to make demands on the military capacity of the UN which vastly exceed anything we were called upon to do as recently as three or four years ago. We will not be able to face the twenty-first century by remaining firmly rooted in the twentieth.

At the same time, there is no question that the heady days of peacekeeping overstretch are over. 'The number of UN operations, the scale of the operations, the money spent on operations cannot keep growing indefinitely', Secretary-General Boutros Boutros-Ghali recently declared. 'The limits are being reached.'[3] At the end of the Cold War, an unprecedented degree of agreement within the Security Council in responding to international crises had plunged the UN into a dizzying series of peacekeeping operations that bore little or no resemblance in size, complexity and function to those that had borne the 'peacekeeping' label in the past. For years, during the Cold War, peacekeeping had worked well, within the limitations imposed upon it by superpower contention – well enough, at any rate, to win the 1988 Nobel Peace Prize. Then, when these limitations evaporated, everything seemed possible. At the same time, the new transcendence of the global media added a sense of urgency to these crises: it is a striking coincidence that the reach and impact of CNN and its imitators peaked precisely at this time of post-Cold War concordance. Television showed that action was needed, and the end of the Cold War meant that action was possible. So 'peacekeeping' became a catch-all term covering not merely the monitoring and implementation of cease fire agreements, but an entire range of tasks including supervising and running elections, upholding human rights, overseeing land reform, delivering humanitarian aid under fire, rebuilding failed states and, as *The New York Times* put it in the same editorial, 'ambitious attempts to impose peace on hostile forces determined to keep fighting'. The widespread criticism, not all of it well-founded or fair, of UN efforts in situations where there was little peace to keep – particularly in Somalia, the former Yugoslavia and Rwanda – lie directly behind the calls for retreat to a simpler era. Amidst so many voices urging the UN to go 'back to basics', it is clear that it will be a long time before the Security Council again authorises another of the hybrid operations whose ever-mounting scope spiralled seemingly out of control in a flurry of SCRs in 1992 and 1993.

But does this mean a return to the brave old world of buffer zones and policing cease fires, the non-threatening application of military skills to defuse conflicts? Not necessarily. The irony of the 'back to basics' appeal is that the UN had already moved successfully beyond the basics before getting embroiled in the controversies of recent years. The operations that brought Namibia to independence, that transformed the society and politics of Cambodia and El Salvador, that restored hope in Mozambique, were all multi-dimensional efforts that demonstrated the effectiveness of a broader concept of peacekeeping – one which combined military functions with a variety of largely civilian undertakings to bring about change and so fulfil the objectives of the operations. The techniques involved worked; the world cannot do without them. In admitting, understandably, that we cannot afford to become part of the problem as we did by taking sides in Somalia; in acknowledging that we cannot easily find troop-contributing countries willing to commit forces to halt genocide, as we had hoped we might in Rwanda; in accepting that we can protect humanitarian aid deliveries, but that we cannot force them through, as we have discovered in Bosnia; in conceding all this, we do not need also to abandon the functions of policing the local police, of protecting ethnic minorities, of upholding human rights standards, of running free and fair elections, of supervising mistrusted local administrations, of creating conditions conducive to political accommodation and national reconciliation, all of which we have done in recent years with success – and all of which take us beyond *The New York Times'* prescription with which I began this chapter.

Yet that too is only a partial answer to the questions that confront us today. For 'multi-dimensional peacekeeping' still rests on the traditional pillars of agreement and consent; the new functions identified above are usually reflected in the terms of comprehensive settlement that both (or all) parties to a conflict want the UN to implement; and none of them involve a threat to the UN's preference for the non-use of force. We can move beyond traditional peacekeeping and still find ourselves on familiar ground. The more difficult problems relate to situations in which agreements are non-existent or short-lived; where the UN does not enjoy the formal consent or the practical cooperation of the parties amidst whom it is deployed; and when the nature of the ongoing conflict obliges us to confront searching questions about the need to use force in order to be effective, with the concomitant risk that doing so will jeopardise the UN's impartiality and thus the very effectiveness we are trying to attain.

The thawing of the Cold War freeze has created the environment in which the world will be making its choices about the management of international conflict. The end of the Soviet Union loosened the straitjacket within which many potential conflicts had been confined. Many erupted amid the disinclination of the big powers to intervene; during the Cold War, both sides had sought to prevent conflicts arising which might engage their interests. Today, the stakes are lower; Somalia is not seen as threatening to lead to Stalingrad, and Sarajevo 1992, for all its emotional

impact, does not carry the globe-threatening resonance of Sarajevo 1914.
In this climate, warring factions, unfettered by bondage to one superpower
or another, pursue their ambitions without regard to an outside world
that clearly cannot summon the will or the resources to intercede decisively.
A post-ideological world stokes its frenzies in the flames of nationalism,
ethnicity, and tribal triumphalism. Old injustices and older enmities are
revived and intensified; history becomes a whip with which to flail those
who are inclined to compromise. Few rules are observed in these wars,
fewer still in the tenuous moments of peace that punctuate them. The
techniques of a calmer era, peacekeeping included, seem inadequate to the
moment.

And yet abstention is not really an option. For most of the crises that
thrust themselves on the UN's agenda, indifference is impossible. This is
not just a moral matter, although the suffering caused by these conflicts –
in many of which the infliction of agony on innocent civilians is a direct
aim, rather than a byproduct, of war – remains an affront to the world's
conscience. In a world of instant satellite communications, with television images of suffering broadcast as they occur, few democratic governments are immune to the public clamour to 'do something'. For a couple
of years the international community, pressed to respond and unready with
an alternative international security mechanism, found in UN peacekeeping the 'something' it could 'do'. Peacekeepers took unprecedented risks,
made foreseeable mistakes, suffered an intolerable level of casualties; governments, accountable politically for the safety of their soldiers, cut their
losses and proved unwilling to risk additional ones. In the process we have
all learned what peacekeeping cannot do; and yet we cannot afford to do
nothing. The challenge of the future is to define that 'something' in terms
of what is doable – in other words, to identify how the UN can be enabled
to respond to future Somalias and Rwandas while retaining the support of
member states.

As a contribution to further reflection on this issue, I would suggest, to
paraphrase the Buddha, an eight-fold path – eight fairly self-evident principles that might demarcate and illuminate the way forward.

PREVENTION IS BETTER THAN CURE

The UN is doubling its efforts in the fields of early warning and preventive
diplomacy, in order to forestall conflicts before they erupt. This is an
activity with a mixed track record; it is fair to say that no one hears of the
wars that did not occur because the UN was able to head them off, but it

is also true that early warning is of little use in and of itself, unless it is accompanied by the political will to act on the warnings received. At the time of writing, this question has been brought into sharp relief by events in Burundi. The Secretary-General has spent weeks urging governments to take preventive action; although some steps have been taken by the Security Council, notably through the despatch of a Mission to take stock of the situation and the issuance of a Presidential Statement calling for restraint, it is not yet clear whether they will prove enough to prevent a looming tragedy.

The Secretary-General's overt preference in the Burundi situation is for serious consideration to be given to the preventive deployment of troops to the area, or at least the issuance of a public warning by governments that they will intervene if a Rwanda-style massacre were to occur. Such a warning alone might prevent a conflagration. It would, however, have to be credible; in other words, the governments issuing it would have to be prepared to back up their threat with action if the parties on the ground decided to ignore them. This implies that effective preventive action requires the same degree of political commitment and agreement as post-conflict peacekeeping. Sadly, governments reluctant to send in troops after a conflict has broken out are usually also reluctant to do the same beforehand. Yet there is no doubt that preventive deployment would be cheaper in lives and resources than anything which might follow.

The one current functioning example of preventive deployment, UNPREDEP (formerly UNPROFOR) in the Former Yugoslav Republic of Macedonia (FYROM), has contributed immensely to the stability of the government and the state of FYROM. But the catch with any preventive deployment is that it is impossible to prove a negative: any such force is a success only until it fails. Preventive deployment may not always, and indefinitely, deter conflict, but there is no doubt that at the very least it raises the political price of any aggression and increases the international community's stake in a peaceful outcome for any conflict that might occur in its area of operations.

A STITCH IN TIME SAVES NINE

If conflict does occur, despite the best efforts of the diplomats and peace-makers, it is vital that it be nipped in the bud before it does the kind of damage that the world witnessed with horrified impotence in Rwanda in 1994. Had the UN's General Roméo Dallaire had 5000 reinforcements within days of the shooting down of the Presidential aircraft that unleashed the carnage in Rwanda, he might have been able to save more than 500 000 lives; but none was forthcoming, and when the Security Council finally approved an enhancement of his Force, Dallaire had to wait more than three months for governments to make them available to the UN.

The future of UN peacekeeping demands a rapid response capacity; the Secretariat is largely agnostic as to how it acquires this. At the moment, the only tool available to it in this domain, the Stand-By Forces Arrangement, is yet to prove itself. In that dreadful summer of 1994, when the UN needed 5500 soldiers for Rwanda, it turned to the 19 governments which at that time had pledged a total of 31 000 troops for future UN peacekeeping operations; all declined to participate. The Arrangement thus turned out to be one for obtaining negative answers more rapidly than in the past, rather than generating forces more rapidly than in the past. Currently, the number of countries enrolled in the scheme has gone up to 37; it is not yet clear whether this implies a parallel increase in the viability of the Arrangement.

The Secretary-General has, in his *An Agenda for Peace* and subsequently, suggested the establishment of a rapid deployment force to serve as the Security Council's strategic reserve whenever emergency situations required peacekeepers to be deployed at short notice. In his *Supplement* to *An Agenda for Peace*, the Secretary-General suggested that battalion-sized units be earmarked by a number of countries for this purpose, be trained to the same standards, use identical operating procedures, share common communications and other essential equipment and train together in regular joint exercises. They would remain within their national armies and be stationed in their home countries, but be maintained at a high state of readiness to be deployed as soon as the need arose.[4] The idea has not so far found favour with member states, and it suffers from the same disadvantage as the current, looser Stand-By Forces Arrangement, i.e. that of requiring a specific decision each time by the offering member state as to whether the unit it has pledged will in fact participate in the proposed operation. An efficiently integrated rapid deployment force would be more vulnerable to disruption by the withdrawal of one of its crucial elements than a force cobbled together, as at present, by the UN from a motley collection of volunteering governments.

A somewhat more ambitious idea that has gained currency in recent years is that of a permanent UN force – a 'standing army' or 'UN legion' – consisting of individuals recruited, paid and managed by the UN as a sort of military counterpart to the international civil service. The principal advantage of this idea is that such a force could immediately be deployed upon the Security Council's authorisation; it would not require further governmental decisions, since the soldiers would belong to the UN, not to their national armies. The principal disadvantages, however, relate to cost, size limitations (how many 'legionnaires' would one need to maintain effective rotations? What would happen if a new crisis found the available forces already deployed in an earlier one?) and the political unreadiness of certain member states to contemplate the existence of what could be seen as a supranational military entity under the command of the Secretary-General.

Whichever solution is eventually adopted, it is clear that if the world wants the UN to serve, even occasionally, as a fire brigade, it will have to do better than the present system, under which the fire breaks out, the aldermen on the Security Council agree it needs to be put out, and the fire chief is then sent out to hire firemen, rent fire trucks, find hoses of the right length and look for sources of water to put into them – while hoping that, when he has what he needs, there will still be enough survivors to rescue.

CONCEPTUAL CLARITY IS ESSENTIAL

The ongoing work taking place in a number of Defence Ministries around the world, as well as at UN Headquarters, to define the terms under which peacekeeping operates, represents one of the most vital developments for the future of peacekeeping. I once remarked, not entirely facetiously, that in the unfolding confusion about whether UN peacekeeping was conducted under Chapter VI or Chapter VII of the Charter, we were all at sixes and sevens. For the truth is that the evolution of peacekeeping – what Marrack Goulding prefers to term the 'forced development' of peacekeeping – in the new world disorder has outstripped the conceptual underpinnings that had girded it during the Cold War years. UN peacekeepers have intervened in crises before the world could find the time to elaborate, or agree upon, the doctrinal justifications or the overall strategy behind each new mandate (or modification of mandate).

Peacekeeping was an activity the UN had been politically reluctant to define (the intergovernmental Special Committee on Peacekeeping Operations, for instance, annually discussed a declaration on the principles of peacekeeping, and annually rejected the idea on the grounds that to define peacekeeping was to impose a straitjacket on a concept whose flexibility made it the most pragmatic instrument at the disposal of the world organisation). Nonetheless, a consistent body of practice and doctrine had evolved over the years: peacekeepers functioned under the command and control of the Secretary-General; they represented moral authority rather than the force of arms; they reflected the universality of the UN in their composition; they were deployed with the consent and cooperation of the parties; they were impartial and functioned without prejudice to the rights and aspirations of any side; they did not use force or the threat of force except in self-defence; they took few risks and suffered a minimal number of casualties; and they did not seek to impose their will on any of the parties. As the Security Council proclaimed 'no-fly zones' and 'safe areas', declared punitive actions against warlords, and acquiesced in NATO-declared 'exclusion zones'; as member states established command arrangements that did not in all cases terminate in New York; as peacekeepers mounted anti-sniping patrols and called in air strikes, all these principles have been strained to breaking point.

Today, there is general recognition that peacekeeping is not peace enforcement, and that the two activities do not mix very well; that, in other words, enforcement action proceeds from different premises and is not merely one more stage in a 'peacekeeping continuum'. As the Secretary-General put it:

> The logic of peacekeeping flows from political and military premises that are quite distinct from those of enforcement; and the dynamics of the latter are incompatible with the political process that peacekeeping is intended to facilitate. To blur the distinction between the two can undermine the viability of the peacekeeping operation and endanger its personnel.[5]

Both the new British doctrine of 'Wider Peacekeeping' and the US Army Field Manual on the subject identify consent as the crucial ingredient in peacekeeping. This is a welcome development. It is to be hoped that the continuing process of reflection and analysis on this question will result in a consensus amongst member states on what peacekeeping is and what it is not. The dangers of conceptual confusion for soldiers in the field (and for the credibility of the UN) clearly outweigh the short-term advantages that doctrinal elasticity might provide governments.

PEACE CANNOT BE IMPOSED

'If there is no political will among the protagonists to solve the problem', the Secretary-General recently declared, 'the UN cannot impose peace'.[6] This firm statement of principle was necessary because, in the heady days after the end of the Cold War, its somewhat obvious truth had eluded many. The experience of the UN in Somalia and the former Yugoslavia has in any case made it clear that those who are determined to fight cannot be prevented from doing so. People who are convinced they have more to gain on the battlefield than at the negotiating table are also particularly unreliable partners for the UN's peace efforts. In any case, as the Secretary-General went on to point out in the same speech, the imposition of peace requires military, financial and political resources that member states are simply not willing to provide for operations other than war; and these resources require a capacity to manage them which the UN Secretariat does not possess and is unlikely to be granted.

Can the UN expect to mix peacekeeping and coercion, as it has been obliged to do in Somalia and sometimes in Bosnia and Herzegovina? UNOSOM's attempts to impose peace led to the loss of political support and its eventual withdrawal; UNPROFOR was blamed for failing to do things it was never mandated, staffed, financed, equipped or deployed to do. Public opinion and political rhetoric have tended to outstrip both the mandate and the means given to the UN. Most of UNPROFOR's critics, for instance, seem to think that UNPROFOR ought to have resisted or repelled 'aggression'. But the answer to aggression is not a peacekeeping operation; it is Desert Storm. In responding to the complex origins of the Yugoslav tragedy, the Security Council chose not to take military sides in the conflict, but rather to use a peacekeeping operation as a means to alleviate the consequences of the conflict – feeding and protecting civilians, delivering humanitarian relief, and helping create conditions conducive to promoting a peace settlement. As a result, a large number of people are alive, and housed, and safe today who would have been killed, or displaced, or in peril had UNPROFOR not been deployed.

Should UNPROFOR have jeopardised these achievements by a greater use of coercive force? Such a question points to a central dilemma in those situations where the UN deploys peacekeepers when there is no peace to keep. Impartiality is the oxygen of peacekeeping; the only way peacekeepers can work is by being trusted by both sides, being clear and transparent in their dealings and keeping lines of communications open. The moment they lose this trust, the moment they are seen by one side as the 'enemy', they become part of the problem they were sent to solve. This was reflected in UNPROFOR's pattern of deployment in a variety of dispersed locations, loosely configured across all the battle lines, full of unarmed or lightly-armed observers and relief workers, and travelling in highly-visible white-painted vehicles. For such a vulnerable force to take sides through the use of force might be morally gratifying – at least briefly – but it would also be militarily irresponsible. Furthermore, no single SCR on Bosnia can be read in isolation from others. Even in those resolutions that allowed for the use of force, the Security Council reaffirmed its previous resolutions on UNPROFOR; in other words, it did not want UNPROFOR to abandon its existing mandates in order to undertake new ones. UNPROFOR thus had the difficult challenge of reconciling its authority to use force with its obligation to perform all other tasks mandated by the Security Council – tasks which require the cooperation of, and deployment amongst, all parties to conflict. The purpose of any UN peacekeeping deployment is, in the last analysis, to help extinguish the flames of war, not to fan them.

So peacekeepers, by definition and practice, cannot impose their will on those who do not wish to keep the peace. Besides, as the Secretary-General has also pointed out, there is an ethical problem with the idea that peace should be imposed on the recalcitrant. Should the UN be devoting its efforts, expending political support and scarce finances, 'in a country where the parties actually do not deserve the assistance of the UN because peace and political will do not exist'?[7] The conditions imposed by the Security Council on the deployment of UN peacekeeping troops in Angola under UNAVEM III, and in particular the requirement that both parties show a tangible commitment to peace and take concrete steps toward honouring their undertakings before the UN operation is fully deployed, suggests that this lesson has been learned by the international community.

TWO HEADS ARE BETTER THAN ONE

If there was any doubt that the UN needs partners in the field, the convening by the Secretary-General of a formal meeting between the UN and 10 regional institutions in August 1994 went a long way towards dispelling it. The meeting explored the nature and prospects of UN cooperation with these organisations, instituting a dialogue which has since continued in various forums. The UN will continue to seek its own 'partnerships for peace', particularly to help ease the financial and resource burden it bears. The regional institutions and arrangements that exist in many, but not all, parts of the world, would provide this partnership, especially since they are also likely to be able both to respond more quickly to problems in their regions and to bring special insights to bear upon them.

Of course, there is certainly a danger that some regional organisations might be too close to the problems they seek to resolve and might be unable to bring to bear the advantages of detachment and impartiality that characterise UN involvement. In such cases, there is a risk that a regional organisation could either become a vehicle for a new hegemony or that its intervention might make it a party to the conflict rather than a means to its resolution.[8] The UN has a valuable role to play in cooperation with such regional organisations to ensure that international standards are met and that the larger interests of the world community take precedence over more narrowly defined priorities. The cardinal principle, from the UN's point of view, should be that cooperation in all cases should be conducted under the authority of the Security Council and in accordance with its resolutions.

There are several types of peacekeeping partnerships possible. In one, other organisations work side-by-side with the UN in the field, using an agreed division of labour. Cooperation between the UN and the Organization of American States in Nicaragua and Haiti, and with the European Commission Monitor Mission in the former Yugoslavia, has been exemplary. A second type of partnership involves turning to an organisation which has capacities the UN does not possess, to support and protect UN peacekeepers in dangerous operations. The principal example of this type of arrangement, that with NATO in the ex-Yugoslav theatre, has been invaluable for the security of the peacekeepers. Although it has admittedly involved a few hiccups, related primarily to differing organisational cultures and mission perceptions, the few problems that have arisen have been resolved without undue difficulty. (Indeed, the late NATO Secretary-General, Manfred Woerner, predicted a future of 'frequent and close co-operation between the UN and NATO'.)[9] Should disaster strike and the withdrawal of the UN peacekeeping forces from either Bosnia or Croatia become inevitable, it is inconceivable that this could occur without the active involvement – indeed, the leadership – of NATO.

A third possibility is for the UN to be superimposed on a peacekeeping operation undertaken by a regional organisation, both to provide it international legitimacy and to ensure that it maintains universally acceptable standards. There are two examples of such partnerships already on the books. Cooperation with the Economic Community of West African States in Liberia and with the Commonwealth of Independent States in Georgia, in both cases involving UN monitoring of the other's operations, is still in its embryonic stages but has so far occurred smoothly.

But this does not exhaust the repertoire. The UN has already, on at least two occasions, turned to 'coalitions of the willing' to involve themselves in situations which are not yet 'ripe' for the UN peacekeeping treatment, asking them to establish the safe and secure environment which would make a handover to a UN peacekeeping operation feasible. In the case of

Somalia, the experiment proved successful only in the short term; in the case of Haiti, the longer-term auguries are more promising. In both cases, the idea of a 'two-stage' operational partnership was established: a first stage of quasi-enforcement action led by member states under national or coalition command, followed by a second in which UN peacekeeping takes over. This pattern could well be repeated in as yet unforeseen situations in the future.

WE MUST NOT ONLY DO THE RIGHT THING, WE MUST DO THE THING RIGHT

We must, of course, 'do the right thing': as the world's television screens bombard the international conscience with new and potent images of injustice and suffering, there is an instinctive tendency to want to respond to each problem, and an inevitable counter-tendency to take the line of *The New York Times* that, since the UN cannot put out all the fires, it should stick to the few it knows it can. If the UN is to fulfil the first purpose enshrined in its Charter – the maintenance of international peace and security – there must be recognition that peacekeeping is not a panacea for every headline-grabbing case of international disorder, but that it can solve certain kinds of problems, provided it is given the resources to do so. Both the determination of mandates, and the resources to implement them, can only come from member states. The fundamental question is: 'what kind of UN do we want?' A vital part of the answer lies in establishing the tasks and methods that member states are ready and willing to approve, support and pay for.

At the same time, we must 'do the thing right'. There are understandable questions about the ability of the UN to deploy and manage peacekeeping operations to the satisfaction of the Security Council and the troop-contributing nations. The Secretariat has taken several significant steps in the last two years to enhance its capacity, notably through the establishment of a 24-hour-a-day–7-day-a-week Situation Centre to maintain constant communications with, and instant responsiveness to, the field; the creation of new units for planning, training, and logistics support; the merger into the DPKO of the former Field Operations Division of the Department of Administration and Management, which has largely eliminated the old dual chain of command from headquarters to the field; and a number of management improvements which have enhanced our ability to mount and manage operations, including the appointment of a new, independent Inspector-General reporting to the General Assembly.

(Even the creation of the Stand-By Forces roster of troops and equipment available for peacekeeping, for all the limitations mentioned above, represents an improvement from the days when no country was even theoretically 'standing by.') If we can function both effectively and cost-effectively, we will have earned the world-wide support without which the UN will be unable to fulfil the responsibilities the world entrusts to it. But note the next point.

THE UN CAN ONLY BE AS GOOD AS IT IS ALLOWED TO BE

I am often reminded of Stalin's line about the moral authority of the Catholic Church – 'how many divisions has the Pope?' One might well ask, how many divisions has the UN? At one level, none: we have no standing army, practically no reserve stocks of basic equipment, not even a replenished Working Capital Fund. But at another level, we have all the 'divisions' we can possibly want, because there is nothing required by UN peacekeeping that member states cannot provide, if they want to.

We are developing the capacity to plan, mount, support and manage peacekeeping operations better than ever before, and to combine the 'gifted amateurism' and inventive idealism of the traditional days of peacekeeping with the technological sophistication, the modern communications and logistics, and the planning skills and response capacity of the military professionals. But we cannot do this without surmounting the endemic problem of the enormous gap between mandates and means. As we learned over Rwanda in 1994 and the Bosnian 'safe areas' in 1993, the Security Council can routinely pass resolutions without having the obligation to provide the troops to implement them. When the troops are found, they too often require to be equipped, usually with unfamiliar equipment, and trained – tasks for which the UN has no infrastructure and which it conducts by improvisation. And when troops are finally found, equipped and deployed, their governments have to be paid, an obligation in which the UN is increasingly falling behind.

The General Assembly routinely exhorts member states to pay their assessed contributions for peacekeeping operations 'on time and in full', but in practice only a handful of states send in their contributions within the stipulated 30 days after the issuance of a letter of assessment (which itself comes at the end of a lengthy process of budget preparation and review by two different governmental bodies, and a vote by the General Assembly). Recent experience has been that, three months after assessments are levied, barely 50 per cent of the required funds have come in.

The result is to tie the operational hands of the UN – which frequently has to deal with commercial contractors, and in some cases government providers, who want cash 'up front' before providing goods and services to peacekeeping operations – and, equally troubling, limits the ability of the Secretariat to reimburse troop-contributing countries. In the case of developing countries, this can cause serious hardship, particularly since governments with hard currency problems tend to await UN reimbursement before paying their troops. The resulting problems of morale in missions like UNPROFOR, where soldiers subsisting on the UN's daily allowance of $1.25 a day serve side-by-side with Western troops earning hardship bonuses in addition to their much higher regular salaries, have contributed to serious operational difficulties on the ground. Even more discouraging are the recent developments in the US Congress, which has already mandated a unilateral reduction of the US peacekeeping contribution from 31.4 per cent to 25 per cent and is now considering legislation which would 'offset' the costs of national military efforts against UN dues, thereby eliminating, for all practical purposes, US financial support for UN peacekeeping if this becomes law.

The problem is all the more ironic when seen against the comparative costs of other military activities – two days of Operation Desert Storm, for instance, would have paid for all of the UN peacekeeping operations that calendar year (1991) – and even against the kinds of military expenditures national governments are usually willing to contemplate out of their defence budgets. An instructive indication of this came in 1993 when NATO planners, asked to prepare for a possible operation to implement a peace settlement in Bosnia and Herzegovina, estimated its annual cost at $8.3 billion – by ironic coincidence the exact figure, at that point, of the UN's cumulative expenditure on all peacekeeping operations since 1948. If peacekeeping is to have a future, governments will have to overcome the syndrome under which legislators are always willing to pay for war, but not for peace.

THERE ARE NO READY-MADE FORMULAE

'One size fits all' doesn't work in peacekeeping operations. Amidst the recent turbulence, some member states have understandably found themselves announcing model criteria and then approving (and in some cases, even proposing) operations that met few, if any, of these criteria. I have already argued that doctrines, concepts and institutions must be developed and applied with as much consistency as possible. At the same time, it is clear that the peacekeeping future we now contemplate will not conform to abstract criteria which neither reflect past experience nor have been applied in subsequent decisions.

Global crises differ in their impact upon international decision-makers; the Permanent Five do not approach every operation with the same stake. The standards applied by the Security Council to Angola in the first few months of 1995 were the opposite of those applied by the same Security Council to the former Yugoslavia at exactly the same time. The Council might well have agreed with Ralph Waldo Emerson that 'consistency is the hobgoblin of little minds'.[10] Or, as the poet Whitman put it:

> Do I contradict myself?
> Very well then I contradict myself,
> I am large, I contain multitudes.[11]

If there is one thing we have all learned in peacekeeping in recent years, it is surely that there are no simple, straightforward, consistent answers to the varied and unpredictable challenges to which the UN has been called to respond. Let us accept that contradictions are unavoidable in the real world, but manage them in ways that reaffirm the integrity of the UN and the global purposes it seeks to serve.

The present, it is sometimes said, is the most difficult to see clearly; the past and the future offer greater certitudes. Clarity has certainly not been a distinguishing feature of the UN's present experience in peacekeeping. But, as I trust the foregoing demonstrates, there is a future for peacekeeping, and it can be made to work.

Notes

1. 'The Future of UN Peacekeeping', editorial, *The New York Times* (8 January 1995).
2. For analyses of these contemporary challenges, see James N. Rosenau, *Turbulence in World Politics: A Theory of Change and Continuity* (Princeton: Princeton University Press, 1990); Lawrence Freedman, 'Order and Disorder in the New World', *Foreign Affairs*, Vol. 71 (1991–2) pp. 20–37; Thomas G. Weiss, 'UN Responses in the Former Yugoslavia: Moral and Operational Choices', *Ethics and International Affairs*, Vol. 8 (1994), esp. pp. 13–14; Survival, Vol. 35 (Spring 1993), special issue on 'Ethnic Conflict and International Security'.
3. 'Managing the Peace-Keeping Challenge', speech by United Nations

Secretary-General Boutros Boutros-Ghali, Yale University (21 March 1995) (United Nations Department of Public Information, Press Release SG/SM/5589).

4. See document S/1995/1, para 44.
5. *Supplement* to *An Agenda for Peace*, report of the Secretary-General (3 January 1995) (S/1995/1) para 35.
6. Speech to the Twenty-fifth Vienna Seminar (2 March 1995) (Press Release UNIS/SG/1310) p. 4.
7. Ibid., p. 5.
8. Such concerns are addressed by the United Nations Secretary-General, Dr Boutros Boutros-Ghali, 'Beleaguered Are the Peacekeepers', *The New York Times* (30 October 1994) p. E15.
9. Manfred Woerner, 'A New NATO For New Era', speech at the National Press Club, Washington DC (6 October 1993). The UN is similarly positive: see Kofi Annan, 'UN Peacekeeping Operations and Co-operation with NATO', *Nato Review*, Vol. 41, No. 5 (October 1993) pp. 3–7.
10. Ralph Waldo Emerson, *Essays* (New York: Scribners, 1864), 'Self-Reliance'.
11. Walt Whitman, 'Song of Myself', 51.1324.

3 Humanitarian Coordination
Juergen Dedring

INTRODUCTION

Humanitarian coordination has always figured as a major issue in the approach to emergency relief. In that sense, the following discussion does not provide a totally different picture as far as the delivery of humanitarian assistance is concerned. Still, the changed international environment and the escalating number and severity of man-made complex emergencies in the years since 1989–90 have deeply affected the nature of relief operations and exacerbated the already difficult process of coordination in humanitarian matters.

This chapter focuses on the patterns and structures of coordination in the UN system, although the analysis also touches upon aspects of the humanitarian instrument which are outside the confines of the world organisation. These outside elements include such distinguished relief actors as the ICRC and the IFRCS of the Red Cross, and several NGOs who prefer to maintain their independence in relief work.

The starting point for this discussion is the appointment of the first UN Emergency Relief Coordinator and the concomitant establishment of the DHA in support of this new function. Despite numerous antecedents, this step taken in 1992 constitutes the first effort in recent years to establish a firm structure and process of humanitarian inter-Agency coordination encompassing the UN system as a whole and reflecting the will of the member states.

The principal questions are: how does the new system work and how effective is it in improving the delivery of relief in crisis situations worldwide? In order to arrive at fair and valid conclusions, this chapter must dwell on aspects of the process before it can successfully take up matters of substance. In particular, details about the composition and organisation of the coordination framework that have been created in the UN system are included in the survey. Once the main features of the evolving coordination system surrounding DHA are spelled out, the evaluation of this policy instrument can proceed. Hopefully, the two basic questions will be satisfactorily answered enabling the observer and analyst to judge the utility of the new machinery.

DHA AND THE UN SYSTEM

In reaction to the massive failure of the international humanitarian community to provide urgent relief assistance to the Kurds in Northern Iraq in Spring 1991, policy-makers, the media and the relief profession itself began a new search for a better way to provide aid to people in need, especially when the crisis results from armed conflict either between or within states or from massive human rights violations or related emergencies. While the initial idea was the appointment of a 'humanitarian Supremo', whose status would place him over and above all other high officials in the relief realm, the multilateral dialogue within the UN eventually resulted in the designation of an Emergency Relief Coordinator by the Secretary-General, under the terms of General Assembly resolution (GA Res) 46/182 of December 1991.

Mandated to improve humanitarian coordination and thus to strengthen the delivery of timely and adequate relief, the new Coordinator was appointed at the level of an Under-Secretary-General for Humanitarian Affairs, accountable and responsible solely to the Secretary-General. A Department of Humanitarian Affairs was created out of existing staff resources in order to support the Coordinator in his challenging task. Its specific functions are carefully spelled out in GA Res 46/182 and in the Annex containing the so-called principles of humanitarian relief, which clearly define the boundaries of the coordination mandate.

For the new approach to humanitarian coordination, the Emergency Relief Coordinator was given four main tools. These are DHA itself, the Inter-Agency Standing Committee (IASC), the Consolidated Appeals Process (CAP) and the Central Emergency Revolving Fund (CERF). The DHA staff working in New York and Geneva consists of more than 200 members, of which a considerable number formed the old UNDRO team dealing with natural disasters only. A significant portion of the current staff is dependent on extra-budgetary voluntary contributions for their salaries. This shows the tenuous nature of the personnel structure underpinning the functioning of the Coordinator.

The most significant innovation is unquestionably the IASC. The Kurdish crisis made clear that the UN system and its humanitarian partners lacked a standing forum in which the leading officials could convene on a regular basis, as well as for emergency reasons, in order to consider common concerns of high priority with a view to seeking a joint decision for quick action without the confusion and waste of the past years. The intent of GA Res 46/182 is clear: the new body is expected to promote efficient decision-making and effective relief action in the field.

Fulfilling his mandate, the Head of DHA initiated the first of numerous meetings of the new inter-Agency body, which consisted of the principal UN Agencies and offices, among them UNHCR, UNICEF, UNDP and WFP, and affiliated organisations, such as ICRC, IFRCS, IOM and NGO councils. In order to guarantee day-to-day consultation and interaction be- tween the headquarters and field operations, a working group was set up to prepare for the IASC deliberations and to follow up on its decisions. With the number of actual crises as high as it has been recently, it must be self-evident that the working group and the various subsidiary task forces for current emergencies or issues lead to many meetings each month. Moreover, this activity itself creates work for the DHA staff assigned to service the IASC machinery.

An issue of importance for all participants in this intensive and lengthy involvement in inter-Agency coordination is the question of value added. Does coordination of this type create a new bureaucratic layer costing time and money or does it enhance the way humanitarian assistance is made available to the people in need? There is no doubt that this question has occupied the minds of many officials, executive and working-level, and the answer so far is not clear. Nobody seems to deny the usefulness of the IASC process; still, the final assessment may have to await a bit more experience of the evolving procedures, which might give rise to reforms by the participants themselves.

The third tool of humanitarian coordination is the Consolidated Appeal Process which is an important innovation resulting from GA Res 46/182. The underlying conception is unassailable: if every humanitarian organ- isation seeks relief-related funding from the donor community, the donors have difficulty getting a clear and comprehensive idea about the critical needs to be satisfied. With the introduction of consolidated appeals for all emergencies in which UN Agencies are engaged, the donor community is able to consider one integrated document spelling out requirements and projects to meet the need. The individual donors, mostly governments, have the chance to review the consolidated document and to pick and choose the projects they wish to underwrite. This approach is certainly a clear improvement in a global situation of rising relief and peacekeeping costs and shrinking national budgets.

The needs assessment itself, a key element of the preparation of the appeal, brings together representatives of the mandated or concerned Agencies for a detailed examination of the gaps and the losses incurred in the course of the crisis. It also creates a dialogue amongst them and with the local authorities concerned about the most pressing needs and appropriate relief measures. A major advantage of this needs assessment is the direct involvement of field personnel who possess a more intimate knowledge of the area under review and who are likely to have formulated approaches and programmes to assist in relief as well as socioeconomic development. It happens quite often that the actual drafting of the appeal starts during the field visit so that the direct input of the specialists closest to the crisis is assured. In the end, when the consolidated appeal document is ready to be launched, there is a sound expectation that the needs identified and the projects proposed will directly reflect the emergency and its humanitarian ramifications.

In view of the turbulence of the current world situation, it should come as no surprise that the number of appeals issued has been growing steadily since the inception of DHA in early 1992. Since all these plans of action and funding requests require a pecuniary response from the donor community, the overall demand for resources exceeds either the ability or the willingness of the donors to pay. This severe shortfall between requests and contributions is illustrated by the fact that in 1993, of about $4 billion of relief funds sought, a mere $2 billion were ultimately received. This negative balance is bound to dampen the effectiveness of the improved appeals procedure. Still, the highly coordinated manner in which most of these appeals are now prepared and launched is undoubtedly a major advance compared to the period before 1992.

The last principal tool of coordination is the CERF referred to in GA Res 46/182 and set at a maximum level of $50 million. Its purpose, as the name implies, is to make available ready cash at the outset of a humanitarian crisis so that relief can arrive long before the assessment and funding phases enable the humanitarian Agencies to start delivering more specifically-targeted emergency assistance. Creating a financial foundation which allows early responses by the humanitarian community is therefore an essential condition for deploying a joint capacity when and wherever needed. However, the rules which guide the DHA's management of the fund are so strict that it lacks the flexibility to handle the often messy situations with such dispatch that human suffering can be mitigated, if not avoided altogether.

The reticence of the main contributors to the CERF became absolutely clear at its inception, as it took nearly a year between the adoption of GA Res 46/182 and the actual setting up of the fund with the total amount pledged, although not fully paid in. Following this tenuous beginning, experience since early 1993 has confirmed the crucial importance of the fund, small though it is. Repeated efforts to increase the size of the CERF to $100 million have so far been defeated by the negative attitudes of most of the Western Group and the United States. The member states pay close attention to the utilisation and management of the emergency fund and are likely to further refine the rules under which the CERF operates.

DHA AND ITS HUMANITARIAN PARTNERS IN THE UN SYSTEM

The group of humanitarian partners among whom coordination is sought is implied in GA Res 46/182, although their names are not listed in its text. The main partners are self-evident: UNHCR, UNICEF, WFP, WHO and UNDP. In addition, one should mention FAO, UNESCO, UNEP and the Bretton Woods Institutions – the World Bank and IMF. Just listing these entities indicates the scope and complexity of the coordination mandate assigned to the Emergency Relief Coordinator. Compared to DHA, most of its partners are well-established and have existed for several decades. Their heads are superior to the Coordinator in status and prestige, and are not subject to the direct authority of the Secretary-General. They are controlled by their own governing boards or assemblies that issue instructions and reviews of their executive roles. If nothing else, these barons of the UN system can conveniently hide behind the undeniable authority of their legislative bodies which may override suggestions or instructions from the Head of DHA.

In order to overcome the status deficit, the Coordinator can, of course, go through the Secretary-General to try and influence his humanitarian partners. Such a course of action, cumbersome and undignified, would definitely not improve the working relationship between the Head of DHA and the Agency chiefs. Therefore, the challenge of designing the right approach to the partners continues unresolved and is beyond facile slogans of cooperation. Most of these UN partners not only possess large staffs and powerful supporters, but they also operate extensive networks of field stations covering most of the Third World and much of Eastern Europe including the former Soviet Union. Their ability to act unilaterally and arrive at separate understandings or arrangements is well known. Humanitarian coordination, as far as they are concerned, will go as far as they want it to go. They neither can nor will allow themselves to be manipulated or coerced. Examples of this assertion of their autonomy are too plentiful to be insignificant.

An underlying basic theme relating to this phenomenon is put forward as a question of 'comparative advantage'. In a system of cooperating partners in which the division of labour can be actively practised, a particular function ought to be assigned to the organisation best equipped to do the job. This pragmatic approach thus helps to avoid duplication of effort and to optimise the outcome. Most humanitarian organisations both inside and outside of the UN system are bound to favour past practice as long as they are satisfied that new challenges will be met successfully. New arrangements will only be made and implemented if the old way of doing things is deficient or if a new situation requires new responses. The term 'comparative advantage' has often been used in the years since DHA's creation to allocate responsibility for the common challenges to one of the existing organisations.

A major concern of the UN partners has been the creation of another bureaucratic layer impeding efficient relief delivery in urgent crisis situations. If a particular agency, such as UNHCR or WFP, to name two principal relief-providing entities, is alerted to an incipient humanitarian emergency where the lives of innocent civilians are at risk, everything should be done to speed up the process of assistance and nothing should stand in the way of swift action. Coordination considerations do not figure much at the front line of humanitarian action. In that sense, the coordinator must be aware of this predicament when it comes to launching and conducting rapid response operations. The experience since 1992 has heightened the sensitivity of the operating Agencies, in the field and at headquarters, to the issue of unnecessary bureaucratisation.

This whole issue is exacerbated by the well-known fact that the humanitarian partners all share the characteristics of large bureaucratic bodies. Hierarchical and inter-departmental procedures are firmly encrusted and will take precedence even in most urgent circumstances. The slow and heavy-handed quality of management in these unwieldy organisations causes delays in executive decision-making and weakens the field operation. The record of emergency relief contains plenty of evidence of the effects of bureaucratic inertia on cooperative humanitarian action.

More specific features of the operational Agencies in the UN system will be noted in the subsequent discussion of field coordination, unquestionably the most difficult part of working together in humanitarian matters. The initial point of departure for this consideration is the simple fact that the operational partners have a more or less permanent field presence, whereas the Emergency Relief Coordinator is not directly or consistently represented at the operational sites. Many of the problems, as far as effective coordination in relief operations is concerned, derive from this fundamental difference between DHA and its partners.

DHA AND ITS UN SECRETARIAT PARTNERS

As DHA is an integral part of the UN Secretariat under the stewardship of the Secretary-General, it goes without saying that humanitarian coordination is directly affected by the nature of the organisational–bureaucratic process shaping the whole institution. The Under-Secretaries-General for Humanitarian Affairs, for Peacekeeping Operations and for Political

Affairs, who share accountability and responsibility to the Secretary-General and a largely overlapping interest in complex field operations, are bound to work together as much as possible so that their specific concerns can effectively be addressed in line with the decisions of the Security Council and the instructions of the Secretary-General.

When examining current field operations, one establishes quickly that most have three components: the political element of searching for an elusive peace; the peacekeeping element which in nearly all cases of this kind is a given; and the humanitarian component resulting from the sad fact that, in most cases, strife and force cause suffering to large numbers of innocent civilians. The high level of connectivity resulting from the same organisational background and the common field responsibility makes it critical that units within the UN Secretariat collaborate very closely. The normal give-and-take of inter-office dealings, especially in a large and un-wieldy bureaucracy such as the UN, further adds to the difficulty of fulfilling the mandate of the humanitarian coordinator. But it could be that while time is lost striving for the maximum collaboration and agreement on how to proceed, disarray and waste might subsequently be avoided in the field. One could justifiably conclude that the gain of such inter-departmental collaboration outweighs the cost in time and effort.

Two specific issues deserve closer attention. It has been the trend since 1992 that the political process focused on the pursuit of peaceful solutions was seen as providing the justification for the DPA to claim overall leadership in the field. Hence, the representative of the political arm of the UN, usually an SRSG, would seek to take charge of all UN staff and activities in the field, while being accountable to the Secretary-General as well as the Head of DPA. Unless the Heads of DHA and DPKO could gain the ear and support of the Secretary-General, they would not be able to influence the decision-making and actions of the SRSG.

Many field operations involve the presence of military personnel under a Force Commander. It stands to reason – and the record confirms this assumption – that such military formations do not always lend themselves to the needs and purposes of humanitarian assistance. Major changes are required to transform soldiers into relief workers. The Head of DPKO has responsibility for the use of multinational military contingents and may find it difficult fully to accommodate the rules and standards of impartial and neutral emergency relief. How the humanitarian coordinator can find complete satisfaction as far as fulfilment of these norms is concerned remains very uncertain. Even under the best of circumstances, the actual presence of military personnel in highly-integrated UN operations can compromise the neutrality of relief workers and might alienate some of the recipients of aid. The occurrence of misunderstandings should not surprise the actors in the field or the outside observer.

DHA AND ITS NGO PARTNERS

With the coordination network widening to include the NGOs, the diminishing ability of the humanitarian coordinator to affect the actual decisions of these partners in the humanitarian field must be accepted as a given. In the enormous range of NGOs or PVOs, one can easily detect large differences in capacity, reach and effectiveness. Wherever humanitarian relief is needed and provided, some alignment of these groups of good-willed helpers will be there. Whatever coordination takes place is not predictable, nor is it foreseeable whether large or small NGOs will know about the UN system's arrangements and, if so, will agree to abide by the understandings governing the interaction of the UN partners. Recent large-scale crises reflect considerable confusion and little order, especially regarding NGO relief teams.

A basic distinction must be made if one wants to do justice to all NGOs involved: on the one hand, there are the ICRC and the IFRCS and, on the other, the many truly non-governmental actors. The proud record of the Red Cross does not need to be reiterated here. It is enough to point out that the Red Cross professionals have achieved many successes under difficult conditions. For the UN system to seek to achieve a sound level of coordination with the ICRC and the Federation is a tremendous challenge, not because these humanitarian partners are difficult to deal with but because they follow their own system of rules and regulations based on the foundation of the Geneva Conventions – the key code of international humanitarian law. Despite their total independence from the UN, the ICRC and the Federation have shown much goodwill and a spirit of cooperation when preparing field action and when standing shoulder-to-shoulder with the UN in emergency situations. DHA and its UN partners enjoy the benefit of this cooperation, but know that when it comes to coordination the best that can be achieved is an agreement between equals and that there is no way that certain measures can be imposed against the will of Red Cross managers and field officers.

The other end of the spectrum of NGOs includes organisations with religious, medical, social and occasionally political programmes, representing such a wide range that any attempt to generalise would end in failure. For all these actors arriving to offer relief assistance in emergency situations, the UN can at best offer close collaboration and thereby advance the common agenda of more effective relief. If, however, as happened in Rwanda, some inexperienced medical group from Europe suffers a fiasco because it failed to pre-plan its operation and acted totally on its own without even attempting to approach or interact with UN Agencies and other experienced organisations, there is very little that the humanitarian coordinator and his partners can do. The only thing that can be tried and might work is an appeal to goodwill, understanding and the sensible notion of teamwork and cooperation. Fortunately, with growing field experience, many NGOs are comfortable in joining UN representatives in striving for the common goal of quick and effective relief for the people in need.

Occasionally, when the opportunity arises, the UN field Agencies contract out to NGOs certain specific tasks and thereby bind these private actors into the larger emergency operation. This has been the case in the ongoing UNHCR relief operation in the former Yugoslavia, as well as in other instances. It is to be expected that the level of collaboration will be quite high, thereby ensuring at least in the field a more or less unified relief presence. Nevertheless, these arrangements are more the exception than the norm in humanitarian work.

The NGOs have organised themselves into a few large councils or associations. In North America, InterAction is the collective umbrella under which many PVOs are assembled. Similarly, the International Council of Voluntary Associations (ICVA) constitutes a worldwide consortium of NGOs, with emphasis on Europe. Many organisations are thus set up to deal with the diverse range of fundamental and operational issues in a collective, self-governing fashion. The task of humanitarian coordination is clearly facilitated for DHA and its UN partners in that they can cover many questions in their dialogue with ICVA and InterAction. To maximise the chance of close collaboration, the IASC and its subsidiary bodies have added NGO representatives as well as Red Cross representatives to the list of guests to whom invitations to its meetings are extended on a regular basis.

DHA AND THE DONOR GOVERNMENTS

Although DHA and its UN partners have no mandate for humanitarian coordination with regard to donor governments, the reality of international relief makes it unavoidable that the UN system must conduct its emergency assistance in closest contact with those member states which underwrite the funding of UN relief operations. With a more than a 50 per cent shortfall in required donations for identified humanitarian needs in numerous emergencies worldwide, the necessity to plead and appeal to the main donors for further contributions is paramount.

The result of this pecuniary dependency is the strengthening of the hand of the donor and the concomitant weakening of the relief agency and of the beneficiary. In the past, funds could normally be spent freely on different aspects of a relief and development package. Nowadays, the donor government will essentially dictate its choices for financial support and demand detailed follow-up from the relief operator on the fulfilment of its instructions. This pick-and-choose policy undercuts the ability of the relief provider and the target country to utilise available donations for a balanced programme addressing immediate relief needs and longer-term rehabilitation and development objectives. Thus, the opportunity to conceive and fulfil a coherent and comprehensive plan of action is jeopardised, if not negated, by the pervasive funding crisis. The symptom of donor or compassion 'fatigue' has become a bitter reality in relief operations, causing havoc in the delivery of emergency aid and leading to abrupt terminations of ongoing programmes because of lack of funds.

Another matter that has considerable ramifications for the impact of the donor governments on the actual delivery of aid is the inevitable bias characterising their foreign policies. One is fully aware of the weight of a global power in international developments. It should not come as a surprise that US support for the UN relief programme in Haiti is, of course, coloured by its policy towards this troubled land. The same is true for British or French policies in Africa, for example. There is a high probability that support for humanitarian relief under UN auspices will be seen as a continuation of national policies by other means. If the aims of a donor government clash with the goals of a UN aid package, the outcome will be either an attempt by the UN to accommodate the governmental partner or the latter's refusal to support the appeal. In view of the chronic resource deficit, it is abundantly clear that the UN system will always be in the position of an appellant begging for a contribution from the donor government.

The recent decline in humanitarian donations has alarmed the relief community. The task of coordinator has become much more difficult in view of the sober realisation that the shortage of donations requires some sort of triage, despite the collective condemnation of such an approach. The severity of the situation is further illustrated by the bitter lesson that at the onset of the Rwanda crisis major donors were unwilling to launch adequate mitigation and prevention efforts, at very low cost, but ended up paying huge amounts of money to provide basic relief once the massacre had cost the lives of half a million innocent people. If donors claim to have no money for incipient crises, where do they find the funds for megarelief in megacrises? Of course, these arguments cannot be put to the group of donor countries on which the multilateral programme of emergency relief totally depends.

This brief review of the relationship between the donors and the humanitarian coordinator reveals the problems regularly encountered by the UN humanitarian community in dealing with its political and financial masters. The power of the purse is as effective in this relationship as in other social and political situations. The inclination of governments to give or withhold support at will cannot be overcome by the argument that in order to be effective, relief needs proper planning and reliable financial backing. The humanitarian coordinator might be able to soften annoyance and impatience on the part of the donor representatives, but he cannot override the inequality between sovereign governments and the dependent multilateral assistance organisations.

DHA AND THE BENEFICIARY GOVERNMENTS

How does the situation look when dealing with the recipients of emergency aid? Are the governments and peoples who stand to benefit from the generosity of the international community easier to deal with than the donor governments? There is no simple answer to that. The reality turns out to be rather complicated. While recipient communities are basically grateful for outside help, the authorities involved tend to insist on their intrinsic rights even when in receipt of massive humanitarian assistance. This means that the relief organisations cannot dictate the terms of the engagement to the beneficiary, but must negotiate the particulars of the actions to be undertaken, including questions of access and sites of assistance.

In most emergency situations, one must recognise the distinction between the people in need and their governments. While the suffering among the needy groups tends to be severe and the urgency of relief is extreme, the ruling elites are in general sheltered from the effects of the humanitarian emergency. Lack of food and shelter remains abstract for the persons not affected, and explains why beneficiary governments tend to manipulate the delivery of aid for their own political purposes. This disjunction between the government and the suffering population automatically makes it difficult for the relief provider to obtain full and impartial access. The government will not beg for relief aid, but instead conveys to the humanitarian partners in no uncertain terms the limits of the engagement so that the power of the local authorities will not be weakened or diminished. Such desire to control the relief action often results in detailed regulation concerning what may go where and with government monitors deployed to keep an eye on the whereabouts of the international personnel.

For these and other reasons, a very skilful use of 'humanitarian diplomacy' is necessary to penetrate the walls of national sovereignty and governmental prerogative, and to bring the relief to the victims of emergencies. The experiences of the humanitarian coordinator in several recent crises, including Myanmar, Sudan and Azerbaijan, illustrate the difficulties incurred by the UN system and other relief operators in their work. Maintaining a close relationship with the governments and other authorities in question and persevering in the pursuit of the essential objectives of humanitarian assistance is a permanent obligation and challenge for DHA and its partners in relief.

DHA AND REBEL GROUPS

This last group in the review of the partners in the coordination of humanitarian assistance is elusive and undoubtedly complicated. The issue is the apparent need for relief personnel to make arrangements with the leaders of rebel factions controlling part of a national territory. A familiar example of this condition is the precarious hold of the Southern Sudanese rebels over a large part of contested territory. Humanitarian staff can enter that part of the Sudan only with the permission of the rebel leadership. If these rebel leaders are under the impression that emergency assistance benefitting people under their effective control would challenge and weaken their authority, they are most likely to refuse access. To avoid delicate situations like this requires much skill and acumen in political matters and personal relations.

The complications are exacerbated in areas where control over territory is directly and actively contested. Much of Somalia and the former Yugoslavia falls into this category, spelling utter confusion. If there is a direct confrontation between opposing forces, the likelihood that relief can reach the victims is very slim. Still, the UN is obliged to try to ensure that people in need are not abandoned and to try to negotiate with both sides over the delivery of urgent aid. It is impossible to calculate the odds of success in a situation like this. A tentative understanding in the morning might collapse by the afternoon, or be denied by other leaders or groups fighting on the same side. Such uncertainty renders coordination of humanitarian assistance in the field a full-time job, but it does not guarantee consistent success; far from it. The record of complex field missions offers plenty of evidence of the difficulties of emergency assistance under these circumstances.

If the opposing forces are fiercely committed to their respective struggles and view their opponent with unremitting enmity, the opportunity for effective humanitarian aid is bound to shrink and might be eliminated. In cases where the two sides view any gain for the rival as a loss for themselves, and vice versa, their aims are absolutely incompatible and the lives of their respective populations become hostage to the struggle for power. This struggle for control results in a total disregard for the victimised civilians who are hit by both sides and who are denied escape or rescue. Such a constellation depicts the outer frontier of humanitarian coordination today. The risk of failure is extremely high, and failure results in the negation of the humanitarian imperative for people in the cross-fire. It confirms that there are no pre-ordained, easy solutions to humanitarianism in war and civil strife. But the search must not be abandoned.

DHA AND FIELD COORDINATION

The issue of field coordination deserves separate treatment since the effectiveness of humanitarian assistance is not felt or measured at the headquarters level but in the field where people in misery need food, shelter and other basic goods and services. From what has been considered above, it follows that the combination of the inherent troubles and impediments afflicting humanitarian coordination in and around the UN system is bound to be felt in an especially marked way in the field.

The most basic difficulty derives from the distance between headquarters and the field. Modern communications have helped bridge the gaps of time and distance in miraculous ways, but the remoteness of emergency sites still weighs negatively in terms of speed and focus of remedial action. The predicament is especially difficult for those humanitarian partners which have no representation in the field and therefore have to rely on others for information and implementation. DHA's role of relief coordinator, explicitly barred from field action, together with its place in the hierarchical structure of the UN Secretariat, establishes its dependence on the goodwill and reliability of others over whom it has no authority and little influence.

Soon after the establishment of DHA in 1992, the impact of the unresolved question of field presence became clear. Over time, certain arrangements have evolved in order to address the links of responsibility and accountability between DHA and its agents in the field. The modality that has so far proven to be most beneficial is the appointment of a 'humanitarian coordinator' for the duration of a humanitarian emergency. While there is an unspoken assumption that UNDP, with its network of field offices and resident representatives, would have the right of first nomination, sometimes the right person works in other parts of the far-reaching UN system and, with the agreement of the IASC, that individual is appointed.

This field coordinator has to work out two essential relations: one with the local head of the UNDP office and other local UN liaison officers; and the second with the heads of the political and peacekeeping arms of the UN in complex emergencies. Frequently, the Secretary-General appoints his SRSG to take overall charge of the UN's approach to a particular crisis, for example in Liberia or Haiti, and instructs other UN staff there to accept his authority. This allows the UN to simplify lines of authority and communications between headquarters and the field. It might, however, cause interference in the line of command between the Head of DHA and the field humanitarian coordinator, since the latter is subordinate to the SRSG who, hierarchically speaking, is accountable to the UN Secretary-General.

Furthermore, there is a clear danger that, if the humanitarian coordinator is not associated with UNDP, this UN entity will be less forthcoming and hold back on office and staff support. In a situation of budgetary cutbacks and shortfalls, such support may be critical for the temporary relief team. Other UN entities, together with the many NGOs and other non-UN actors, will each determine their relationship to the humanitarian coordinator in the field and act according to their own agenda. While most will make an effort to liaise with the coordinator, only a few will agree to be fully coordinated. This is especially the case when the personal chemistry does not work and the people in question avoid close contact.

The difficulty of the field assignment is further exacerbated by the tenuous relationship with the government of the recipient country, the donor representatives and, possibly, with the leaders of a rebel or secessionist faction. Much of what was said about these links at the executive level is applicable to the field situation. It is safe to suggest that it will take all the time and commitment of the field coordinator to succeed in these critical relationships. Even under the best conditions, there is no assurance that agreement will be granted by government representatives to enable the humanitarian teams to carry out their relief task. Since the humanitarian workers usually lack powerful supporters, they are ill-equipped to argue against narrow-minded office-holders and devious bureaucrats who give preference to their own needs and interests.

Much has been written about the actual field conditions and the unavoidable human shortcomings and failures. In this context, one must try to be as realistic as possible in assessing the actual delivery of humanitarian assistance under adverse conditions. Looking at major crises such as Somalia, Bosnia or Rwanda, it must be conceded that what can be achieved and what has been achieved falls significantly short of the ideal outcome. One individual, appointed humanitarian coordinator with few staff or little administrative backing, is physically unable to carry out all the actions and make all the contacts that would put him into total control of what is going on in his relief operation. Moreover, as was referred to above, the political and peacekeeping components of the UN field presence are also beyond the reach of the humanitarian coordinator. Numerous examples document the clashes between peacekeepers and relief workers. Such difficulties can only be resolved by the SRSG or by the Office of the Secretary-General. The success of the relief coordinator in the field depends on the goodwill that can be generated by the individual, and cannot be built on the essentially hollow authority he has been given.

CONCLUSION

Despite all the built-in barriers and hurdles, the DHA's record in its first three years shows considerable progress in the way humanitarian assistance has been coordinated both within and without the UN system. The improvements in terms of speed of response, integrated approaches and unified field action are measurable and confirm the validity of the intent of GA Res 46/182. Compared to the fiasco of the Kurdish crisis of early summer 1991, the treatment of humanitarian emergencies since 1992 has been characterised by the determination to rectify the faults of the past. While capacity issues and funding gaps prevent the full application of the relief tools available to the UN humanitarian community and its partners, the prospects for further gains in coordination and actual relief delivery continue to be good.

The discussion throughout this chapter has focused on the realities affecting the mandate of coordination given to the Head of DHA and his staff. The range of clients and partners is far too wide to allow close-knit relations with all the actors relevant to the political, military, socioeconomic and humanitarian dimensions of the complex emergencies of our time. The weak starting position of the Emergency Relief Coordinator as a member of the UN Secretariat reporting to the Secretary-General and lacking the status to be accepted as a full partner by other Agencies, programmes, NGOs, and governments, is a powerful limit on his actual authority. But even if the position was more elevated in the international hierarchical order, the innate complexity of the world would continue to hinder the effective execution of the steering and coordinating mandate.

How to remedy the mistakes and improve the humanitarian assistance system? A sober review of the recent weakening of UN multilateralism allows only one conclusion: while the world community is aware of the shortcomings of the current relief machinery, it lacks the collective will to make the necessary changes and put the system on a sound financial footing. This might require a revision of the principles of GA Res 46/182 and of the tools provided for a strengthened approach to relief. Unless a large majority of UN member states adopt such a pro-active plan and see to it that it is faithfully carried out, the future will bring new tales of half-baked successes and near-failures. The attempt at better humanitarian coordination will not be abandoned, although it often appears to detached observers as nothing better than muddling through.

4 The Hidden Costs of Better Coordination

Neill Wright[1]

As the title of this volume suggests, there is considerable evidence to support the argument that the genocide in Rwanda in the second quarter of 1994 marked a turning point in international responses to humanitarian crises.

This tragic episode in Rwanda, witnessed around the world at a time when the most visible international presence – the UN peacekeeping force, UNAMIR[2] – was being reduced from 2500 to just 270 personnel, gave new impetus to the debate on the whole question of when and how best the international community should act in response to such crises. The complexity and confusion of the subsequent humanitarian response within Rwanda added to the momentum. Despite rapid and innovative humanitarian action in the surrounding countries, the result was a growing demand for more effective and coordinated use of the limited resources available to humanitarian actors.

From the perspective of UNHCR, the genocide, and the resultant outflow of over 1 million Rwandans into eastern Zaïre within two weeks in July 1994, created another in a series of crises in the Great Lakes region – the precursor to which had been the outflow of 250 000 refugees from Burundi into the Ngara region of northwest Tanzania during April 1994. This latter outflow occurred with overwhelming speed following the deaths of Presidents Habyarimana and Ntaryamira on 6 April 1994 when their aircraft crashed on approach to Kigali airport. The greatest challenge in seeking to provide relief and protection to those who sought refuge in Zaïre that July was that the international community's humanitarian emergency response capacity was already at full stretch responding both to ongoing operations elsewhere in the region and to other demanding missions, including former Yugoslavia.

Once again, UN member states were asked to respond to a crisis situation where there was little prospect for a politically-negotiated peace. Having learned from many ongoing UN missions, particularly large-scale missions such as those in Somalia and former Yugoslavia, donor governments might have been understandably weary of the seemingly endless demand for contributions to UN peacekeeping operations and humanitarian programmes, as

51

well as justifiably concerned about yet another open-ended commitment. With the UN's annual peacekeeping budget running at over $US3 billion, and humanitarian budgets[3] rising sharply as a result of the increasing number of humanitarian crises stemming from the spread of internal conflict since the end of the Cold War era, such contributions as were made available might have been driven more by limited altruism rather than by investment in regional stability or the maintenance of international peace and security. Despite the Secretary-General's continuing pleas for the necessary resources to match the profligate resolutions of the Security Council and the General Assembly, frequently stated and clearly evidenced in his later *Supplement* to *An Agenda for Peace*,[4] the 17 May 1994 Security Council Resolution[5] authorising the expansion of UNAMIR to 5500 troops fell largely on deaf ears. The rapid deployment and presence of an expanded international military force might have deterred many acts of violence.

A French-led multinational peacekeeping operation did establish a 'Humanitarian Protection Zone' in southwest Rwanda. SCR 929 authorised the operation, including the French national command – which undoubtedly contributed to making possible its rapid deployment. This intervention, named Operation Turquoise,[6] while largely successful, had mission objectives which were more closely aligned with simple protection through the provision of physical security than with humanitarian relief to the victims of the genocide or the protection of human rights under international humanitarian law.

Within the humanitarian community, the lessons learned of the risks in carrying out humanitarian operations in 'failed state' or emergent state situations, where consensual activities, neutrality and impartiality are easily jeopardised, led to a cautious, though highly visible, involvement with the recently-victorious RPF-based Government (which established the BBGNU[7] in July 1994) but a noticeably greater willingness to allocate resources to the relief and protection of refugees in the surrounding countries. Given the likelihood that the ongoing tribal tensions would lead to abuse of humanitarian relief for the advantage of the new Tutsi-dominated administration in Rwanda, the caution of many international organisations within Rwanda may be understandable, although it can be argued that it delayed activities likely to result in a durable solution. It did highlight once again the moral dilemma of how effectively to protect human rights in life-threatening situations, when to do so means intervening in the affairs of a sovereign state.

If the international community failed to respond effectively to the genocide in Rwanda, was this a failure of early warning? Given the small size and the relative unimportance of Rwanda to the international community, were governments overly dependent on the UN and NGOs for such warning? There is considerable evidence to demonstrate that the genocide came as no surprise to many governments. The systematic murder of between 500 000 and 1 million members of the population of Rwanda was, to some extent, an anticipated if unexpectedly severe result of generations of political violence. Amnesty International, Human Rights Watch and other organisations gave clear warning of the likelihood of Tutsi retribution.[8] What failed, therefore, was not the early warning system, but the translation of such warnings into preventive action or better preparedness to respond to events. There is a clear need to ensure that influential bodies both in the UN and in its member states act on early warning signals, and pursue investment in greater preparedness.

In Rwanda, out of a pre-war population of 7.75 million people, over 50 per cent were estimated to be refugees or internally displaced as a result of the genocide. By October 1994, the number of internally displaced was assessed to be as many as 1.8 million, approximately 724 000[9] of whom were within the area of southwest Rwanda which had been the Humanitarian Protection Zone established by Operation Turquoise. The DHA[10] initially deployed a small team of staff to Nairobi to form a coordinating office known as the UN Rwanda Emergency Office (UNREO). This team moved to Kigali in August 1994, and started to work closely with the newly-appointed SRSG, Ambassador Khan, and with the UNAMIR Force Commander, Major-General Dallaire. UNREO and its UN Humanitarian Coordinator established close links with the new government, which set up a Humanitarian Unit Coordinating Centre in the Ministry of Rehabilitation. While the Ministry of Foreign Affairs was the first point of contact for all international organisations, it was the Ministry of Rehabilitation which provided liaison with relevant UN Agencies and NGOs. UNREO has since provided coordination through regular inter-Agency meetings, prioritisation of humanitarian activities, and through its reports to the UN Office in Geneva and to UN Headquarters in New York – which have helped to keep donors aware of events and have formed the basis of the consolidated inter-Agency appeals for Rwanda.[11] While Kigali remains the obvious choice as a focus for regionalisation of the international response, security within Rwanda and the independent agendas of neighbouring member states of the OAU, have made both a more influential involvement and regional coordination of international activities difficult to achieve thus far.

Outside Rwanda, complete Hutu societies set up home in some 'refugee camps'. The humanitarian response to these outflows, driven by the suddenness and scale of the influx, was remarkably well coordinated at the field level in April 1994 in Tanzania. UNHCR, NGOs and local govern-ment authorities worked closely together, pooling resources in shared warehouses and coordinating their efforts to meet the humanitarian crisis. Within the camps in Tanzania, law and order remained the responsibility of the police and armed forces of the sovereign state. However, in eastern Zaïre, Hutu leaders, including those responsible for the genocide, controlled events within the camps – exercising considerable influence over whether or not the refugee population could return to their homes in Rwanda. The already weak infrastructure and lack of Zaïrian capacity to support the massive influx of Hutu refugees from Rwanda, often referred to as being of 'biblical proportions', exacerbated the initial conditions in the camps, quickly leading to very high mortality rates from dysentery and malnutrition.

Recognising a huge shortfall in the necessary capacity and resources to respond effectively in eastern Zaïre, UNHCR identified eight sec-toral response activities, ranging from water treatment and distribution to airport management, which rapidly brought additional resources to bear in alleviating the high mortality rate in the refugee camps around Goma. Donor governments were asked to undertake one or more of these sectors, which became known as 'Service Packages'. This approach was warmly received by major donors, who saw an opportunity to play a highly vis-ible and relatively independent role which did not require them to subor-dinate their efforts to an international humanitarian organisation. At the same time, this concept also integrated donor governments more closely in the overall response. Donors retained the right to choose how to meet the overall objectives set by UNHCR as a result of daily inter-Agency meetings in the field, including whether to deploy national military or civil-ian expertise. Most military resources, such as the 2500 US personnel deployed on Operation Support Hope, were known to be available for only a short period until traditional civilian implementing partners could be identified to take over the tasks they performed. Much of the operational responsibility for each sectoral activity was relinquished by UNHCR, although UNHCR still attempted to provide over-arching coordination, objectives and priorities. The UNHCR Service Package mechanism had several initial flaws – lacking clear definition of the parameters of each package, and establishing packages of a size that was beyond the capacity of most nations. A follow-up study by UNHCR is under way, seeking to refine the concept for future use in large-scale emergencies.

The availability of international support for the Rwanda emergency was once again influenced by the presence of the world's media. While graphic images of machete attacks against innocent civilians walking the streets, and of truckloads of refugee corpses being taken to mass graves filled the lenses of the CNN cameras between April and September 1994, the conscience of the international community ensured a readiness to resource at least the most-needed humanitarian action, if not the Security Council's approved expansion of UNAMIR. Once again, humanitarian action was effectively substituting for the political will necessary to find a solution to the Rwandan crisis.

As the High Commissioner for Refugees, Sadako Ogata, said later that year to support her view that humanitarian action cannot be a substitute for political solutions:

> Humanitarian action can [only] buy time and space for political action. It can create an environment conducive to political negotiations. While political initiatives are essential for our work, we must not become a hostage to politics. Nor must we be politicized ... The non-political, impartial and neutral nature of our mandate must be preserved and perceived as such by all. This is essential to the credibility of humanitarian action and hence to our ability to protect human beings and find solutions to their plight.[12]

Other 'newsworthy' international events soon focused global public attention elsewhere, with events in Haiti and Chechnya replacing the ongoing crises in the Great Lakes region. International support for the necessary humanitarian action dwindled along with the fading spotlights. The problem of insecurity in the refugee camps in eastern Zaïre, where the military and militia of the former Rwandan regime were disrupting the delivery of relief, obstructing voluntary return to Rwanda and endangering the lives of both the refugees and humanitarian workers, no longer had sufficient visibility to mobilise the necessary political will to contribute a small peacekeeping force to assist the Zaïre authorities in maintaining law and order. The lack of contributors caused the Secretary-General to write to President Mobutu of Zaïre in January 1995 admitting that he was unable to muster an effective response. UNHCR was requested to explore alternative options, which has resulted in an additional appeal for humanitarian funds to equip and pay bonuses to a security force of 1500 Zaïre troops, monitored by a Civilian Security Liaison Group comprised of international police officers, and under the control of an experienced Canadian peacekeeper. This may reflect a growing donor preference for voluntary humanitarian contributions rather than assessed contributions for peacekeeping.

Action to at least monitor respect for human rights was also long delayed, given that human rights abuse in Rwanda had been reported for several years by, among others, Amnesty International,[13] Human Rights Watch, and the International Centre for Human Rights and Democratic Development (ICHRDD).[14] Prior to the creation of the Office of the High Commissioner for Human Rights (UNCHR) under General Assembly Resolution 48/41, the Centre for Human Rights had no mandate to carry out its own investigations. Equipping and deploying the Human Rights Field Operation in Rwanda (HRFOR) took many months. A Special Rapporteur was subsequently appointed. It was agreed with the new government of Rwanda that a maximum of 147 human rights field officers could be deployed within the country. The lack of resources for this operation resulted in a special appeal on 2 August 1994. Since then, the number of field officers has gradually increased to 80. The work and reports of these personnel has been made available to the Chief Prosecutor of the International Tribunal for Rwanda.

The limited number of human rights field officers has led to considerable dependence on the ICRC (which had remained present throughout the conflict) and other humanitarian actors to extend their limited visibility of events. One danger of such a close relationship between those providing humanitarian relief and those responsible for human rights issues is the restriction it can create on consensual humanitarian access to the victims. Human nature dictates that there will always be a greater acceptance of neutral relief operations than that afforded to human rights investigations. In this respect, the under-resourcing of UNCHR, and its lack of trained operational capacity, remain serious limitations on its ability to address human rights abuses. More fundamentally, while external humanitarian aid and support for human rights can help a collapsed society like Rwanda, it cannot long substitute for the national action to rebuild local civil authority, justice and the rule of law.

The General Assembly has already expended considerable time and funds on improving the strategic coordination of the political, military and humanitarian responses to such complicated emergencies. Improvements to date[15] in coordination within the UN Secretariat among the DPA, the DPKO and the DHA include sharing of early warning information, joint assessment missions, joint planning fora, regular sharing of desk-level information, and establishing a 24-hour situation centre within the expanded DPKO. These activities, coupled with a growing understanding of the requirement to return much-needed integrity to the recently beleaguered principles, concepts and operational doctrines of both peacekeeping and humanitarian action could go a long way towards resolving the imbalance between longer-term issues addressed by the General Assembly and the priority given this decade to security issues addressed by the

Security Council. On a more operational note, it should also improve the clarity of mandated mission objectives and keep member states better informed throughout the planning and implementation phases of UN Missions. As a further move towards better preparedness, other initiatives are addressing stand-by or rapid deployment forces, rosters of qualified SRSGs and Humanitarian Coordinators, and improvements in training to achieve a higher standard of performance.

The majority of UN humanitarian Agencies, including UNHCR,[16] depend largely on governments' voluntary funding for the majority of their finance. NGOs broaden the scope of humanitarian fund-raising by including the public amongst their donors. While this is advantageous to the beneficiaries, it also creates a need for the NGOs to maintain considerable independence. Experience has shown that the NGOs' need for independence is in some ways analogous with the relationship between DHA and the major operational Agencies. The latter, in fulfilling their part of the common objective, will only look for operational coordination if there is a clear benefit to the performance of their individual humanitarian programmes.

At the operational level, the international humanitarian community will seek to put its limited resources to use where they are most needed and where they are most likely to promote a durable solution in terms of protection of human rights and an end to suffering. Unfortunately, these logical aims are frequently incompatible – since the greatest need most often arises where durable solutions are unlikely to be achievable in the short term. This dilemma is compounded by the loss of humanitarian neutrality experienced in situations where there is no political solution in sight and the presence of international peacekeepers, while often required to provide a secure environment or to protect humanitarian actors, can also jeopardise neutrality if they are drawn into using force (even in self-defence) by the parties to the conflict.

The basic principles and mandated responsibilities of international humanitarian organisations, in many cases underwritten by international humanitarian laws and conventions, have stood the test of time and appear to be fundamentally sound. Improvements in preparedness (given adequate early warning) require an investment in emergency capacities, training, management, and planning capabilities. Experience has shown that funding is considerably more difficult to obtain for preparedness than for ad hoc crisis response. The insecurity which stems both from the majority of staff members being on short-term contracts and from the annual competition for an ever-larger slice of the limited donor funding makes it understandably difficult to extend the horizon of planning and budgetary cycles, or enhance preparedness measures within UN humanitarian organisations.

In this environment, investment in future competence will continue to be constrained.

To draw on the lessons learned in the Rwanda crisis or in other recent or ongoing humanitarian operations, and to identify areas where the effectiveness of international humanitarian responses can be improved through better coordination, is a considerably easier task than to bring about the necessary improvements without increasing administrative overheads or reducing the percentage of the annual budget needed to carry out mandated responsibilities for an ever-increasing global caseload. The responsibility for better coordination lies not only within the community of international humanitarian actors, but also with those charged to coordinate that community. At the end of the day, whoever pays the piper, calls the tune.

Finally, they key lesson from Rwanda (as from former Yugoslavia) must be that preventive political action, and where that fails, action to remove the causes that make humanitarian aid necessary, is likely to be much less expensive, and save more lives, than even the best-coordinated humanitarian operation.

Notes

1. The text of this chapter is not attributable to the Office of the UNHCR and represents only the views of the author.
2. The UN Observer Mission in Uganda and Rwanda (UNOMUR) was created in June 1993 to resolve peacefully the conflict between the Government of Rwanda and the RPF. In October 1993, the UN created a larger mission, the UN Assistance Mission for Rwanda (UNAMIR), into which UNOMUR was integrated.
3. As examples, the 1 January–31 December 1995 UN Consolidated Inter-Agency Appeal for Persons Affected by the Crisis in Rwanda totalled $US229 million, and both the 1993 and 1994 UNHCR annual budgets were approximately $US1.3 billion.
4. UN General Assembly Resolution A/50/60-S/1995/1.
5. SCR 918/94, passed unanimously.
6. Operation Turquoise was mandated by SCR 929 of 22 June 1994, which limited the duration of the operation to two months.
7. Broad Based Government of National Unity.
8. AI report on 'Rwanda, persecution of Tutsi minority and repression of Government critics, 1990–1992'. HRW reports, 'Rwanda, talking peace and waging war: human rights since the October 1980 invasion'; and 'Beyond the rhetoric: continuing human rights abuses in Rwanda'.
9. Estimate taken from the UNAMIR British Contingent's displaced persons list of 14 October 1994.

10. DHA was established in early 1992 as a result of GA Res 46/182 of December 1991, in which UN member states sought improvement in the coordination of humanitarian assistance.

11. The Overview section, Volume 1 of the UN Consolidated Inter-Agency Appeal for Persons Affected by the Crisis in Rwanda, January–December 1995, provides more detail of DHA's coordination role.

12. In her statement to the 3rd Committee of the General Assembly, New York, 9 November 1994.

13. The AI report 'Rwanda, persecution of Tutsi minority and repression of Government critics, 1990–1992' (Afr 47/02/92) alleged over 1000 untried executions, over 8000 'political prisoners', and repeated RPF murders of prisoners and 'traitors'.

14. ICHRDD has participated in the International Commission of Inquiry on Human Rights Violations in Rwanda since 1 October 1990. The Commission visited Rwanda on 7–21 January 1993, hearing extensive testimonies and going to the sites of mass graves. It concluded that the then Government had participated or sanctioned the killing of over 2000 Tutsi as well as Hutu moderates, while the RPF had killed or kidnapped civilians, and looted or destroyed property.

15. The General Assembly has repeatedly called (GA Res 48/42 of 10 December 1993 and 48/57 of 14 December 1993) for closer cooperation and the involvement of the Emergency Relief Coordinator (Executive Head of DHA) in the overall planning of UN responses. This has been carried forward in an ongoing joint DPA/DPKO/DHA project.

16. GA Res 428 (V) in 1950 led to the creation of UNHCR as a subsidiary organ of the General Assembly, which fulfils responsibilities in accordance with the 1951 Convention Relating to the Status of Refugees and its additional Protocol of 1967.

Part III
Intra-Community
Perspectives

5 The Integrated Operations Centre in Rwanda: Coping with Complexity

Randolph Kent

No one was quite sure of the numbers killed on that day in late April 1995. Estimates ranged from 250 to 8000. Nor was anyone ever sure about the incidents that immediately precipitated the massacre although it eventually became the subject of an international inquiry. Most eyewitnesses agree that large numbers of internally-displaced persons (IDPs) in a camp called Kibeho in southwest Rwanda just panicked. Deprived of food, shelter and basic sanitation for almost four days and uncertain about the future that lay before them, a large group of camp occupants tried to break out of the cordon created by the Rwandese Patriotic Army (RPA); and the army, undertrained and on edge, let loose with vollies of automatic weapons and rocket-grenade launchers into the terrified crowds.

The Independent International Commission of Inquiry that reviewed the brutal killings at Kibeho camp less than one month later concluded that 'the reactions of the RPA soldiers to the threat [posed by IDPs attempting to flee the camp] were disproportionate and, therefore, violative [sic] of international law'.[1] The Commission's findings on this point were clear and unequivocal. Nevertheless, after almost half a year of seemingly close collaboration between the government and the humanitarian community to address the complex problem of the internally displaced, one was left wondering how the events at Kibeho had ever happened.

Six months earlier, on 3 November 1994, two flights crossed paths over Nairobi. One was heading towards Rwanda with the newly-appointed United Nations Humanitarian Coordinator, who had been directed to assist with the safe return of IDPs.[2] The second flight was on its way towards Geneva, with a UNAMIR officer on board who had instructions to deliver a confidential plan – Operation Rondaval – to the Secretary-General. Operation Rondaval was indeed sensitive. It concerned a programme for the closure of 20 camps in which an estimated 350 000 IDPs had taken refuge from the chaos and confusion that was post-genocide Rwanda.

The new Government of Rwanda that had taken power in July 1994 was determined to see the IDP camps closed. It saw them as an affront to

Rwanda's sovereignty – 'little Rwandas within Rwanda' – and increasingly was concerned that the concentration of IDPs posed a major security threat. In the words of the Minister of Rehabilitation and Social Integration (MINIREISO), the camps were a potential 'spearhead' of revenge attacks from the fallen government and its forces encamped along the borders of Zaïre. There were of course other reasons why the Government was so insistent that the IDP camps be closed. The camps themselves occupied valuable agricultural land. Moreover, the level of assistance that they were receiving from a well-intentioned humanitarian community was creating grave disparities between local populations and camp dwellers.

Yet, while these were all perceived as legitimate concerns, the Government's hostility to the camps was more profound, more visceral. It stemmed from their link to the genocide. The camps were regarded as one of the products of Operation Turquoise, the French Government's attempt in late June 1994 to stem the continuing progress of the victorious RPA into southwest Rwanda, for reasons purportedly humanitarian. A large portion of those who had taken shelter within Zone Turquoise were seen by the Government and the RPA as perpetrators of the genocide. The longer the camps remained after the French withdrawal in August 1994, the greater the Government perception that a large proportion of IDPs were 'guilty'.

PERCEPTIONS AND CONTENDING MANDATES

The plight of IDPs is perhaps one of the most sensitive problems that the humanitarian community must confront. IDPs more often than not are a symbol of government failure. They all too often reflect a government's inability to control its own population and represent an essential breakdown in the legitimacy of the state. For the humanitarian community, IDPs frequently pit the legitimate aspirations of governments for stability and state sovereignty against the rights of individuals for protection from undue persecution and for survival assistance. In the case of Rwanda, the conflict between state aspirations and individual rights was even more complex.

The humanitarian community felt itself increasingly burdened by the genocide. The standard rules of protection and assistance seemed to lack a certain relevance when faced with a reality that in the course of three months, from April to June 1994, a plan of the previous government, almost incomprehensible in terms of its cruelty, cold-bloodedness and efficiency, had been implemented, resulting in the torture and murder of between 500 000 and 1 000 000 supposedly-ethnic Rwandan Tutsis.[3] The humanitarian situation was further compounded by the fact that after July 1994 the new Government of Rwanda never failed to remind the humanitarian community that in refugee camps along the nation's borders perpetrators of the genocide were being fed and maintained by UN Agencies and NGOs alike.[4]

This 'fact' not only complicated relations between the Government and the humanitarian community, but it also pointed to the different imperatives of each side. On the side of the Government, security and state sovereignty as well as the right to post-genocide justice were all-consuming considerations. From the perspective of the humanitarian community, responsibility and obligations were clearly defined by mandates that required assistance to all in need, whatever the political context.

The position of the peacekeepers, represented by UNAMIR, was also not free from seemingly irreconcilable complications. The Government pointed to UNAMIR as the symbol of international indifference to the genocide. At the outset of the turmoil in April 1994, the Security Council had reduced UNAMIR forces from 1515 to 270.[5] Many Rwandese, in and outside government, firmly believed that had UNAMIR's capacity not been reduced, hundreds of thousands of lives might have been saved. Indeed, these same critics maintained that had the remaining UNAMIR forces been properly deployed, they could have saved significant numbers of people.

These accusations intensified with the new mandate given to UNAMIR on 17 May 1994.[6] UNAMIR's new mandate provided for 6000 formed troops, military observers and civilian police, with a relatively wide-ranging responsibility for protection.[7] Yet, for many in the new Government, the victorious RPA and amongst 'old caseload refugees',[8] the protection responsibilities of UNAMIR were regarded as a cruel irony. 'Who needs UNAMIR protection?' was a frequent refrain, the response to which was 'those who were involved in the genocide'. UNAMIR was therefore tarred by its detractors with the brush of harbouring the guilty. UNAMIR was also regarded by many Rwandese as too affluent, possessing too many vehicles and too much equipment, and with too many privileges in a country seriously damaged by conflict and profoundly poor. Such perceptions also added to tensions between the peacekeepers and those for whom the peace was being kept.

Nor were NGOs immune from the tensions created by the provision of humanitarian assistance to the perceived perpetrators of the genocide. Over 130 NGOs had rushed to assist the many vulnerable groups that arose out of the Rwanda crisis including an estimated 2 million refugees in camps in Tanzania, Zaïre and Burundi. At one stage, others were assisting an estimated 900 000 IDPs within Rwanda. Therefore, in common with UN Agencies and UNAMIR, NGOs had to contend with the opprobrium associated with providing assistance to IDP camps in the former Zone Turquoise. And like UN Agencies, the work of the NGOs in the refugee camps outside Rwanda was regarded by many within the country with a degree of suspicion if not open hostility.

NGOs had an additional problem with which to contend. It was clear that the Government felt very uncomfortable with the number of NGOs that had descended on Rwanda at the end of the conflict. Officials were uncertain about the benefits many NGOs were providing, and were also suspicious about their motives for wishing to assist. The Government seemed to feel that it lacked control; that it was inundated with NGOs whose utility and motives frequently did not seem apparent.[9]

In the final analysis, for the NGOs at large as for UNAMIR and the humanitarian community, there were two issues that profoundly affected their relations with the Government. The first was the genocide; the second was what might be described as contending mandates. As for the former, the genocide, like the slow unfolding of a horrific nightmare, began to be understood – slowly, painfully. This understanding brought with it a host of emotions: a sense of guilt that one was part of an international community that had shied away from this abominable event; a certain unease that a proportion of the IDPs and the refugees whom one was assisting might indeed have been killers; and an inclination to support in any way possible all those who had survived the appalling tragedy.

And yet, with all the inclinations to make common cause with the survivors of the genocide and their Government, even in seeking ways to make amends for deeds that were almost incomprehensible, the reality of contending mandates more often than not set the course of relations between the Government and the humanitarian community. No issue reflected the tension between the two issues – the genocide and contending mandates – more than that of IDPs.

THE INTEGRATED OPERATIONS CENTRE: PURPOSE AND PRACTICE

The plan for Operation Rondaval that the UNAMIR officer was to present to the Secretary-General, through Ambassador Shaharyar Khan, the SRSG for Rwanda, was an attempt to address these tensions. The plan proposed a comprehensive scheme to move what was estimated by then to be the 350 000 remaining IDPs back to their communes of origin.[10] The Rondaval

initiative was important for UNAMIR. It was clear that there were growing tensions between UNAMIR and the RPA. By late September 1994 it
was also becoming increasingly clear that if the Government did not get
some assistance in moving the IDPs in a relatively humane way, the RPA
might very well move them in a less humane fashion. Such action would
be a direct rebuff to UNAMIR's mandated responsibilities to protect civilian populations. By October, it was apparent that time to resolve this
matter was running out.[11]

Operation Rondaval was not UNAMIR's first initiative to assist the
Government in closing the IDP camps, but it was its most comprehensive. Two months before the Rondaval plan, UNAMIR, in conjunction
with UNHCR, had transported some IDPs back to their home areas but
although the intention was good, the numbers involved were relatively
small.[12] A more dramatic initiative was needed. UNAMIR's new operational plan came only partly as a surprise to the humanitarian community.
By August 1994, UNAMIR had become the focal point for assisting the
Government's efforts to return IDPs to their home communes. Initially,
the UN humanitarian Agencies were quite willing to let UNAMIR take
the lead, as they were still regaining their foothold in the country, preoc-
cupied with establishing their own emergency programmes and relatively
wary about entering into this extremely sensitive area. Furthermore, given
the enormous demands for assistance both within and outside the country, the return of IDPs was not seen as a priority. This, however, was to
change as the Government's frustrations about 'little Rwandas in Rwanda'
increased.

Operation Rondaval reflected the Government's growing concern. The
plan had been described as essentially a 'trucking operation', designed to
provide transport for the IDPs back to their communes. And, while there
was reference to the humanitarian needs of IDPs once they returned, the
predominant emphasis was on the physical journey and not on their requirements once home.

Despite the seeming reluctance of the UN Agencies to get involved in
the return of IDPs, it nevertheless reportedly came as a surprise that there
had been no consultations between them and UNAMIR about Operation
Rondaval during its formulation. UNAMIR attributed this lack of consultation in part to the sensitive nature of the issue and the operation; but
there were other reasons as well. One of the reasons might be described
as 'institutional'. The principally military-oriented UNAMIR had its own
standard operating procedures that ran essentially in a self-contained
way; there was a planning office and established chains of command and,
generally speaking, these did not incorporate procedures for external

consultations. There was also the fact that, while cooperation between the
UN Agencies and UNAMIR was ostensibly good, UNAMIR had become
quite accustomed to taking the lead in the international response to Rwanda.
It was a habit that had evolved in the still unstable aftermath of the war,
when the Agencies' need for protection as well as transport and other
forms of support made UNAMIR a relatively dominant actor. It also reflected a certain clash of cultures between the military and the humanitarian communities, where the military seemed a bit bemused by the apparent
lack of a 'chain of command', let alone order, amongst the humanitarian
organisations. The military appeared frustrated that when faced with a job
to do, it had to deal with a large and seemingly amorphous group of UN
Agencies and NGOs whose direction was hard to pin down. UNAMIR had
collaborated with Agencies in a hastily formed IDP task force towards the
end of October, but the work of the task force seemed neither to reflect the
dimensions nor the urgency of the problem.

Thus, by the beginning of November 1994, the issue of IDPs was fraught
with complexity. The Government of Rwanda was more and more determined to see the closure of the IDP camps, and UNAMIR felt commen-
surately obliged to take action. The UN Agencies, along with many NGOs,
were extremely concerned that the Government's determination to see the
camps closed would conflict with fundamental humanitarian principles,
including that of protection. At the same time, they were all too aware of
the Government's own moral stance on the issue as well as the practical
problems caused by the camps. The Government saw the slow response
to its requests for assistance to move the IDPs as further evidence that
UNAMIR and, to a lesser extent, the UN Agencies and NGOs were more
concerned with protecting the perpetrators of the genocide than with assisting the 'victims'. A mechanism was required that would bridge these growing perceptual gulfs and would be able to reconcile the schism between
the objectives of the Government and the mandates of the humanitarian
community. This mechanism would have to be a radical departure from
the normal interaction between both. It would have to encompass physical
and intellectual cooperation if either side were to achieve its objectives.

THE CREATION OF THE IOC

The Integrated Operations Centre (IOC) was in one sense more a concept
and a process than an *ad hoc* institution. In practice, it was all three. By
early January 1995, the physical structure was in place.[13] A vast hall was
sub-divided into communications rooms, offices for seconded officials,

an operations room and a conference room, each filled with appropriate equipment, including computers, maps, telephones and office furniture. Seconded officials from the main operational Agencies were designated, and commitments to participate from the Government's ministries were ostensibly forthcoming.

The purpose of the IOC was to address four critical issues:

- *The political dimension of IDPs.* In one sense, there was safety in numbers. Any agency that would take the 'lead' for responsibly addressing the problems of the IDP camps could well have run the risk of being singled out by the Government for failure, or by the humanitarian community for complicity in violating fundamental humanitarian principles. While the tensions were inherent, it was thought that the best course was for all UN Agencies to commit themselves to a common approach and action.

- *Engaging the Government.* It was essential to bring the Government not only into the planning process, but also into common implementation arrangements. If this were not the case, the likelihood would be that the Government would either act on its own – possibly forcing a significant rift between itself and the humanitarian community – or would leave the issue to the humanitarian community which, in turn, might well leave the UN Agencies exposed to accusations either of connivance with the perpetrators of the genocide or of incompetence.

- *Restoring the balance between peacekeepers and the humanitarian community.* Given the contentious nature of closing the IDP camps, the entire matter might well have been left to UNAMIR. However, on several levels it was increasingly evident that the humanitarian community felt obliged to become engaged in this issue, whatever the potential hazards. The humanitarian community was acutely aware of the relationship between the return of refugees and camp closures, was concerned that the political role of UNAMIR would dictate the methods used to deal with the IDPs and also felt that, with relative peace in the country, the time was right to make it clear that the peacekeepers were in place to support the work of the humanitarian organisations.

- *Dealing with the practical dimensions of the IDP problem.* In a world grown all too used to providing humanitarian assistance to millions of people in any single emergency operation, dealing with the estimated 350 000 IDPs might seem a relatively simple exercise. In fact, while the numbers were relatively large, the complexity of the operation necessitated as fully integrated an approach as possible. The operation not only involved humanitarian assistance to the IDPs in camps but

also preparations in the communes that were to receive them and publicity campaigns that would induce the IDPs to return to their homes.
This sort of effort required the combined resources of all major actors
to provide essential information and resources.

In mid-November 1994, with these four objectives in mind, it was agreed
that an IOC would be established in the MINIREISO.[14] The objectives of
the IOC were to serve as a mechanism for planning IDP return, information and data collection and dissemination and materiel resource exchange.
The key issue was the composition of the IOC membership and, at a meeting in November, MINIREISO agreed that it should consist of all UN
operational Agencies, two representatives of the NGO community, representatives of two major donors (i.e., the USA and the European Union) and
representatives of his own Ministry and the Ministries of Plans, Interior,
Justice and Defence.

THE IOC IN PRACTICE

A sense of joint ownership of the IOC was essential. Yet, the logic of the
IOC structure and its potential as a mechanism to deal with IDPs had to
contend from the very outset with a sense of the unknown and conflicting
interests. There was considerable uncertainty about the degree to which the
humanitarian community should be tied to the institutions of the Rwandan
Government. There was concern that proximity would trap the Agencies
or at least hamper their freedom of action and flexibility. At the same
time, the initiative was new; the idea of an integrated process in which
all participants would be committed to lend personnel, share information
and resources was a venture rarely tried. That, too, was disconcerting for
some. However, the ultimate test of the concept was the sense of ownership that participants brought to the effort. Individual ministries, other than
MINIREISO, maintained even into the beginning of 1995 that they were
not certain about the IOC's function. In part, this was due to the poor
communication structure within the fledgling Government itself. More
significantly, the attitude of some ministries, such as the Ministry of the
Interior, reflected specific concerns about the seeming expansionist role of
MINIREISO.[15]

There was also the all-important factor of the Government's limited
capacity during this period. It was generally recognised that the civil service structure was extremely weak and that virtually all ministries and departments lacked even the most basic requirements to fulfil their functions.

And, while this was recognised, there were still expectations that the various officials would be able to attend the endless number of meetings that were set up not only within Government but with the many international organ-isations in-country, and still make themselves available to the IOC. Yet in the final analysis the Government's attitude towards the IOC concept was determined less by capacity and inter-ministerial turf battles than by divisions within the Government about how best to close the IDP camps. There was little doubt amongst Government officials about the need to close the camps, but considerable division over the methods to be employed. The subject of methods reflected a far-reaching division between those who might be regarded as moderates and those more extreme.[16]

The moderates recognised the legitimate fears of many IDPs that return to their home communes would spell arbitrary revenge and harassment. There was no system of justice through which accusers and accused could give vent to their positions.[17] There would also be questions over land rights, since old caseload refugees and, in some instances, the military had taken over the houses of those who had fled.[18] For the moderates, the solution to the IDP issue was linked to a process of confidence-building and commune rehabilitation. The former would require extensive 'informa-tion campaigns'; the latter a semblance of basic assistance for those who returned to their communes. On the other hand, there were those who took a more extreme position. The IDPs who were not guilty of the geno-cide should have no fear of returning to their homes. Almost by defini-tion, those who did not return were guilty. Nor did those in the camps require the extensive assistance that the humanitarian community was pro-posing, particularly transport – the IDPs came on foot, and could return on foot. The humanitarian community, according to those of this persuasion, did not understand the make-up of the Rwandese; for the Rwandese were compliant peoples, and once ordered to abandon their camps would readily do so.

Only on one level did the two views meet. During late 1994, both mod-erates and extremists were willing to play the game of the humanitarian community. Neither were willing to risk alienating the international com-munity since the Government and the nation desperately needed the full weight of outside assistance to restore the country. The brief accommoda-tion between both positions rested upon the urgent hope that substantial rehabilitation and development assistance would be forthcoming. In this sense, only the time necessary to close the camps separated the two.[19]

The Government, principally the Vice President and the Minister of Defence,[20] initially set 30 November and subsequently 31 December 1994 as the deadline for camp closure. However, the SRSG was able to persuade the Vice President that ill-prepared action might lead to a human rights catastrophe that would rebound upon the international support that was increasingly accruing to the Government. In his discussions with the Government, the SRSG gave full assurances that the humanitarian community could assist the Government to close the camps in a way that would avoid recriminations. He stressed that the resources of the humanitarian community would be at the disposal of the Government to support a safe, humane and expeditious closure of the camps – and, indeed, that was the intention. The Government backed away from rigid deadlines and, while never agreeing to an alternative time frame, seemed willing to test the commitment of the SRSG and the humanitarian community. Throughout November and December, the planning phase of what was to be called Operation Retour was underway, and by 29 December 1994, the UN Agencies, UNAMIR, participating NGOs and Government representatives had completed the planning for Operation Retour.

There were four essential components to the plan. The first was an information campaign to inform the camp populations about the conditions in the home communes and the procedures that would provide those returning safe passage. Linked to the first was a system of escorts for the returnees – a combination of UNAMIR and RPA forces that would guarantee the safety of the returnees from the camps to the communes. Thirdly was the creation of 'open relief centres' (ORCs). The ORCs were to be way-stations that would provide assistance on the outskirts of the home communes to those returnees who wanted to 'test the waters' before making the final decision to return. Finally, there was a programme to provide assistance to the home communes to support vulnerable groups as well as the returning IDPs.

OPERATION RETOUR UNDERWAY

The initial stages of Operation Retour were successful for reasons due as much to good fortune as to good planning. This major exercise in restoring normality to Rwanda was fraught with hazards. In early December 1994, the UN Agencies made it very clear that they would have to withdraw their cooperation if the Government decided that essential services (e.g., provision of water) were to be withdrawn from the camps. On the other hand, it was abundantly clear that the RPA in the field were becoming increasingly frustrated that the IDPs were showing no signs of wishing to move, and were making it abundantly clear to UN Agencies and NGOs alike that only by withdrawing essential services would the IDPs leave the camp. Added to these tensions was the all too evident fact that the expertise and resources required to initiate the information campaign in the camps were not available. Nor for that matter had there been any significant steps taken to prepare the home communes for the return of the IDPs. On the other hand, with substantial support from NGOs, the ORCs were rapidly established and the RPA showed increased willingness to assist UNAMIR in the convoy procedures. In addition, the imminent planting season led large numbers of IDPs to consider the losses that would result in delaying their return home.

By early January 1995, Operation Retour was underway.[21] Between the first week of January and the middle of February, an estimated 82 000 IDPs had left the remaining camps in the southwest. Of this total, 40 000 had been moved to their communes by a combination of UNHCR, IOM and UNAMIR vehicles and an additional 26 000 had gone home without any formal assistance. Approximately 16 000 had either gone to other camps not initially targeted for closure or across the border to refugee camps in Zaïre.

By February 1995 there was considerable optimism that the entire operation to move 350 000 IDPs would be completed by the end of May. However, two weeks into February, optimism began to wane. A growing number of reports were coming in from the home communes about harassment of not only returnees but also of many now suspected of participation in the genocide. Without any formal system of justice, and with very weak communal government structures, insecurity in the communes was reversing the returnee flow. It seemed that many who had recently returned from the camps were now trekking back. Even worse were clear indications that more and more people who had never been IDPs were swelling the camp numbers. As it happened, this reverse trend did not result in substantial numbers of former IDPs and others going back to the camps. However, the fear created in those who might have been considering returning to their home communes was considerable. By the third week of February, Operation Retour had come to a virtual standstill. The fear about the dangers of returning to the communes intensified, and the arguments of the IDPs against leaving became hysterical in many instances. Operation Retour – or at least the initial stage – was *de facto* over.

OPERATION RETOUR REVISITED

Whatever the successes and failures of Operation Retour during mid-February, it was clear that a new approach would be needed to close the camps. However, with the growing resistance of the IDPs and with the commensurate frustration on the part of the Government, a renewed phase of IDP return had an additional level of hazard. From the Government's perspective, whatever the reasons for the slowdown of IDP returns, the fact of the matter was that the humanitarian community had had its chance to demonstrate its approach to camp closures. And, while some in Government acknowledged the reason for Operation Retour's loss of momentum, there were still nine camps remaining, containing approximately 250 000 IDPs.

Once again, the humanitarian organisations found themselves confronted with the Government's hardening attitudes towards camp closure, and once again they were forced to determine how far they could reconcile the Government's wishes with the limitations imposed by their respective humanitarian mandates. Yet, in so saying, it was increasingly clear that they were, like the Government, becoming more and more frustrated with the IDP issue. At the beginning of 1995, it had seemed that the IDP issue was being resolved and that the aid agencies would be able to move on towards the much needed tasks of recovery and rehabilitation. Now that this was no longer the case, it was difficult to resummon the enthusiasm for an issue that all had hoped would disappear.

Far more significant was the fact that a new initiative would require much firmer action. The relatively gentle persuasion of the previous two months had only worked in part, and any new approach would most likely require measures that might confront the aid organisations with the prospect of forced camp closures.

From implementing Operation Retour, the IOC found itself back to devising new plans at the beginning of March 1995. However, this time the Agencies and NGOs were wary about how much further they might be asked to go. It was clear that the Government's patience was running out, and that the camp populations would no longer respond merely to information campaigns. Hence, the month of March was devoted to an even more intense struggle to reconcile the mandates of the humanitarian community with the imperatives of Government,

'Forced closure' can be a matter of perceptions. The term was never used, but it was clear that the camps had to be closed quickly. The strategy that finally emerged from the IOC on 5 April 1995 was based on a combination of the new and the old. There would be intensified information campaigns and another effort to reinvigorate rehabilitation in the home communes; there would be convoy protection for the returning IDPs and assistance packages for IDPs leaving the camps. However, there were now three new elements that changed the dynamics of the original conception of Operation Retour.

Camp populations were to be separated into their home communes and, based upon an agreed sequence, each of these commune-targeted groups would be informed that they would receive three weeks of food rations and then they would only receive food assistance in their home areas. Services would not be cut off, but rather shifted to the communes. To that extent, it was clear that the aid agencies had accepted that the camps would be closed, and that the IDPs had no choice but to move. The sequence of camp closure was to be announced to all nine camps. While the revitalised information campaign would in no way seek to deceive the IDPs about the varying conditions in their home communes, it would at the same time not propose any alternative but leaving. The final and critical element to the new approach was an implicit concession to the Government – namely, that those who did not leave according to the proposed timetable were to be assumed to have something to hide; that is, that they were quite possibly implicated in the genocide. Therefore, the IDPs who did not leave the camps would find themselves in closed camps, subject to investigation by Rwandese officials. In addition to these measures, UNAMIR agreed to provide additional observers in the home communes to work with the RPA to provide security. In reality, the capacity of UNAMIR and the topography of the home commune areas made any effective security undertakings of relatively limited value.

The new operational strategy took approximately one month to complete. This time was the price that had to be paid to get full consensus for the proposal, and yet the lengthy efforts at consensus-building were done with a growing awareness that time for a 'safe, humane and expeditious' return home of the IDPs was running out. The RPA, which was represented at a very low level within the IOC and even then only sporadically, was becoming ever more restless, reflected in a variety of rumours coming from the southwest. In Butare, the local RPA commander indicated on 8 April that camp closures would begin on 16 April 1995. A few miles away, the Préfet of Gikongoro was reported to have agreed on 16 April that 24 April would be the date that the camp closure operation was to begin. Uncertainty was everywhere. Rumours abounded; did they reflect a different 'strategy', one devised by the RPA alone?[22]

When MINIREISO was queried about these rumours, he maintained that he had no knowledge of such a decision. Similarly, the Minister of the Interior asserted that he certainly would know if such a decision had been made, and he had heard nothing. According to the former, his only wish was that on 18 April he, and the UN Humanitarian Coordinator and the heads of UN Agencies, would go to Butare to launch the new strategy's information and commune rehabilitation campaigns. This was consistent with the agreed plan, and would cohere with the understanding of the humanitarian community.

KIBEHO

In the early morning of 18 April 1995, two RPA battalions surrounded a camp called Kibeho, Kibeho held an estimated IDP population of 100 000, and was regarded by the RPA as a 'hard-core' camp containing a large number of Interahamwe, former RGF soldiers and other perpetrators of the genocide. As a military operation, it was reported that the RPA had been efficient in its initial manoeuvres. With the knowledge of very few, it had cordoned off the area sufficiently tightly so that no IDP could escape without going through RPA checkpoints.[23] Tens of thousands of people who had been spread over five sweeping hills were now compressed on one hill – men, women and children bunched together as if in a rush-hour subway.

Whatever military laurels the RPA might have gained for its initial operation, Kibeho was a humanitarian disaster. Seemingly, no attention had been paid to essential logistical support to take people from the camp to home communes. Clearly, no provision had been made to provide even a minimum of survival assistance to the thousands now trapped on the hillside. In the midst of the rainy season, there was no shelter; nor was any consideration given to basic sanitation requirements.

Agencies, both UN and NGO, were not allowed to provide any assistance for the first three days, although the camp's water system was not cut off.[24] It was all too apparent that the dire conditions in the camp were increasing tensions amongst the IDP population and that these tensions, in turn, were raising the temperature amongst the young soldiers of the RPA. The volatile admix finally exploded on 22 April. Hundreds of IDPs tried to break out of the tight cordon and the RPA responded with automatic weapons and rocket-propelled grenade-launchers. Estimates of the dead ranged from 250 to 8000. Whatever the actual number, there was no question that the moral high ground of a Government that prided itself in having stopped a genocide nine months earlier had been severely eroded.

The UN Agencies and NGOs were faced with a tremendous dilemma. Despite the Government's insistence that it was only following the strategy as agreed on 5 April, no Agency or NGO had ever agreed to the precipitous and unilateral action undertaken by the RPA.[25] The RPA's initiative was totally unexpected, and for many it was a betrayal, a profound and fundamental sign of bad faith. To what extent should the humanitarian community now respond to a humanitarian crisis provoked by the disingenuousness of the RPA? Would a response by the Agencies and NGOs be seen as sanctioning an action that was contrary not only to an agreed strategy, but also contrary to the very humanitarian mandates that they were responsible to uphold? And yet, the fact of the matter was that tens of thousands of people initially trapped in the camp and now forced out were in need of massive humanitarian assistance.

The suffering that Kibeho and other camp closures generated allowed the humanitarian community little choice. Within 24 hours, the main logistics organisations (UNHCR and IOM) had moved their fleets of vehicles to the operational centre of Butare and, along with UNAMIR, began transporting the IDPs that crowded the rough roads from the camps to their home areas or to half-way stations. Food distribution and nutritional feeding were effectively handled through the efforts of WFP, the ICRC, UNHCR, UNICEF and a variety of NGOs. Along with UNICEF and several highly efficient NGOs, medical attention and basic shelter and household goods were provided. Operationally, the emergency response of the humanitarian community was extremely impressive. Coordination mechanisms were in place and functioning; resources, material and transport, were shared amongst implementing partners and, from the very outset, information about the operation flowed to the outside world, as well as within Rwanda. But despite the operational success of the humanitarian response, the integrated humanitarian approach and its mechanisms – the IOC and the Integrated Task Force – had failed in one fundamental sense to cope with the complexity of the IDP issue.

As envisaged when the IOC was formed, a uniquely strong bond between the UN peacekeepers and the humanitarian community had certainly been achieved. The peacekeepers provided considerable support to the humanitarian community's efforts through their involvement in the IOC and by the operational assistance given in the wake of the Kibeho incident. The balance between the peacekeepers and the humanitarian community had been restored.

When the unanticipated events of Kibeho occurred, the machinery of the IOC moved quickly into action. Coordination between the centre in Kigali and the operational focal point in Butare led not only to effective sharing of information, but also to the timely and efficient sharing of resources. But the IOC had failed in two very fundamental ways. Despite the protestations of the Government, the reality was that the IOC mechanism had been unable to engage the Government effectively. In part, the lack of full Government commitment might have been due to its own internal weaknesses or to the inter-ministerial rivalries that were becoming evident by the end of 1994. Second, it might have been the result of the Government's own sense of inadequacy when faced with the disproportionate strength of its international counterparts within the IOC, or partly because of the Government's resentment at being pressured into dealing with IDPs in ways that were contrary to the faster approach it most likely would have preferred. In any event, the Government was a marginal actor, on board but never fully committed, allowing the humanitarian community to assume responsibility for an 'integrated' approach that in reality never existed.

The IOC concept failed for another reason as well: the mandates of the humanitarian agencies were never reconciled with the Government's strategic and political interests in moving the IDPs quickly. Many in Government never really believed that the IDPs would move 'voluntarily' from the camps; the instruments of protection and relief services that were so essential to the obligations of the humanitarian community were regarded as an irrelevant luxury to those in Government who regarded the IDPs as an army-in-waiting and an affront to sovereignty. The Government was willing to play the international game until more important interests demanded more drastic solutions.[26] The camp in Kibeho was the result of these irreconcilable tensions.

COPING WITH COMPLEXITY

There are many lessons that can be drawn from the experiences that led to the creation of the IOC and its subsequent operations. It is clear that the initiative took too long to set in motion, and that the full commitment of all the central players – Government as well as humanitarian – remained too weak for the IOC really to fulfil all its potential. Here, the lessons are both conceptual and institutional. Conceptually, it became all too evident that much greater clarity was required about the rules under which joint collaboration should take place. The oral agreement that was received from the Government for the principle of 'safe, humane and expeditious return' was neither sufficiently explicit nor clear enough to warrant any sense of guarantee. Even if these rules were eventually to be violated, their very existence would have at least established an important basis for a parting of the ways. Institutionally, the capacity to garner the commitment and resources to implement the IOC initiative was to some extent lacking. The UN system certainly did not have what has subsequently been described as effective 'command and control' that would have enabled senior officials to bring the IOC into action quickly and efficiently. Persuasion was ultimately the only effective, albeit slow, means of coordination.[27]

The situation was further complicated by a lack of clear institutional roles. The UN's operation in Rwanda was guided by an SRSG who took a determined and active interest in humanitarian affairs. The SRSG's deputy was the UNAMIR Force Commander, who by his mandate also had substantive responsibilities for humanitarian affairs. At the same time, there existed a UN Humanitarian Coordinator who, although not part of UNAMIR, was ultimately responsible to the SRSG, but accrued no institutional benefits from the SRSG's structure. Neither the SRSG nor the Humanitarian Coordinator had resources available to undertake humanitarian initiatives and while UNAMIR had resources to place at the disposal of activities such as the IOC, the Force Commander always had to weigh these requests against contending requests for his own immediate peacekeeping objectives.

In similar situations in the future, there must be greater institutional clarity. The fact that the IOC initiative worked in so many instances was due to the good fortune of having cooperative colleagues. The requirements of effective coordination cannot always depend upon such vagaries. Clear lines of authority, agreed to by all partners, are essential, and resources to support coordination efforts must be available.

In addition to these familiar lessons learned, there are others. Perhaps the most fundamental problem that had to be faced in addressing the issue of IDPs in Rwanda was the inherent tension between the mandates of humanitarian agencies and the objectives of the Government. The Government made some gesture towards resolving this tension by extending the time limit for the closure of the camps at least three times. The humanitarian organisations in turn tried to bridge the gulf by seeking in every way permissible within their respective mandates to comply with the Government's objectives. However, the gulf was too great. This gulf reflects the dilemma posed by a certain lack of political will on the part of the international community. Fundamental political issues were thrown in the lap of humanitarian organisations that did not have the power, authority or mandate to resolve them. UN Agencies and their NGO counterparts are increasingly asked to assume political tasks that demand the concerted and coherent influence of interested UN member states. In the future, the international community must either make a greater effort to support the mandated responsibilities of the humanitarian community or must clearly accept the limits of humanitarianism. Humanitarianism, though, cannot be an alternative to political pressure and persuasion.

Linked to the necessity of greater political support for humanitarian objectives is the need for more sensitive and speedier support for the 'victims' of nation states traumatised by events such as genocide. There might have been a greater chance to reconcile the positions of both sides had the Government been more convinced that the international community was indeed responsive to its needs. This in turn would have required the international community, principally the donor community, to appreciate more fully the practical consequences of the genocide.

The victims of the 1994 Rwandan tragedy were the society and its capacity to govern. The type of assistance that was required did not fit into the conventional categories of either relief or development. The situation in Rwanda demanded greater risks and greater imagination than the international community felt willing to give. Resources to stabilise the military, to recreate the police force, to build prisons and to rebuild the justice system were essential but few donors were initially willing to accept the domestic political consequences of such assistance. And when some did, the procedures for providing such assistance were all too slow and cumbersome.

The Government's frustration and disillusion with the slow and often irrelevant response of donors became increasingly evident, and spilled over into its dealings with the humanitarian community. It was difficult to engage a government that felt more and more that words rather than action were the net result of efforts at accommodation. Here, the lesson must be that in future we will have to develop a greater understanding about the impact upon societies of events similar to those suffered by Rwanda. Concern must be reflected in the practical measures taken by donors to address the unusual needs of the victims.

In the final analysis, the events that took place in Kibeho might not have been inevitable. In so many respects, the humanitarian response stemming from the IOC worked. And yet, the inability to fully engage the Government and at the same time to bridge the gulf between the obligations of the humanitarian community and the imperatives of Government must in part explain the untold numbers of deaths that took place on that day in late April 1995.

Notes

1. *Report of the Independent International Commission of Inquiry on the Events at Kibeho, April 1995*, p. 10. The Commission was formed at the official request of the President of the Rwandese Republic, Mr Pasteur Bizimungo, in a speech of 27 April 1995, five days after the Kibeho massacre. The Commission was officially established on 27 April and completed its report

on 18 May 1995. The Commission consisted of 10 members, representing France, Canada, Belgium, Germany, the United Kingdom, the United States, the Netherlands, Rwanda, the Organisation for African Unity and the UN.

2. While the responsibilities of the UN Humanitarian Coordinator extended beyond the internally displaced, the importance of addressing the problem of IDPs was paramount, as evidenced in the briefings received by agencies prior to the Coordinator's assignment. Not only was the resolution of the IDP issue a vital element in bringing a sense of normality back to Rwanda, but it was also closely tied to solutions for bringing an estimated 2 million refugees back in to the country.

3. While the number of people killed in the genocide is still uncertain, it is clear that moderate Hutus also numbered amongst the victims of the regime of President Juvenal Habyarimana. The death of President Habyarimana along with the president of Burundi in a plane crash on 6 April 1994 led almost immediately to widespread killings for both ethnic and political reasons which in turn led in a matter of two weeks to deaths in the tens of thousands.

4. The number of refugees who fled Rwanda during this period was approximately 2 million, representing a cross-section of the society as a whole, including senior civil servants and former government officials, farmers, businessmen, engineers, medical practitioners as well as an estimated 10 000 troops of the former regime. Prior to the genocide, Rwanda's population was 7 526 000.

5. The authorised military strength of UNAMIR was 2548 military personnel, including 2217 formed troops and 331 military observers. As of 31 March 1994, UNAMIR had 2539 military personnel. With the withdrawal of the Belgian battalion in early April after the murder of 10 Belgian soldiers, the force level was reduced, and by 20 April UNAMIR strength stood at 1515, with only 190 military observers. The Secretary-General reported to the Security Council that UNAMIR personnel 'cannot be left at risk indefinitely when there is no possibility of their performing the tasks for which they were dispatched'. On 21 April 1994, SCR 912/94 reduced UNAMIR numbers to 270.

6. On 13 May 1994, the Secretary-General reported to the Security Council that UNAMIR had been reduced to 444 personnel in Rwanda, with 179 military observers in Nairobi pending repatriation or redeployment. He stated that the situation in Rwanda remained 'highly unstable and insecure, with widespread violence'. Four days later, the Security Council demanded that all parties to the conflict immediately cease hostilities and agree to a ceasefire. It expanded UNAMIR's mandate to enable it to contribute to the security and protection of refugees and civilians at risk. In so doing, it authorised UNAMIR's expansion to 5500 troops, plus military observers and civilian police (SCR 918/94).

7. UNAMIR would, *inter alia*, support and provide safe conditions for displaced persons and other groups in Rwanda and help with the provision of assistance by humanitarian organisations. It would work on behalf of displaced persons in the interior of the country as well as on the border. It would also monitor border crossing points, and could be required to take action in self-defence against those who threatened protected sites and populations and the means of delivery and distribution of humanitarian relief.

8.   The 'old case load refugees' represented an estimated 600 000 Tutsi refugees who had fled the country principally for Uganda from 1959 onwards. They were a significant political force given that many in the RPF originated from this refugee population and they provided significant financial and material support to the RPF/RPA. The complications in resettling this population in Rwanda, after almost 30 years, has proven to be one of the greatest tests of the new regime, involving fundamental principles of land rights and the like.

9.   The Government's attitude has to be seen in the context of earlier experiences that the RPF had had in its efforts to overturn the former Government between 1990 and 1994. In allowing NGOs to work in areas which they had overrun, the RPF took a very *dirigiste* approach to NGOs. One NGO official remarked that the RPF/RPA not only told NGOs what to do and where to do it, but also 'gave us periodic report cards on our activities'.

Upon assuming power, the new Government appeared equally determined to continue to maintain control over the NGOs. There was inevitably tension between many of the traditionally independent-minded NGOs and Government authorities. This tension was exacerbated by three factors. The first was the sheer number of NGOs seeking to work in Rwanda. With limited institutional capacity, the Government found it difficult to imitate the approach of the RPF/RPA during the civil war.

Adding to the problems faced by the Government in their dealings with NGOs was an additional problem, namely, that within the Government there was considerable uncertainty about which Ministry had responsibility for NGOs. During November 1994, a rather heated debate ensued between the Ministry of Foreign Affairs and MINIREISO about the focal point for NGO registration. There was also some difficulty between sectoral ministries and MINIREISO about NGO registration. Such 'territorial disputes' are by no means uncommon, but in this instance posed an additional burden for all.

10.   The number of IDPs in Rwanda presented a most difficult definitional problem. Many people had fled the terror between April and July 1994 to the homes of relatives or friends, and remained in such temporary accommodation for many more months. Were they to be counted as IDPs? Operationally speaking, however, one was more immediately concerned with those IDPs in formal camps and, here, numbers were also difficult to determine. Food distribution figures would suggest that towards the beginning of November 1994, there were an estimated 350 000 people. Using health and medical figures, there was a clear case for suggesting that the numbers were approximately 20 per cent less, or 280 000. Complicating the issue even further was the fact that during the day, many IDPs left the camps for surrounding villages and towns or went off to other camps. By mid-April 1995, figures for the nine remaining camps in the southwest ranged from a maximum of 250 000 to 180 000, with greater evidence that the latter figure was correct. The Government always maintained that the camps held far fewer people than many in the international community assumed.

11.   The Government had issued a deadline in late October 1994 that all camps would have to be closed by 30 November. This deadline was extended in late November to 31 December 1994.

12. An estimated 20 000 people had been moved under this programme, many of whom were Tutsis.

13. The IOC initially held its meetings in the Amohora Stadium, near UNAMIR headquarters. This temporary accommodation was used until the facilities in MINIREISO were completed, which they were on 11 January 1995.

14. Even the location of the proposed IOC was a source of considerable debate. UNAMIR was concerned that the location of the IOC in an exposed and unprotected ministry would present a security risk. Some agencies believed that to place the IOC in a Government ministry would mean that the neutrality required by humanitarian organisations would be compromised. Others insisted that the only way to empower the Government as well as to engage it in this common effort was to bring the IOC into the centre of the Government's focal point for IDPs, MINIREISO.

15. As in most emergencies, the international community in Rwanda tended to flock towards the Government's emergency focal point, MINIREISO. There was a perception that MINIREISO was acquiring resources at the expense of normal line ministries, such as the Ministry of the Interior. This was particularly galling for some, since MINIREISO was not regarded within Government as a normal line ministry, but rather a temporary ministry that had been established to fulfil a specific and time-bound function.

16. The use of terms such as 'moderates' and 'extremists' in the context of post-genocide Rwanda tends in all too many instances towards gross over-simplification. The use of such terms in the context of this chapter is limited to attitudes on ways to close down the IDP camps.

17. The 'justice issue' was one of the most fundamental concerns that faced the Government. Not only had the physical structures of courts, records, legal texts and office equipment been substantially destroyed, but also many of those who were trained to uphold justice had fled as refugees to neighbouring countries. The process of re-establishing the justice system had been in train for many months after the new Government's assumption of power; however, a combination of bureaucratic procedures on the part of international donors, a sense of uncertainty about where one should start both on the part of Government and the international community, as well as the sheer enormity of reconstructing a justice system led to inaction and long delays.

18. The Government had established a Commission on Land Rights. However, the sheer complexity of the issue made progress extremely slow, and would require years rather than months to resolve.

19. During this same period as pressures were increasing to address the IDP issue, the Government, supported by UNDP, began to make preparations for a Round Table for international assistance to Rwanda. The Round Table, initially scheduled for November 1994, was eventually held in Geneva in January 1995. Though there was a strong body of opinion within as well as outside Government that felt that the Government was not prepared at this early stage for a major resource mobilisation effort, the urgent need for immediate and large-scale international assistance propelled the Round Table process.

20. Vice President and Minister of Defence, General Paul Kagame, was regarded as a national hero not only for directing the campaign that brought the new

National Government to power in July 1994, but also because he was seen as the leader who had brought a halt to the genocide.

21. On 3 January 1995, a squad of RPA soldiers attacked a small IDP camp known as Busanza near the Burundi border killing 12 people. The reason for the attack was never made clear. Some reports indicated that it was in revenge for grenades being thrown at RPA patrols; others maintained that the RPA attacked because the camp population had not heeded the RPA's earlier demand that the camp should be closed within one week. It seemed apparent that the attack was not sanctioned by RPA headquarters in Kigali, and the officer in charge of the squad was reported to have been arrested soon after the incident. Nevertheless, the psychological impact of the attack was felt in IDP camps throughout the southwest, and delayed the implementation of Operation Retour by at least one week.

22. On 13 April 1995, a small satellite camp, Kivu Gizza, was shut down by the RPA. The official explanation for the closure of this satellite was that Kivu Gizza was merely an offshoot of a camp that had already been peacefully closed, and that the Government/RPA was merely ensuring that this site would not become an IDP camp once again. The Government's explanation made sense in the context of the original Operation Retour and, hence, did not seem to diverge from previous agreements, nor the 5 April strategy.

23. While no one in the international community purportedly knew about this operation prior to 18 April 1995, it was clear that many within the Kibeho camp had received prior warning. A large though unknown number of IDPs had fled the camp as early as 16 April, many of whom reportedly crossed the borders into Zaïre and Burundi. Some observers suggest that by 18 April Kibeho camp contained fewer than 80 000 people, and that would in turn suggest either that the original estimate had been wrong or that almost 20 000 people had left the camp in the few days before 18 April. In all likelihood, it was probably a combination of both factors.

24. Discussions at the highest levels in Rwanda took place between the UN and the Government by 19 April 1995 about the urgent need to provide at least minimum assistance to the camps. The Vice President and Minister of Defence reportedly concurred completely; and yet despite this concurrence, General Kagame's instructions for assistance to the IDPs were not implemented for a further two days. One of the practical difficulties during this period was that of finding someone in authority in the camps themselves. A great deal of time was spent by UN officials and NGOs in tracking down a sufficiently high-ranking RPA official who was willing to implement decisions made in Kigali.

25. The RPA maintained that the details of the military operation had to be kept secret through 18 April 1995, while maintaining at the same time that it was only following the broad intentions and timing of the 5 April strategy. At a hastily assembled press conference on 18 April, MINIREISO insisted that the international community was aware of the camp closure strategy, and that it had been working with the Government closely. The Minister went on to say that 'there is a schedule of camp closure as outlined under the strategy for the closure of the camps. However, this schedule need not be followed rigidly. Camps will be closed as soon as they are ready for closure'.

26. From February through July 1995, the Government continued to complain about the slow rate of international assistance that it was receiving. It had made a significant effort to prepare for the Round Table that was launched in Geneva in January 1995; and, though US$537 million had been pledged at the Round Table, the Government maintained that little of that assistance had been received. Many members of the Government took the position that the Government won the war and stopped the genocide without international help, that the normalisation process that Rwanda had witnessed since July 1994 was done without any significant international involvement and that it would now continue to rebuild the nation on the assumption that it would have to do so on its own. Hence, the Government became less inclined 'to play the game' as it had done in late 1994 and early 1995.

27. *The Report of the Independent International Commission of Inquiry on the Events at Kibeho* called upon the UN system to review its chain of command and its operational procedures to make sure 'that in the future an entire operation is not held hostage or bogged down by one or several agencies and organisations with limited mandates and responsibilities' (p. 14). While the Commission might be correct to suggest that the UN review its chain of command and its operational procedures, there is no evidence to suggest that 'an entire operation' was held hostage or bogged down by one or several agencies. To the contrary, one of the most impressive aspects of the response to Kibeho was the way that agencies responded so coherently to a humanitarian emergency that took them to the very edge of their mandated authority.

6 NATO and its New Role
David Lightburn

NATO's emergence as an important contributor to international peace-keeping and humanitarian operations is still a relatively new phenomenon. Expectations have been generated that NATO's political and military strengths, developed over 40 years to ensure the security and to protect the territorial integrity of its members, can now be applied in close coopera-tion with its partners, other organisations and institutions, and other UN member states in promoting and supporting international peace, order and stability, especially in the European area of interest.

Peacekeeping and humanitarian assistance are not specifically addressed in the Alliance's Strategic Concept but the emphasis on crisis manage-ment, the recognition that unforeseeable, diverse and multi-faceted risks will emerge, and the opportunity to improve stability in Europe with the end of the Cold War, all suggest that Alliance support for international peacekeeping and humanitarian objectives and efforts is fundamental to Europe's security. Also, and particularly at this juncture, the Alliance has a specific role to play given the complexity of some security and humanit-arian situations which demand a more organised, multifunctional and effect-ive response from the international community.

NATO first agreed to contribute to international peacekeeping in 1992. During that year NATO foreign ministers agreed to support, on a case-by-case basis in accordance with existing procedures, peacekeeping and other operations either under the authority of the Security Council or the respons-ibility of the OSCE – including the provision of Alliance resources and expertise. NATO operations in support of UN objectives in the former Yugoslavia began in mid-1992; but the Alliance has made it clear that, although peacekeeping operations are an important new task, the primary objective of NATO remains the security of its member states. There is also a clearly accepted policy that the Alliance is not seeking a role as a world policeman. A further fundamental tenet is that the Alliance will not act on its own responsibility. Rather, NATO's collective security interest is restricted to the OSCE area, and realistically even narrower, and it will only act in support of UN or OSCE mandates. In supporting such man-dates, the Alliance has also made it clear that even when committed it will not act alone; it seeks no monopoly and is ready and willing to act in cooperation with other UN member states. Any unilateral action by the

Alliance could only realistically be contemplated in light of threats to the territorial integrity of member states, and are therefore outside the commonly accepted understanding of peacekeeping operations.

THE ALLIANCE'S CAPABILITIES IN SUPPORT OF PEACE AND HUMANITARIAN OPERATIONS

The Alliance can contribute to international peace and humanitarian operations in several ways. First and foremost, the 16 Allies can bring proven structures, procedures, capabilities and experience to bear in complex security and humanitarian situations in a timely fashion. As a functioning multinational security organisation, NATO has developed common procedures, effective command and control systems, effective logistics systems and capabilities, substantial transportation means, extensive modern infrastructure and well-trained, modern and inter-operable military forces. In addition, many of these forces have extensive experience in both peace-keeping operations and humanitarian assistance and intervention. In addition to military forces, the Alliance has the structure and expertise to coordinate humanitarian relief operations.

Second, NATO has a number of strategic resources and unique capabilities. Some of the more obvious include the NATO AEW aircraft, extensive European supporting infrastructure, standing naval forces, and self-contained, rapidly deployable air assets. These resources can provide the UN with a range of supporting capabilities for humanitarian or peace-keeping operations. They also have a deterrent capability in certain more difficult circumstances.

Third, NATO and its member nations can provide a range of military forces on a scale and degree of readiness not available elsewhere. The Alliance can support large and complex military operations (including humanitarian emergency assistance or intervention) which exceed the UN's capacity. For example, the core of any implementation force to support either a peace plan or a contested UN withdrawal from the former Yugoslavia could well be a NATO force; indeed, such options have been offered to the UN. NATO readiness forces which have been made available to the UN include: the deployment of NATO's Standing Naval Force Mediterranean (and at one point the Standing Naval Force Atlantic) to the Adriatic for UN sanctions monitoring and enforcement; the deployment of air forces to monitor and enforce no-fly zones, to protect UN forces, and to conduct air strikes in support of UN objectives; and the formation of the bulk of the UN headquarters in Bosnia-Herzegovina.

Fourth, NATO can provide international organisations with an extensive and experienced multi-dimensional planning capability. Alliance draft plans for support of a peace plan in Bosnia-Herzegovina and concepts for the protection of humanitarian convoys are examples of assistance already offered to the UN.

Fifth, NATO can develop and contribute an essential core political consensus on difficult issues – including harmonising and influencing the views of three of the Permanent Five members of the Security Council. The NACC forum provides an even wider opportunity to apply the consultation process to such international humanitarian and security issues, engaging a fourth member of the Permanent Five.

NEW PARTNERS IN SUPPORT OF INTERNATIONAL PEACE AND HUMANITARIAN EFFORTS

In addition to NATO's resolve to contribute its own capabilities, the Alliance is working with its new Partners as a part of an extensive programme of cooperation to improve common understanding of peacekeeping and humanitarian issues and to enhance inter-operability in peacekeeping, humanitarian and search and rescue operations. Since 1993, NATO has been working with the 22 states of the former Warsaw Pact in the peacekeeping and humanitarian fields. Peacekeeping definitions and principles, based on *An Agenda for Peace*, were agreed in mid-1993. More recently, together with Austria, Finland, Malta, Sweden, Slovenia and Ireland, the Cooperation Partners have worked on a range of practical measures, including the promotion of a better understanding of humanitarian aspects of peacekeeping. In early 1994 Hungary hosted a seminar on this subject and, later in the year, UNHCR and the ICRC contributed to the work of the 44 PfP nations in furthering the understanding of the complexities of contemporary peacekeeping and its humanitarian dimension.

In addition to the foregoing cooperative work, most of the PfP nations are working on the more operational aspects of the peacekeeping and humanitarian fields. When NATO heads of state and government established the PfP in January 1994, they set a number of objectives. Two of these specifically encourage international responsibility and inter-operability:

maintenance of the capability and readiness to contribute, subject to constitutional considerations, to operations under the authority of the UN and/or the responsibility of the CSCE and

the development of cooperative military relations with NATO for the purpose of joint planning, training, and exercises in order to strengthen their ability to undertake missions in the fields of peacekeeping, search and rescue, humanitarian operations, and others as may subsequently be agreed.

Today, some 44 nations are working on these PfP objectives through a variety of means: training and education courses, seminars, exchanges of experience, and, in particular, a wide range of military exercises with a peacekeeping and/or humanitarian operations theme. Three PfP exercises were held in 1994, and more are scheduled for 1995. In addition, many Alliance and Partner nations are hosting and organising similar exercises, with the same PfP objectives, on a bilateral or multilateral basis. In many of these, the humanitarian dimension is either simulated by using military personnel or, more frequently, by international relief agencies and NGOs providing advice or even participating in the exercises. Since these nations currently provide more than 50 per cent of the peacekeeping and humanitarian forces deployed by the UN, the net result of this PfP effort will be a much greater inter-operability of forces – in particular for the more complex peacekeeping operations that have a strong humanitarian dimension. Procedures, equipment, rules of engagement, logistics, communications, transportation and command and control are but some of the many inter-operability areas currently being addressed, and these efforts will intensify as more nations either join the programme or become progressively more active.

MAJOR PEACEKEEPING AND HUMANITARIAN ISSUES IN 1995

But all of this cooperative effort is developing against a background of increasing complexity in the pursuit of international peace and security and the preservation of human rights. NATO and its Partners have come to realise that humanitarian assistance and intervention has become much more difficult than traditional peacekeeping operations. Today, the main challenge to the international community tends to be complex emergencies – the delivery of humanitarian assistance and the protection of civil populations in the midst of civil conflict during the long search for a peaceful political solution. Meeting this challenge requires humanitarian, political and, increasingly, military participation. The most striking current example is where NATO, its Allies, and some NATO Partners are working side by side in the difficult circumstances of the former Yugoslavia.

This new complexity, evident in Somalia, the former Yugoslavia, Rwanda and, to some degree, Haiti, is often referred to as the 'grey area' in peace-keeping. It lies somewhere between traditional or classic peacekeeping under Chapter VI of the UN Charter and enforcement action under Chapter VII. Purists attempt desperately to maintain such clear-cut differences, but reality points to a new and different category. A better understanding of this phenomenon is required, together with a concept of operations, appropriate training for troops and civil officials, enhanced operational coordination and other items on an ever-growing list.

A further complication is the need for a much more rapid response to humanitarian crises, especially one that emerges from conflict and where anarchy and the breakdown of law and order are principal characteristics of the situation. Rwanda and Burundi illustrate the international community's inability to react rapidly and effectively under such circumstances.

UN relief operations have sometimes been used by all parties to a conflict as bargaining chips resulting in delays and lives lost. Moreover, in certain conflicts food aid is itself perceived as a weapon, as it sustains military forces as well as a civilian population. Most recently, even the UN itself has used relief supplies as a bargaining tool in an attempt to improve political and security situations; UNHCR, for example, withheld food from certain areas in northwestern Bosnia following the Bihac blockade.

Other challenges to humanitarian objectives include inconsistencies in the international responses to humanitarian crises (no consistent rationale for priorities?); a failure to engage local structures or over-dependence on weak state structures; and the treatment of humanitarian emergencies as temporary crises after which 'society will return to normal'. Conflict, hunger, displacement and economic hardship can last for many years and become a feature of life for whole generations. There is a need in any humanitarian relief situation for a thorough and honest analysis of the crises that created the need for aid in the first place, and then the development of policies to address them.

A principal concern of humanitarian organisations is the difficulty of conducting impartial aid operations in a military environment. A great deal of misunderstanding and confusion exists between military communities and civil relief organisations. Generalities such as 'military operations and aid must be kept separate' could well be applicable on the Golan Heights or in Cyprus, but they fail miserably in the volatile circumstances of a Yugoslavia. This misunderstanding and ignorance can lead in turn to a form of 'turf war' in which organisations, military and humanitarian, each exhibit an unreasonable level of rigidity over their rules and procedures, papered over with concepts of 'cooperation, on the ground', when in reality the security situation demands authoritative coordination, prescribed, agreed and practised in advance.

These are but some of the issues that NATO faces as the Alliance continues to grapple with the complexities of this new task. Others include the pressures on resources, the need for better training of civilian members of relief organisations, the requirement for a better understanding by the military of civil aspects of peacekeeping and humanitarian operations, and the need for real coordination between civil, political, military and humanitarian elements of a complex operations.

ADDRESSING THE ISSUES IN 1995 AND BEYOND

There are four major areas where international effort needs to be focused and coordinated, and in each NATO and/or its Allies and Partners have a potential role to play: the lack of an adequate conceptual basis for contemporary peace and humanitarian operations; the resource problem and the potential of regional organisations; the problem of response times, and the UN stand-by arrangements system; and the need for inter-operability in complex situations. These will be dealt with separately in successive paragraphs.

Concepts

One of the difficult challenges is that the type of peace support operation that has been applied in situations such as Somalia and the former Yugoslavia has not been adequately defined. There is no clear framework beyond *An Agenda for Peace* and its January 1995 *Supplement* to guide political, military, civil, humanitarian and academic development of what is widely referred to as the 'grey area' in peacekeeping. While the *Supplement* to *An Agenda for Peace* begins to address the extension of peacekeeping, no framework has been set in the same way that *An Agenda for Peace* offered a conceptual basis for peacekeeping and security activity. During a NACC/PfP peacekeeping seminar at NATO HQ in October 1994, the UN speaker, the Director of the Europe and Latin America Division of the DPKO best summed up the situation by observing that 'the conceptual development of peacekeeping is an area crying out for attention',

Table 6.1 Proposed Conceptual Framework for Contemporary Peacekeeping

Objective and concept	Principles	Variable criteria	Military forces required	Military tasks	Nature of humanitarian assistance
Conflict Prevention through Peacemaking *and* Traditional Peacekeeping	Consent Impartiality Non-use of force	Threat – minimal Environment – stable Government – cooperative Public – welcomes UN	Any, with appropriate training	Observation Truce supervision Preventative deployment	Some humanitarian assistance possible
Conflict Mitigation through Multi-functional Peacekeeping (UK – 'wider peacekeeping'; and France – 'active impartiality')	Limited consent Impartiality strictly to objectives of mandate Use of appropriate (measured, minimal) force to accomplish mandate	Threat – probable, unpredictable, irregular and undisciplined forces Environment – unstable Government – minimal cooperation Public – tolerates UN	Well-trained, generally inter-operable and protected	Interposition Protect humanitarian intervention Protect safe areas	Humanitarian *assistance* and *intervention* are a characteristic of such situations
Conflict Resolution through Peace Enforcement	No consent Partiality Use of overwhelming force	Threat – severe Environment – hostile Government – hostile or non-existent Public – perceive UN as enemy	Professional, ready, highly inter-operable, and heavily-armed and protected	Suppress aggression Re-establish secure environment	Generally, not possible or desirable during conflict
Conflict Rehabilitation through Peacebuilding	Consent Impartiality Non-use of force	Threat – minimal Environment – generally stable Government – cooperative	Specialised and tailored	Disarming De-mining	Humanitarian *assistance* a major component

adding that the UN had neither the time nor resources to devote to such an effort.

NATO Allies and their Partners are now examining conceptual issues, as a complement to *An Agenda for Peace* and related work in the UN HQ. Accordingly, as one attempt to devise a conceptual basis for Yugoslavia-type conditions and operations, Table 6.1 sets out a simple framework for further work in the peacekeeping area. It is intended as a structure and a reference, and demonstrates some of the variables in peace and security situations. The area of Multi-functional Peacekeeping is where, conceptually, NATO might usefully concentrate its efforts. While Peace Enforcement too could usefully engage the capabilities of the Alliance, neither the principles nor concepts have been developed for such missions, and most certainly the Alliance has no political commitment to such operations. Individual Allies did, however, use the procedures, common training and inter-operability, gained over many years in NATO, in their contributions to the Gulf Coalition Force.

It makes little sense for NATO to focus on traditional peacekeeping; that is done well by the UN. Similarly, activities at either end of the peace operations spectrum, namely preventive diplomacy and peacebuilding, are best left to other organisations. The OSCE is developing a considerable expertise in preventive measures and contributions to peacebuilding. Other regional organisations have the capability to develop similar expertise. The UN is best placed to focus on, and to take the lead in, peacebuilding. But this work needs to go further. Concepts, such as 'safe areas' and 'exclusion zones for heavy weapons' need to be carefully thought through and elaborated in practical, workable terms. There is a tendency to blame poorly-conceived mandates; the reality is that there is no conceptual basis for many of the notions that find their way into current mandates.

Resources

The UN itself requires assistance as peace and humanitarian needs increase in number and complexity. As one possible solution, the UN is seeking assistance from regional and international organisations. Many of these organisations are capable of assisting; others have the will but lack certain capabilities; and some can assist in only a very limited manner.

NATO and its Partners potentially can contribute in a variety of ways. In addition to the capabilities already described – structured approach, readiness, unique capabilities, planning and consultative forums – a more recent initiative taken at the 1994 NATO Summit is the concept of a Combined Joint Task Force (CJTF). The CJTF is intended to facilitate contingency operations, including operations with participating nations outside the Alliance. Further development and implementation of this concept could provide the type of headquarters needed for complex humanitarian and peace support missions. In order to be effective, CJTFs would have to develop capabilities to coordinate and work closely with UN Agencies, international relief organisations and NGOs. Given the void in mutual understanding between military and civil communities, much training is required to promote such a coordinated team effort. This could begin with a structured exchange of views, experience and problems amongst key players, and continue through seminars, training, exercises and the development of practical working procedures.

Another way that NATO might contribute is through further examination of the whole concept of regional organisations providing assistance to the UN. In a narrow sense, it might be possible to offer assistance to a neighbouring region, the OAU for example, or perhaps the CIS. NATO has already stated a willingness to assist the OSCE. Indeed, such inter-regional cooperation already exists elsewhere; for example, the WEU is currently assisting the OAU. Perhaps NATO infrastructure could be used to support individual Allies in any efforts to assist other regional organisations. France, the UK and the USA are currently assisting the OAU. Could certain NATO infrastructure or other means be of assistance in these efforts? Similarly, NATO, together with NACC and PfP Partners, could also assist the UN in developing its approach with regional organisations. The UN Secretary-General held his first gathering of regional and international organisations on 1 August 1994 to explore possibilities for cooperation in the peacekeeping and humanitarian fields.

Another area where NATO could contribute to complex peace and humanitarian operations is logistics. The types of movement, resupply and maintenance problems that might arise in any support of a comprehensive peace plan in Bosnia-Herzegovina could be resolved efficiently using NATO logistics procedures and arrangement – designed in another time and for a different purpose.

A final point on resources and humanitarian operations is that of specialised capabilities. In December 1992, NATO was instrumental in hosting the initial conference that began the process of developing guidelines for the use of military and civil defence assets for international responses to sudden emergencies. Moreover, NATO itself has already used its specialised civil emergency planning capability to assist in coordinating the delivery of humanitarian aid. Taken together, these could contribute to assisting the NATO military authorities in developing and better understanding the humanitarian dimension of peacekeeping operations.

Reaction Time

The response time of the international community to humanitarian crises must be improved, in particular because the effectiveness ascribed to preventive diplomacy and early warning are suspect. In Rwanda there was ample early warning; the problem is that it was not heeded. Moreover, there was plentiful 'diplomacy' through gatherings of ministers, ambassadors and the like. The UN's efforts to develop a system of stand-by arrangements for use in emergencies will not alter the political willingness of states to commit in specific instances; nevertheless, information gathered from over 50 nations on their military forces, services and other capabilities might still improve response times in some instances, since there remain significant shortfalls in the UN's support, logistics, transport, health services, and communications categories – areas of particular relevance to the humanitarian dimension of multifunctional peacekeeping. Two NATO nations have initiated major studies in this regard, in an attempt to assist the UN in enhancing its stand-by concept. One study deals with the possibility of creating a UN standing force for a range of peacekeeping and humanitarian contingencies; the second deals more with the wider enhancement of the stand-by arrangements themselves. Thirteen of the 16 Allies have committed themselves to the UN stand-by system. Moreover, eight Partners have also committed themselves to the process.

Accordingly, it should be possible, given the degree of interest and commitment amongst many of the NATO Alliance and its Partners, to exchange views on ways of enhancing the emerging UN standby system. Consideration might be given to the following:

- Identifying shortfalls in capabilities in the current arrangements and discussing amongst the group practical ways of meeting such requirements;
- Exchanging views on national response arrangements with a view to then improving them through national legislation, military preparedness, civil and humanitarian preparedness, and parliamentary approval procedures;
- Developing a clear conceptual response framework, to include a generic military structure (and options), the necessary civil humanitarian response elements, specific command, control and coordination arrangements, logistics concepts and transportation and other memoranda of understanding;
- Enhancing national non-military response capability and creating the necessary civil–military coordination; and linking such conceptual arrangements clearly with the UN decision-making process.

Inter-operability

In the past, it mattered little that equipment, procedures, languages, and other facets of operations were not wholly compatible. In operations such as in the former Yugoslavia, where the situation is volatile, where the climate is hostile, where many different organisations must work towards a common goal, and where the humanitarian situation often demands innovative measures, inter-operability becomes crucial – inter-operability between national contingents, between civil and military elements, and amongst the many disparate civil elements themselves.

NATO's PfP programme is beginning to address this problem, but it will be a long and deliberate process. The many military exercises in the programme have already been mentioned. It should also be noted that extensive cooperation in training and education is taking place. The many courses in peacekeeping and humanitarian operations offered by the 44 countries are being catalogued; the availability of course vacancies, of instructors and of other training assistance is likewise being collated; and NATO itself has developed specific courses in this field. In addition, NATO and its Partners are pooling training experience and developing proposed minimum training standards for soldiers, staff officers, civil police and others, as a complement to similar work in the UN.

One of the related areas requiring particular attention is the training of civil elements for use in multi-functional peacekeeping operations. While a great deal of national and collective effort is currently being devoted to the basic and specialised training of military forces, the same is not true for the essential civil components. Some UN Agencies and some international organisations arrange some training, or at least pre-briefings, but the standards are sometimes low and the efforts are sometimes less than satisfactory. Many such civil personnel are simply well-intentioned volunteers but, with the closing of the Missions in Mozambique and Cambodia, a certain expertise has become available. The new 900-man civil police force for Haiti will demand that members of the force have a minimum of seven years' national or international police experience. Similar standards, and their development, need to be adopted nationally, or even collectively within regional and other relevant international organisations.

CONCLUSION

NATO with its NACC and PfP programmes provides a key element of stability in Europe. Over and above this emerging new security partnership, the Alliance can also adapt its capabilities in support of multi-functional peacekeeping – including its humanitarian dimension. NATO has hard-earned experience in enforcement operations, in humanitarian assistance and in the protection of UN personnel and objectives in the former Yugoslavia. While the Alliance is still predominately a military organisation, this is only a part of the political/military/humanitarian capability package that it can bring to bear in support of the UN or the OSCE in its general area of interest. Time will show that NATO can be a major contributor in the international response to new multi-functional peacekeeping requirements.

7 Humanitarian Assistance Intervention in Complex Emergencies: Information Requirements in the 1990s
William J. Garvelink

In any humanitarian response one of the most routine but critical activities is the collection and dissemination of accurate information about the emergency. During the Rwanda response in 1994, the US Agency for International Development established within the US Government the Rwanda Information Center (RIC) to receive, synthesise and disseminate information on the crisis. It was highly effective and may serve as a prototype for information dissemination for other governments and organisations in future humanitarian responses.

INFORMATION REQUIREMENTS

Information is always a critical element in any emergency humanitarian response. Capturing as much of the available information as possible and channelling it to the correct decision-makers, planners and field operatives is a formidable mission. The international community, individually and collectively, has not been particularly effective in managing the flow of information, thus detracting from an effective emergency response. Either key pieces of information do not reach the right decision-makers and the response is degraded, or perceptions often arise that actions have not been taken and hence field operatives are diverted from their response duties to provide information to correct their headquarters' misperceptions.

More often than not, the problem is not a lack of information but too much information, so that the most relevant pieces of intelligence do not filter their way up to the humanitarian response decision-makers. Just as the uncoordinated arrival of relief supplies can clog a country's logistics and distribution system, the onslaught of unwanted, inappropriate or unpackaged information can impede decision-making and a rapid response to an emergency. The key is to determine what kinds of information each level in the humanitarian response process needs, from the executive heads of Agencies to the relief worker in the field. Likewise, it is important that information and reporting from the field makes its way up to the decision-makers, and that decisions and other information are relayed back to the humanitarian response implementors.

Within each organisation responding to an emergency, there are several levels of participation, each with its own information requirements. These information requirements are generic to almost all organisations responding to humanitarian emergencies: donor governments, UN Agencies and NGOs. But all of these players need their information presented in a clear and uncluttered format, and in a timely fashion to carry out an effective emergency response. Rarely does one receive information from the field, from other donors, or from one's own organisation in such a neatly segmented way that it can be easily digested and transmitted quickly to the individuals who need it.

Heads of Agencies need general information on: the overall situation and political developments; progress of the humanitarian response; their Agencies' activities and funding levels; other relief organisations' participation; and impending issues. This information is used for briefing other senior officials and policy-makers. The information requirement is not only for managing the emergency, but also for championing the effort. Facts and figures must be made available in anticipation of questioning from the other senior officials involved in policy-making, and, of course, the media.

Decision-makers and planners need the same types of information, but more specific and in greater detail. These participants also want detailed information on the humanitarian operations in the field and reports on all levels of coordination activities. Detailed donor funding information is also a high priority. Decision-makers and planners use the information to make policy recommendations to senior officials in headquarters and to offer policy guidance to the field staff.

Field staff, emergency managers and technical experts have another set of information requirements. Coordinating and implementing the humanitarian response in the field, they need information which enables them to make tactical decisions. Field operatives need some basic types of information: an understanding of the emergency and how it might change; the arrival schedule for incoming assistance; basic data on the technical sector (health, water/sanitation, food) in which they operate to assess progress; knowledge of other organisations operating in their sector and geographic area; procedures for working with local authorities and other emergency response organisations; and, finally, they need to know the types of information the headquarters requires for its needs and how frequently it must be reported.

EMERGENCY HUMANITARIAN RESPONSES IN THE 1990S

The number of humanitarian crises which have taken the form of 'complex emergencies' has been steadily increasing since the end of the Cold War. A 'complex emergency' is defined as a long-term humanitarian crisis resulting from internal or external conflict, usually compounded by the breakdown of economic and political order in the country. Another factor that adds to its complexity is that this type of humanitarian crisis requires an international response that goes beyond the mandate or capacity of any single Agency and requires coordination among various UN Agencies, donor governments, international organisations, NGOs, and groups from within the affected country.

Humanitarian and military interventions cannot resolve complex emergencies; only political resolution can bring them to an end. By their very nature, complex emergencies tend to last for years rather than the weeks or months of natural disasters. In addition to humanitarian assistance programmes, diplomatic initiatives and military peacekeeping operations are involved. Along with life-saving relief efforts, one now finds conflict mitigation activities, de-mining efforts, combatant demobilisation and re-integration programmes, and a concerted effort to link relief activities with rehabilitation, reconstruction and development programmes. Information requirements for responses to complex emergencies increase dramatically as the range of the response (degree of military and political involvement) and the number of humanitarian actors increase. Diplomats and emergency planners at all levels require some of the same information mentioned earlier, but they also require additional data unique to their roles in the emergency response.

Technological advances in information delivery, and an increase in the number of complex emergencies in the 1990s, have complicated the way humanitarian crisis information is managed. As the amount of information has increased significantly, its synthesis and dissemination have become more difficult. Humanitarian response organisations are being forced to devise new ways of collecting, analysing and distributing the information they receive in a timely manner to respond to immediate emergency requirements and to participate with diplomats and policy-makers in a coordinated effort to resolve these complex emergencies.

At the outset of humanitarian crises, some relief organisations now dispatch emergency response teams equipped with satellite communications with fax capability and high-powered laptop computers with E-mail connectivity. If organisations operate from more than one location, each site usually has at least some of these capabilities. As communication technologies advance, organisations are searching for ways to harness them to improve emergency response capacities.

Abundant information on emergency situations is wonderful for the media and historians, but quickly becomes a nightmare for information specialists who must collect, analyse, and disseminate only the relevant information to the appropriate individuals in their organisation. Much of the additional information is not relevant to the needs of either the headquarters or the field, and sifting through data takes valuable time away from actual response activities. Most response organisations now suffer from information overload and are struggling to find methods and procedures to cope with the increasing traffic on the information superhighway.

ORIGINS OF THE RIC

The Rwanda crisis brought together several factors which forced USAID to tackle the information overload problem. Following the events of April 1994, US government relief officials initially were prohibited from working inside Rwanda. The USAID mission and the American Embassy in Kigali were closed. USAID's Office of US Foreign Disaster Assistance (OFDA) dispatched a Disaster Assistance Response Team (DART) to establish offices in Kenya, southern Uganda and Burundi to coordinate the US government's humanitarian response to the Rwanda refugee exodus. The Rwandan refugees in western Tanzania were monitored from Nairobi; the Goma tragedy was still in the future. Information flowed in from the DART offices, UN Agencies and NGOs to the OFDA office in Washington where it was analysed and disseminated throughout USAID and the US government. OFDA issued public situation reports to keep the various US government offices and external audiences informed.

In June and July 1994, the information flow and the urgency of the humanitarian response increased rapidly. USAID DART representatives were permitted to work inside Rwanda and immediately opened an office in Kigali at the same time that approximately 1 million Rwandan refugees fled to Goma. French forces were in southwestern Rwanda and US forces were deployed to Entebbe, Goma and Kigali to assist in the airlift of relief supplies, and to help establish a potable water system in Goma. DART offices were also opened in Kampala, Entebbe, and Goma.

In Washington, the unfolding tragedy in Rwanda and eastern Zaïre continued to increase in importance. Senior USAID officials briefed the White House and other high-level civilian and military officials almost daily. But the information requirements of the Departments of State and Defense continued to expand, and requests for information from within USAID, from the State and Defense Departments, as well as from Congress and the public, soon overwhelmed OFDA's information reporting system.

In addition to the increased reporting coming in through US government cable traffic, valuable information was also being received from various UN humanitarian response Agencies, NGOs, and human rights groups. At the peak of the crisis, thousands of pages of reports were being transmitted to the offices of the humanitarian relief organisations on a daily basis. Critical information on refugee movements, numbers of affected populations, security incidents, health conditions, mortality rates, logistical bottlenecks and the like was becoming lost in a tidal wave of incoming reports and documents. A clearing house operation of some sort was required to assist overburdened OFDA information specialists. This concept of an information clearing house eventually evolved into the RIC.

The RIC was initially created by the USAID Administrator's office in response to his need for information to brief the President and the National Security Advisor. The responsibility for managing the RIC fell to OFDA and the USAID Africa Bureau. The remit of the RIC extended to routeing incoming information to appropriate offices and individuals, responding to both external and internal inquiries, generating situational and financial reports and tracking donor assistance. It should be noted here that the objective of the RIC was to provide relevant information to the Administrator of USAID and to decision-makers and planners in USAID and other government departments. The information prepared by the RIC was provided to field operatives but they were not its primary client. Consequently, the RIC only addressed a portion of the information requirements.

The RIC served as the central clearing house for all information concerning the Rwanda crisis in the weeks after the refugee exodus to eastern Zaïre. Because several US government agencies and numerous NGOs participated in the humanitarian response effort, it was essential that information clarifying the scope, location, and nature of each organisation's work be widely available to facilitate the coordination process.

Participants in the RIC included staff from both USAID (OFDA and the Africa Bureau) and the Department of State's Bureau for Population, Refugees and Migration, with additional input from the Department of Defense, the UN and NGOs. This wide access to information allowed the RIC to produce concise summaries of the most current reports when the plethora of information regarding Rwanda was far too great for any one person to assimilate.

HOW THE RIC OPERATED

It quickly became apparent that two primary types of information were necessary successfully to facilitate the aid effort. First, the quantity of information generated in the early days of the crisis was far too great for any one individual to manage and analyse on a daily basis. Some form of consolidated report was necessary to give officials in USAID and the government a means to assess the situation quickly. Such a report would offer those responsible for providing accurate analysis a means of getting a broad overview of the most important day-to-day events. It would also provide a summary of the situation to members of the public interested in the relief effort. Second, accurate financial information was a key to the coordination process since it enabled all involved agencies to be aware of US government assistance by region and sector.

The RIC produced two special documents to meet the needs of its Washington-based constituency. The Consolidated Rwanda Report (CRR) compiled excerpts of field reporting and public information by sector (Refugees, Health, Security, etc.) and by region. The CRR, produced twice weekly during the crisis, was a compilation, not an analysis, of reports submitted by a wide range of sources with the citation and date included. Two versions were prepared: one was an all-inclusive classified version, containing excerpts from both classified and unclassified sources, and distributed internally to appropriate officials in USAID, the State and Defense Departments, and other government offices. This gave decision-makers within the US government an easily assimilated summary document that provided the latest information on the rapidly-changing situation. A public version was also prepared and distributed to the NGO community and interested individuals via the Internet. A survey conducted of various public recipients of the CRR found that the Report served a useful purpose in informing the expanding number of groups and individuals who were monitoring the Rwanda crisis.

The second document produced was a US government financial assistance report, reflecting all sources of US government activities by cost, implementing agency and funding source. Additionally, in conjunction with the DHA, the RIC unit contributed to a Donor Contribution Report, which tracked all reported donor contributions to the Rwanda crisis.

Initially, personnel from various USAID and State Bureaus and Offices were drafted into the RIC on an ad hoc basis. But as the magnitude of the crisis emerged, it became apparent that the RIC required dedicated individuals to respond to the demand for information on a daily basis. During peak crisis periods, up to 20 staff members pooled their expertise to produce the reports required by the National Security Council and senior White

House Advisors, and the USAID Administrator, his senior managers and the USAID Bureau for Legislative and Public Affairs (LPA). LPA in turn distributed the information to Congress and the media, the DHA and other UN Agencies, and the general public.

OTHER HUMANITARIAN INFORMATION SYSTEMS

At the same time as USAID created the RIC, a Brown University graduate independently developed a World Wide Web site called 'Crisis in Rwanda'. By scanning the Internet and making contact with individuals in most of the major relief organisations, he collected public access documents which were then posted on a hypertext and hypermedia electronic bulletin board. By the summer of 1994, the 'Crisis in Rwanda' Web site contained over 60 megabytes of data, including documents from USAID, various UN Agencies and departments, the ICRC, numerous NGOs, Voice of America, the Canadian Broadcasting Corporation, Amnesty International, Human Rights Watch, and many others. The site not only included textual documents, but also radio broadcast transcripts, graphic images, and thematic and geographic maps of the region. At the peak of interest, thousands of users from 45 countries accessed the site, retrieving thousands of documents.

The UN is presently exploring the creation of a reliable, high-speed communications network for both the preparedness and response phases of complex emergencies and natural disasters. The DHA, in partnership with the US Department of State, is undertaking the development of an electronic information and communications system, tentatively known as Reliefnet. As currently envisaged, this will be a practical information management system and communications network for the international relief community which will enhance its ability to prepare for, prevent, and respond to emergencies. The system will utilise and complement existing crisis information collection and analysis mechanisms and be easy to use, publicly accessible, and scalable. Essentially, Reliefnet will be a databank composed of individual databases on countries believed to be 'at risk' from natural disasters and/or complex emergencies. Information available will include background data on the social, economic, political, and health environments, as well as current data on relief operations already under way, data on the transport details of commodities shipped to specific areas, interactive map services, etc. This information could offer comprehensive background information for contingency planners and disaster managers.

LESSONS LEARNED

The first lesson learned was that access to continuous, accurate and comprehensive information is vital to policy- and decision-makers during complex emergencies. The RIC's role in collecting and making up-to-date information available was widely acknowledged, particularly in the acute stage of the crisis when it was difficult to maintain an overview of the fast-changing events. However, while the RIC was able to summarise and disseminate raw information received from a wide variety of sources, it did not have the capacity or expertise to validate, cross-check and evaluate it, or to determine opportunities for humanitarian action. This is an area worthy of review.

Also, information exchanged between the US government (via the RIC) and DHA's financial tracking section in Geneva was extremely important in compiling and disseminating information on all sources of humanitarian assistance. Based on the RIC model, USAID is considering institutionalising the US government's all-source financial reporting by establishing a permanent humanitarian assistance reporting centre. Its purpose would be to compile and disseminate information, current and historical, on US government assistance to all countries, on a country-by-country basis.

Finally, information needs at the headquarters are markedly different from information needs in the field. To improve the information exchange at all levels, field operatives should be surveyed to determine their information needs, and how best they can be served.

CONCLUSION

The Rwanda crisis, like many other post-Cold War complex emergencies, has shown that the international relief community requires a comprehensive and coordinated information network to manage the response. To improve decision-making within government, NGOs and UN Agencies, there is a critical need to increase the flow of information between headquarters staffs and field operatives. Each organisation must make decisions about the movement of resources, money, and personnel based on its own mandate, but these decisions can be greatly improved if based on information available from multiple sources and verifiable throughout the crisis.

8 Humanitarian Emergencies and the Role of NGOs

Peter Shiras

INTRODUCTION

During the worst days of the humanitarian crisis in Somalia, before the US Marines came ashore in the glare of television lights, the only humanitarian presence in Somalia was a handful of NGOs. The UN had pulled all of its personnel out of Somalia in early 1992, and the US and all other nations had evacuated their diplomatic and aid missions at around the same time. Only the ICRC, several American and European NGOs and some very committed Somalis were present to feed the hungry and heal the wounded.

Nothing could better dramatise the increasingly important role which NGOs now play in humanitarian relief than their singular presence in Somalia. NGOs are not only present in every humanitarian emergency, but they are usually in place long before an emergency begins and remain after the crisis fades from the public view. The number of NGOs involved in humanitarian relief is growing, as is their overall contribution to relief efforts.

Not only are NGOs growing in size and number, but they are also assuming new roles and exerting greater influence than in the past. Whereas NGOs traditionally limited their role to direct humanitarian relief and consciously defined that role as apolitical, the response of NGOs today to 'complex emergencies' is multi-faceted. NGOs now see the critical link between relief and development, and so attempt to build developmental elements into their relief programmes. As NGOs examine the root causes of humanitarian emergencies, they are forced to look at the political dimensions of conflict and consider programmes of reconciliation and post-conflict peacebuilding. As NGOs gain more experience working in war zones, they are beginning to understand the uses that warring factions make of humanitarian assistance and how not to become unwitting participants in that process.

In a growing number of cases, NGOs are assuming roles usually filled by governments or international organisations. In Ethiopia, NGOs brokered agreements between warring factions to get humanitarian assistance across the front lines of war from government-held to rebel-held territory. NGOs have increased the scale of their operations in some instances to become major forces in markets, in running trucking companies, and in providing health services.

What explains the change in roles that NGOs are playing? Are they filling a vacuum left by others? Are they encroaching on areas better left to governments or international organisations? Or are they responding to changes in the world environment more quickly than other types of organisations and thereby leading the way for others?

THE CHANGING INTERNATIONAL CONTEXT

The post-Cold War era has ushered in a period of tremendous upheaval in the world at a time when many expected 'a new world order' and the long-awaited 'peace dividend'. Instead, since the fall of the Berlin Wall and the dissolution of the Soviet Union, we have witnessed major conflicts in the Gulf War, northern Iraq, Bosnia, Somalia, Haiti, and Rwanda. The number of significant conflicts around the globe has skyrocketed, numbering over 160 in 1992 and 1993. This reality is reflected in the increase in UN peacekeeping Missions around the world, as well as in burgeoning emergency aid budgets, often at the cost of development aid.

The world community has also become more willing than ever before to respond to internal conflict. Many of the forces unleashed to cause conflict today were ones long held in check by superpower competition. The international response to internal conflict before 1990 was constrained, but international structures are now being utilised, albeit with a great deal of trial and error. It would have been unimaginable, for example, to have a UN-authorised peacekeeping force in either Central America or Afghanistan during the Cold War, as these were both conflicts where either the USA or the Soviet Union would have vetoed a Security Council Resolution.

However, in recent years the Security Council has been authorising peacekeeping Missions at a dizzying pace, far outstripping the UN's capacity to either manage or fund all the operations. Since the perceived failure of the Somalia operation, personnel and financial constraints among major donors have dampened enthusiasm for peacekeeping and humanitarian intervention.

Nonetheless, the implications of the changes at the UN for NGOs, and humanitarian operations in general, are enormous. Internal conflicts, and the humanitarian crises they create, have become central issues in the foreign policy debate. In northern Iraq, Bosnia, Somalia and Rwanda, humanitarian issues have been propelled to the top of the foreign policy agenda and have either influenced or dictated whether and to what extent military force is used, and how it should interface with diplomatic initiatives and humanitarian aid.

The results have by no means always been salutary either for humanitarian interests or for diplomatic ones. In former Yugoslavia, humanitarian action has been used as a fig-leaf to cover up the inaction by the West on the diplomatic front. Worse still, the presence of relief workers on the ground has been used as a justification not to take more aggressive action to resolve the conflict. In Somalia, what began as a limited humanitarian intervention to get food to the starving was transformed into a military effort to punish one side in the conflict, and to a political effort to re-establish a nation. When that effort failed and the peacekeeping mission took substantial casualties (including 18 US personnel), the entire mission was declared a failure. The 'Somalia syndrome', a fear of committing international forces to ill-defined missions of humanitarian intervention, now largely frames the thinking of US policy-makers, despite the fact that the humanitarian element of the initial US intervention under UNITAF was highly successful.

A second major change in the international context affecting humanitarian operations is the growing involvement of the military in relief efforts. In the past, the military's involvement in 'humanitarian' activities related to internal conflict was usually seen in the context of pacification programmes intended to win the hearts and minds of the civilian population in pursuit of military victory. Thus, the US military carried out civic action programmes in Vietnam, the Guatemalan military proposed 'development roles', and the Ethiopian military carried out forced resettlement, all in the name of humanitarianism. NGOs, sensibly enough, shunned all contact with these military programmes. Those that did cooperate did so at considerable risk to their own credibility within the NGO community.

In the past five years, however, the military has been called upon to play a new role in humanitarian operations. Beginning with Operation Provide Comfort in northern Iraq, through Operation Restore Hope in Somalia, to further actions in Rwanda and Bosnia, military forces are now present in many humanitarian emergencies. The US military has begun to provide training to its forces on involvement in 'situations other than war' and is developing a manual on 'Multi-Service Procedures for Humanitarian Assistance Operations'. For the first time, the US military has revised its main statement of military strategy to reflect its involvement in peacekeeping and other non-combat operations.

Given the perceived failure of the use of force for humanitarian purposes in Somalia, as well as budgetary pressures in the US and other Western countries, the trend towards use of military forces in humanitarian operations may be a short-lived one. The rejection of the UN Secretary-General's appeal for military forces to police the Rwandan refugee camps in Zaïre is a recent example. Thus, military forces may continue to be present but in a more limited role, such as providing logistics – as US military forces did in Rwanda – rather than trying to provide security for an entire country.

The third major change in the international context is the new willingness on the part of governments and the UN to challenge the inviolate nature of sovereignty when the state is found to be either unwilling or unable to protect the fundamental human rights of its people, or a portion thereof. While for years relief organisations have worked in cross-border programmes, often in violation of a country's national sovereignty, they are now receiving more direct support from governments and the UN to do so. This is most easily accomplished when there is no functioning government as in Somalia, but in other instances as well, the international community has acted without the express request of a sovereign state.

OPERATIONAL CHALLENGES FOR NGOS

For the sake of simplicity, the roles that NGOs play can be divided into two categories: one is the field operational role which they perform in providing direct assistance in emergencies; the second is the policy advocacy role in which NGOs, both operational and those devoted exclusively to advocacy, are becoming increasingly involved. Both roles, and the interface between them, present opportunities and challenges for NGOs as they become more active players, and as complex emergencies become an important foreign policy and security issue.

Professionalisation of the NGO Mission

As an increasing number of humanitarian emergencies become 'complex', the operational roles of NGOs become correspondingly more difficult. Both the pressures on NGOs to assume new roles and the scope and intensity of complex emergencies demand of NGOs a renewed emphasis on professionalism and a careful consideration of their mission in relief situations.

NGOs have several comparative advantages relative to other types of relief organisations in their response to emergencies. These include

flexibility, quick response capacity, personal and institutional commitment and grassroots contact. At the same time, new complex emergencies
are taking NGOs to countries where they have never previously worked
and where the scale of the problems they face is sometimes overwhelming. These factors tend to limit the natural advantages of NGOs and call
instead for high degrees of professionalism, specialisation in mission, and
coordination – none of which are necessarily NGO strengths. In the camps
of Rwandan refugees in Goma, for example, there was a tremendous disparity in the skills of NGO health efforts, some of which were considered
by health experts from the Center for Disease Control to be potentially
harmful.

Similarly, in Somalia, the food distribution techniques used by NGOs
varied dramatically, some of which resulted in losses of less than 1 per
cent of food and others which resulted in losses of up to 80 per cent. The
food losses were a major factor contributing to the famine, fuelling the
war and influencing the decision to intervene militarily. It is not clear that
better food distribution methods could have stopped all of the looting and
diversion which took place – nor were 80 per cent losses widespread – but
significant disparity did exist in the methods and results of food distribution.

In both Somalia and Rwanda, many NGOs were drawn to the emergency situation not because of any long-standing involvement in the country, experience working at the grassroots, or appreciation of the social and
cultural norms, but simply because of the scale of the crisis. They were
very much needed, but their operations also caused unintended consequences
which might have been prevented.

These facts demand of relief NGOs a reassessment of their role. First,
NGOs need to define their mission: are they going only to work in relief
and specialise in that area, or are they going to work in both relief and
development? In either case, they need to be cognisant of the important relationships that exist between relief and development programmes.
Development programmes should reduce a community or a country's vul-
nerability to emergencies; relief programmes should lay the foundation for
effective development. Relief organisations can bring more sectoral expertise
to their work while relief and development organisations can bring in-depth
knowledge of the local conditions if they have been working previously
in development programmes in the area where the emergency occurs.

Second, NGOs need to decide whether they are going to respond to
emergencies anywhere in the world under any circumstances, or whether
they are going to limit their involvement either geographically or sectorally.
Relief and development agencies may limit their response to emergencies
to places where they have ongoing development programmes and, therefore,

a good understanding of the area. Of course, emergencies might erupt in places where few NGOs have been working and, in those instances, NGOs wishing to respond must at least have strong sectoral expertise if they lack in-depth experience of working in the country.

Third, NGOs need to decide whether they are going to specialise in a certain aspect of relief response and hence develop the sectoral expertise needed to operate professionally in that area. If an NGO decides that it has a worldwide mission to respond to emergencies anywhere at any time, the necessity of sectoral expertise is even greater. To think that an organisation can operate proficiently in any sector of emergency response anywhere in the world is simply foolhardy and, worse still, is a disservice to those the NGOs seek to aid. In a world of increasing complexity, NGOs are most effective when they operate in territory that they know, and when they limit their activities to sectors in which they have technical and social know-how. For example, Oxfam-UKI is considered to be one of the best NGOs in the field of emergency water supply; the International Rescue Committee (IRC) only operates relief programmes and is considered a leader in the area of sanitation.

NGOs are growing more aware of the need to upgrade their professional capacities. In an initiative begun by a small group of US NGOs, researchers, and trainers and then assumed by InterAction, a coalition of 160 US-based NGOs has begun a process of training in emergency health and security. The health training will concentrate on key measures necessary for providing public health programmes. The security training will cover a spectrum of issues including the principles of humanitarian response, international humanitarian law, principles of conflict management, mine awareness, relationships with peacekeepers, personal security and stress management. In a survey conducted by InterAction of its members involved in relief operations, 100 per cent of respondents felt the need for further training, 67 per cent identified security issues as their highest priority and 41 per cent named emergency health as a high priority.

On the one hand, NGOs need to understand the environment in which they are working, even if they limit their own activities to the provision of relief. In complex emergencies, the environment comprises political, military, economic, social, cultural, religious and, sometimes, ethnic factors. It also consists of local institutional forces (governmental and non-governmental), national institutions, international organisations and donor governments concerned with the relief operation. The most successful NGOs are those which limit the scope of their activities, specialise in a particular area and work where they have an in-depth knowledge of the people, institutions and culture.

Coordination of NGO Activities

As the number of NGOs involved in relief activities increases, and as they begin to take on new roles, the need for effective coordination both amongst NGOs themselves and between NGOs and other institutional sectors is greater than ever. While one of the great strengths of NGOs is their flexibility and quick response capability, one of their weaknesses is their inherent nature as small, fragmented organisations dedicated to their own particular purpose. While flexibility and quick response are essential qualities, particularly in the early stages of an emergency and in responding to changes in the nature of the emergency, they are not necessarily positive attributes for establishing a well-functioning, large-scale, long-term relief operation.

In Somalia, for example, a number of problems could have been overcome with better coordination among NGOs. First, many NGOs established operations in areas which were easier to operate in or areas of media interest, but eventually this led to an over-concentration in these areas and neglect of other areas. Thus, south Mogadishu, where the airport was located, became the headquarters of most NGOs and not north Mogadishu. Similarly, most NGOs worked in either Mogadishu or Baidoa, but vast areas of the countryside were neglected.

Second, many NGOs which had never worked in Somalia entered the country after very little consultation with other NGOs already established there, or with Somalis themselves. Often driven by headquarters pressure to set up shop and start doing something, valuable consultation with others, which might have led to much more effective programmes, was sacrificed. Third, this lack of consultation and coordination had a direct affect on NGO security. Each new NGO had to negotiate with the Somalis for protection and for rental of housing, office space and the like. By not coordinating these negotiations, NGOs not only paid exorbitant rates, but the failure of one or another NGO to meet Somali demands could result in security problems for the whole NGO community. Without a coordinated NGO position Somalis, who were often directly linked to the warlords, were able to extort large sums from NGOs which were then used to fund their war efforts.

Finally, on programme issues, NGOs failed to develop common procedures which undermined the effectiveness of their work: some NGOs attempted to distribute food to specific recipients while others simply turned large amounts over to village elders; some NGOs insisted on distributing high-value rice while others preferred low-value sorghum; and some NGOs stipulated conditions with local elders for providing assistance (such as a guarantee of security), while others would work anywhere they could. At times, there were substantive disagreements amongst relief organisations on programming issues, such as ICRC's insistence on distributing rice for nutritional reasons, when other NGOs believed that it invited looting. Nonetheless, all these divergent practices, while perhaps justified at the earliest stages, eventually undermined a tightly-controlled relief effort and were, in part at least, responsible for the ultimate resort to military intervention.

All NGOs recognise the need for coordination – some more readily than others. In Somalia, there were mechanisms for coordination with the military forces of the US-led UNITAF and both UN-led initiatives, UNOSOM and UNOSOM II. The establishment of a DART, with the ability to coordinate US government assistance, was one of the most effective mechanisms developed in Somalia. In Rwanda, a new mechanism was attempted to try to improve NGO coordination through the establishment by ICVA of a coordinating office for NGO activities. While this effort was handicapped by personnel problems in its early stage, it later proved to be a useful mechanism to correct some of the problems identified from the Somalia experience. However, in Rwanda other issues surfaced as humanitarian NGOs became increasingly concerned about, and tried to address, the human rights problems in the country. This, in turn, suggests the need for better understanding of and coordination with international human rights' NGOs by humanitarian organisations.

NGOs have an near-genetic aversion to having their activities curtailed in any way by outside authorities. They see themselves as free from bureaucratic regulation and, therefore, find the notion of external interference in their activities to be just that – interference. However, NGOs must take a hard look at their operations and recognise that a strength here today might be a weakness elsewhere tomorrow. Greater adherence to certain standards and greater willingness to come together and act in concert will strengthen the overall impact of NGO relief efforts, not diminish the good NGOs can do.

Do No Harm: The Unintended Consequences of Relief Programmes

One of the major challenges facing humanitarian relief organisations is to recognise and minimise the unintended negative consequences of relief programmes; hence, practitioners often face ethical dilemmas which cannot easily be resolved. The current dilemma facing relief groups providing relief to the Rwandan refugees in Goma is a case in point. By providing sustenance to the camps controlled by the Hutu militia, relief groups might be aiding the military preparations of the militia. Yet by cutting off relief, innocent people would suffer. However, relief groups can adopt principles, policies and practices which will minimise negative outcomes.

The negative consequences of relief operations might include: the diversion of relief supplies to warring factions; purchase of security services from warring factions, thereby supporting and financing their activities; working with one faction, thereby legitimising that party to the conflict; or channelling aid through authorities which violate basic principles of humanitarian law and response. In addition, by providing aid to people internally-displaced by forced resettlement or by policies not directly related to the conflict, such policies might, in effect, be abetted.

Examples of the negative consequences of relief activities abound. In Somalia, looting occurred in part at least as a result of inadequate food distribution mechanisms. This raises the question of accountability and transparency. NGOs have, often rightly, insisted that the normal accounting requirements for food and other materiel aid items be relaxed during emergencies, because it is impossible to meet these standards. But when material aid is being diverted to support a war effort, the issue is much more serious than simply accounting irregularities. In this context, aid organisations should insist on as much accountability, if not more, in war zones than in other contexts.

Somalia also provides a good example of how the purchasing of security services can be harmful to relief efforts. Somalia was the first time in its history that the ICRC hired armed guards to gain access for humanitarian purposes. In addition, many NGOs agreed to use some of their food or other supplies as 'payment' either for access or for security. The effect of these arrangements was not only to finance the Somali war effort, but also to absolve local authorities of responsibility. Much of the looting which took place in Somalia was done by the armed guards themselves, in collusion with local officials. Those organisations which placed security responsibilities in the hands of local officials, and cut off food aid if they did not maintain security, had a much better track record – keeping losses down to less than 1 per cent in some cases. However, this strategy of 'tough love' requires that the organisation be prepared to carry out its threat if necessary.

Many observers have long maintained that working only through official channels on one side of a conflict compromises the neutrality of a humanitarian relief operation. This was the case with many relief organisations in Ethiopia in 1984–6 at a time when most either worked in government-controlled areas with Ethiopian government acquiescence or in rebel-controlled areas, but few if any worked on both sides as an expression of neutrality. Much the same was true in Central America in the 1980s, where most NGOs sided with the 'people's' organisations and shunned working even with refugees or displaced persons viewed as sympathetic to the repressive governments of Guatemala or El Salvador, or antagonistic to Nicaragua's Sandinista government.

Finally, aid that is provided in support of government policies that violate basic human rights may also be said to support those policies. Most refugees and displaced persons are created by policies that violate human rights, but many governments and rebel groups engage in forced resettlement activities after civilians have already been uprooted, or for other than war-related reasons. For example, the Ethiopian government's resettlement programme in the 1980s involved bulldozing displaced persons' camps – a clear violation of human rights. By taking a stand not to provide assistance to those forcibly relocated, relief organisations run the risk of penalising innocent victims of government policies, but to provide such assistance aids and abets the violations of human rights.

NGOs must recognise that sometimes they cannot fulfil their mandate; that upholding a principle or the practical inability to carry out a humanitarian mandate might take precedence over saving a life at any cost. One of the principles that NGOs must uphold is their independence from conditions imposed on them either by donors or by host authorities. When host authorities intervene to such an extent that the basic humanitarian mission of NGOs is compromised, they must decide if they can operate under those conditions and, if not, withdraw. For example, if host authorities dictate which populations may be helped or if they arbitrarily confiscate supplies or vehicles used for relief purposes, NGOs should decide that their operations no longer meet basic humanitarian standards. While some lives might be lost as a result, more lives could be lost if NGOs do not uphold such principles.

TOWARDS MORE EFFECTIVE ADVOCACY FOR NGOs

While there are a number of NGOs which exist solely to advocate on behalf of refugees and displaced persons, a relatively new trend is the involvement of traditional relief organisations in the field of public policy advocacy. Much of the advocacy work of these organisations focuses not on the need to secure additional governmental resources for their work, but rather on the need to affect government policy related to humanitarian emergencies. Often, these groups find themselves spending as much, if not more, time with the Pentagon and the DPKO as with their more traditional partners such as OFDA, UNICEF, and the DHA.

The primary reason that NGOs have become involved in advocacy is the lack of political will on the part of Western governments to respond early and responsibly to humanitarian crises. Without leadership from Western governments, problems become emergencies and emergencies become crises. Much of the advocacy efforts of NGOs are focused on an early response to crises by Western governments and on the formulation of effective policies for dealing with the many elements of complex emergencies.

The involvement in advocacy by field-oriented relief organisations is a natural evolution of their work. particularly as they realise that, acting alone, they will not be able to alleviate the effects of complex emergencies. Given the growing need for an outside military presence in order to gain access to populations at risk, relief groups are finding it ever more important to lobby for the support of their domestic governments. However, it has not always been easy for humanitarian organisations to make the transition from walking the hills of refugee camps to walking the halls of Congress.

The most successful NGOs in advocacy are able to translate their field experience into policy recommendations in Washington or New York. What this requires is a field presence that sees not only the minutiae of relief, but also comprehends and reports on policy issues which are constraining the overall relief effort. In addition, NGOs must have staff at headquarters who are willing to listen carefully to the field reporting and use it to formulate policy positions which are both realistic and credible to policy-makers. This requires an understanding of the policy-making environment in national capitals or New York.

An interesting new trend is the greater number of NGO senior staff who have served in government, not only after retirement but also in the middle of successful careers. Three former directors of OFDA are currently senior executives with major US NGOs, and the current director of OFDA comes from an NGO background. The president of the largest US relief and development organisation, CARE, served briefly as the coordinator for humanitarian relief for the UN in Somalia. This cross-over experience assists policy advocacy for NGOs, as long as NGO advocacy remains rooted in its strengths of field-based information and promotion of humanitarianism.

A concern among many NGO practitioners is whether or not NGO advocacy efforts are compromised by the funding which most of the major relief organisations receive from government sources. This concern may increase as more former government officials begin to work for NGOs. However, the reverse seems to be the norm. Those organisations which receive major government funding are often the most outspoken, as are former government officials, on humanitarian policy matters.

Another area where NGOs need to be more effective in their advocacy efforts is in their use of the media. Most NGOs see the media as a vehicle for publicity and fund-raising, but it can also play a key role in influencing policy-makers. Effective use of the media requires that NGOs train their staffs on using the media not only for dramatising the needs in an emergency situation, but also for advancing policy recommendations.

As NGOs begin to coordinate more effectively on field operations, the need is just as urgent for greater coordination on advocacy and 'internationalising' advocacy efforts. What happens in Rwanda or Burundi, for example, might be more a product of French and Belgian influence than US policy. Thus, it is critical for American NGOs to have strong links to their counterparts in Europe.

Similarly, more and more NGOs in the developing world are playing a role in advocacy and these organisations must coordinate their advocacy with that of Western NGOs. Some of the major NGOs are now developing international networks to facilitate this and the religious-based NGOs already have a worldwide network that they can call upon for this purpose. Coalitions such as InterAction and ICVA are also seeking ways to coordinate public policy advocacy.

Not only must NGOs coordinate more effectively within their community, but they must also form more effective coordination mechanisms and broader coalitions with other types of NGOs, such as those which focus on human rights, conflict resolution and broad foreign policy issues. Advocacy on humanitarian assistance has long been viewed primarily as an issue of resources, and not one of policy. As a result, links to human rights groups in particular have not been as strong as they should. The relationship between human rights, humanitarian law and effective humanitarian assistance programmes is too close for it to be ignored by advocates. By broadening their coalitions, internationalising their networks, using the media more effectively and integrating field reporting into their policy recommendations, NGOs can have a much greater impact on policy than they now do.

9 Coordination is the Key
Sir David Ramsbotham

Anyone attempting to evaluate the contribution that the military can make to coordinated UN humanitarian assistance operations has to take two 'givens' into account. First, the deployment of the military to assist with UN humanitarian operations will always be determined and conditioned by the appropriate political authority. Secondly, the size and equipment of national armed forces are fixed by what individual nations assess they need and can afford for national defence purposes. These practical realities condition the contribution that any national military can make towards a UN Mission with a humanitarian mandate. This chapter will proceed on the assumption that the necessary political will for any type or degree of national involvement is straightforward – would that it were so! – thus removing one of the two biggest impediments to effective UN action. The other – lack of coordination – is the subject of this chapter.

To their credit, a number of people with peacekeeping responsibilities within the UN have already made many qualitative and internal organisational changes; nevertheless, to be truly effective every individual development should be part of the larger whole, encompassing all aspects of all UN activities. In other words, an individual improvement is only as valuable as its contribution to a coordinated aggregation.

Despite there being no provision in the UN Charter for peacekeeping there is ample precedent for its 'classic' variety, and legal provision through the agency of the Security Council to address the full range of what the Charter terms 'threats to international peace and security'. However, legal sanction is only the beginning, as the UN and its member states have learned painfully with the rapid expansion of peacekeeping-related activities since 1988. In addition, there now exist a multiplicity of non-military threats to the way of life, safety and wellbeing of all peoples extending well beyond the bounds of the inter-state conceptions which informed the framing of the UN Charter. One need only cite ozone-layer depletion, the threat of global warming and the multiple risks which follow in the wake of large-scale environmental degradation. National security is becoming increasingly inseparable from international and global security, and threats to the security of nations and peoples now include matters which threaten their health, economic wellbeing, social stability and political peace – now likely to arise from novel and unexpected sources. Such threats can only be countered by the peoples of the world – for which the UN remains the principal agent.

But the coordinated response and political will represented by a General Assembly or Security Council Resolution requires its counterpart in implementation. This is most clearly the case with the new range of peace support operations mounted by the UN in recent years to combat communal violence, to safeguard the delivery of humanitarian aid through or within war zones, or to assist countries devastated by years of conflict to find a way toward the re-establishment of civil society. What is required in situations like the Rwandan tragedy is not peacekeeping or peace enforcement, but rather a multi-functional operation, in which the key requirement is that the activities of all military and civilian elements involved, including national militaries, UN Agencies and NGOs should be coordinated. In other words, what is required is a structured military–humanitarian interface, capable of ensuring that the best use is made of all dedicated contributions.

In his *Supplement* to *An Agenda for Peace*, UN Secretary-General Dr Boutros Boutros-Ghali describes six instruments for peace and security: preventive diplomacy and peacemaking; peacekeeping; post-conflict peace rebuilding; disarmament; sanctions; and enforcement action – but here I shall not consider sanctions and disarmament (arms control). As a 'doer' rather than a diplomat, I shall use the terms preventive *action*, conflict or crisis *resolution* and post-conflict *reconstruction* to cover the remaining themes, examining one over-arching coordination requirement in each. I shall then look briefly at UN HQ itself, and conclude with the pattern I should like to see adopted in all future multi-functional operations.

To those who accuse me of suggesting impossible military tidiness, I answer that where coordination has been tried it has proved efficacious, because all concerned had the will to make it work. The least attractive characteristic of much of what happens at present is that, all too often, abundant goodwill is dispersed by a proliferation of turf battles, inter-Departmental and Agency jealousies, and obstacles put in the way of common sense – all of them unworthy of the organisations in whose name they are fought. Since UN Agencies will admit openly that they are prepared to collaborate but not be coordinated; inter-NGO jealousies are legion; and humanitarian impulses are harnessed to national interests – it is hardly surprising that any talk of coordination meets with varying degrees of alarm and despondency. Transformation might not be within the bounds of the politically possible, but progress is.

THE INSTRUMENTS

Preventive Action

The essential prerequisite for effective preventive action is the provision of early warning, or intelligence. Much has been written and said about the incompatibility of the UN ethos and military intelligence, but any early indications are invaluable – whatever their source – given that turbulence in states or regions could, if not recognised and addressed, lead to threats to international peace and security. Such intelligence must be gathered and passed to decision-makers by all those in a position to assess political, economic and social indicators of potential problems – which might well include NGOs and the UN Agencies themselves (see also Chapter 7). Although the ICRC is often in a better 'gathering' position than any other organisation, the neutrality and impartiality upon which it is founded and operates is well understood.

Dr Boutros Boutros-Ghali has concentrated on preventive diplomacy, which can be subsumed under the broader heading of preventive action, which itself could include preventive deployment (as currently in FYROM), and some form of humanitarian deployment with the aim of preventing the occurrence of potentially destabilising social or economic disasters, such as famine. Many UN Agencies, such as UNICEF, are already engaged in this work with their programmes to improve health 'league tables' around the world by, for example, increasing the percentage of people vaccinated. It is noteworthy that those countries listed by UNICEF as falling most behind in this area are also those listed as potentially unstable in terms of possible conflict by the International Institute for Strategic Studies (IISS). The correlation is obvious; the need self-explanatory.

But to be effective, preventive action requires UN Agency, military and NGO elements to be on call and on hand, which in turn suggests the need for a full register of the human and materiel resources available for humanitarian operations, and under what conditions. This parallels the work already done in the DPKO Stand-by Forces Study in 1994, which listed military assets which could be requested from member states. Many other UN Departments and Agencies have compiled their own registers of response potential, but these are not currently coordinated. A complete humanitarian register must contain all Agencies and NGOs, and their resources. This will require them to share information with the UN, within which I suggest that it be maintained by the DHA, which has been given a coordinating responsibility in the field as well as for a number of other activities. Further on the DHA, and to refer to both resolution and reconstruction as well, to date only the Mission to Rwanda has had a DHA humanitarian coordinator with responsibilities delegated to him by the operational Agencies. In the case of preventive action, it could be appropriate for individual Agencies and NGOs initially to act independently but, in general, I believe that the Rwanda precedent of DHA field coordination (long advocated by those with experience in the field) should be followed in future. In cases where one Agency's contribution is dominant, it might well continue to make sense to appoint it as lead Agency, but where several Agencies interact on a more equal basis then there is obvious scope for DHA to exercise its coordinating function.

It is becoming increasingly apparent that the field operations of humanitarian Agencies cannot count automatically on their name, or that of the UN, to guarantee their security – particularly if they enter a conflict situation before a UN Mission is firmly established. For example, the situation in the UNHCR refugee camps for Rwandan Hutus in Zaïre shows what can happen when a crisis of this scale produces risk and volatility which goodwill cannot resolve. In these circumstances, if humanitarian aid is to be guaranteed, precautions must be taken that Agencies would once have deplored. First, all those deployed must be made aware of the security rules that they should observe for their own protection: anti-kidnap precautions, evacuation plans, and the like. Secondly, and acknowledging that the presence of military guards could raise rather than lower the profile of a humanitarian operation, it might be sensible for them to employ professional security advisers, or some form of guard force, to protect themselves and their supplies. The point is that preventive humanitarian action is now almost invariably dangerous and must be provisioned accordingly. If there is an accompanying military deployment, the military must be prepared to assist those with humanitarian responsibilities in any way they can. Here, familiarity and the common cause of humanitarian ideals has done much to diminish prejudice on all sides.

Conflict Resolution

The military have a natural concern with *C3I* – Command, Control, Communications and Intelligence. I have mentioned the importance of intelligence under preventive action, but C3I is an essential to any UN Mission. In traditional peacekeeping operations, this was carried out by ad hoc headquarters, manned by representatives from the contributing nations. However, *ad hoc* headquarters have no place in peace enforcement operations, because they lack the training or experience to command troops committed to high-intensity conflict. In this case, it is better to employ an existing operational headquarters, supplemented as appropriate, as was done for Operation Desert Storm.

In multi-functional operations the lead rests not with a military commander but with an SRSG who has a much wider mandate than merely to maintain or restore peace. This requires a C3I structure that includes all elements at all levels, command and control being exercised throughout a structured organisation by means of an effective communications system, with intelligence collected and disseminated as required. Multi-functional operations require a command and control triumvirate of an SRSG and his secretariat, a military Force Commander with his headquarters through which all military contributions are channelled, and a Humanitarian Coordinator with a staff appropriate to the coordination of all humanitarian contributions. I submit that the Humanitarian Coordinator should come from DHA and that this Department should have responsibility for developing a staff of experienced field coordinators. But there is one other important group of contributors whose activities must be coordinated, and that is NGOs. At a recent count in former Yugoslavia there were about 200 NGOs active there, of whom only 41 had agreed to be affiliated to the UN. In effect, this means that there are many 'loose cannons', operating independently, perhaps hampering the UN Security Forces and inadvertently aiding the combatants rather than the victims. I accept that some have moral qualms or ideological views that inhibit them from working with the military but in the name of humanity and common sense this must change, not least in the interests of their donors, whose chief interest is the alleviation of suffering. If a UN Mission has been deployed, this might mean offering up their particular contribution to be coordinated within an overall plan if scarce resources as well as their own motivation and goodwill are to be employed to best advantage. This applies to any emergency, and not just UN operations.

POST-CONFLICT RECONSTRUCTION

Apart from gathering the necessary forces, the most difficult task facing those responsible for mounting any UN operation is the determination of the 'exit strategy'. This is not helped if there is no coherent aim around which to determine such a strategy. UNTAC was an exception, because the election of a new government determined both aim and timing of the UN's withdrawal. However, in hindsight, it could be said to have been less than entirely satisfactory because national reconstruction was not included in the plan.

All post-conflict reconstruction programmes need a strategy, which should be mandated by the Security Council in the same way as conflict resolution. This will require a thorough consideration of what a country needs and will almost certainly require inputs from the following: the government of the country concerned (assuming one exists); the UN and its relevant Agencies; the World Bank and IMF; bilateral national donors interested in funding particular ventures; NGOs with skills in areas of identified need; and private sector elements which can take over a variety of tasks from the military, such as disarmament, and reintegration of combatants linked to job creation.

To begin this process early, I would appoint a fourth person to the team responsible for conflict resolution, namely a Director of Post-Conflict Reconstruction, from either DHA or UNDP (in Rwanda, DHA was given the responsibility for short-term reconstruction). The Director should be responsible for developing the reconstruction strategy, reporting to the SRSG and working with the Force Commander and Humanitarian Coordinator. Indeed, it might be that the reconstruction strategy will have an impact on the exit strategy, by indicating developments which impact on the nature and duration of the political and practical commitment of donors. Current UN thinking is that the UNDP Resident Coordinator should become the UN Coordinator, once responsibility has been handed over by the DHA. This will ensure that there is a seamless transfer from resolution to reconstruction, and that the country concerned sees immediate action in areas such as de-mining and infrastructure regeneration, while longer-term projects are put in place. The Coordinator would be responsible for implementing agreed strategy in the longer term, remaining in country to oversee it and being the chief point of contact for anyone with a role to play in the process.

The aim of any reconstruction strategy must be to enable a country to undertake or resume its position as a fully independent member of the world community. A properly conceived reconstruction strategy will define, limit and inform the less protracted crisis resolution phase which it will follow. The reaction of the NGO community to being invited into such strategic thinking is uncertain and unlikely to be uniform in any event, but it is to be hoped that they will have the good sense to appreciate the opportunity as well as the requirement. Reconstruction also represents an opportunity for individual nations to demonstrate their commitment to helping beleaguered parts of the world, not only by the amount of resources they are prepared to donate to the process but also by the effort they make toward coordinating efforts on a national basis. That is why they must be included in strategic thinking and planning.

THE REQUIREMENTS

I have concentrated chiefly on three separate groups of players: the military, UN Agencies, and NGOs. Each has a different role to play in each of the three types of activity that I have described, but if one looks at the mechanics of how they determine what they could and should do, one is struck at once by the similarity of the process: planning, logistics, the establishment of resources, sustainment, communications and long-term strategy all differ little in their essentials between the civilian and the military, and from one organisation to the next. If there is no substantial difference in their planning procedures then, in theory, there should be no difficulty in coordinating their activities. What is required for a successful military–humanitarian interface to be created is coordination machinery – and the political will that I assume to exist – capable of operating at all levels and amongst all players. I believe that the tone for this should be set by UN HQ itself, which is why I now look at six major improvements that I would like to see.

The Secretary-General and the Secretariat

While much has been written about the internal organisation of the UN, I believe that reform of the position and responsibilities of the Secretary-General must be implemented. At present, in theory, every Department and every Agency reports directly or indirectly to him; in addition he has responsibilities in the Security Council and as a global ambassador. I favour Sir Brian Urquhart's proposal;[1] it is practical, delegates responsibility sensibly and would ensure coordination at the top. Since the deputy Secretaries-General would have to liaise with each other in the course of their work, as would their staffs, coordination would be implicit in the organisation of the Departments. What is more, the major Specialised Agencies would be linked to the Departments, and more links could follow. The deputy Secretary-Generals' responsibilities would empower and require them to take coordination action without having to refer everything to the Secretary-General. Such delegation would be more efficient, as well as freeing the Secretary-General for other responsibilities. I would like to see this reorganisation formalised, and included in a revised Charter.

The Economic and Social Council (ECOSOC)

One coordinating body that is not properly used in the UN is ECOSOC, whose functions and powers are set out in Chapter X of the Charter. In particular Article 63.2 states that '[ECOSOC] may co-ordinate the activities of the specialised agencies through consultation with and recommendations to such agencies'; while Article 71 empowers ECOSOC to

> make suitable arrangements for consultation with NGOs which are concerned with matters within its competence. Such arrangements may be made with international organisations, and, where appropriate, with national organisations after consultation with Members of the UN concerned.

In other words, the political means to achieve the coordination that I advocate is already enshrined in the Charter. What we need now is the political will.

The Military Staff Committee (MSC)

The Charter also allows for the regeneration of the only subsidiary body it names, the MSC, which is described in Article 47. However, I do not subscribe to its composition as stated in Article 47.2, comprising the Chiefs of Staff of the permanent members of the Security Council, nor do I see a revitalised MSC as comprising the Chiefs of Staff of the permanent and rotating members. Rather, I would appoint a distinguished UN Force Commander as Military Adviser to the Secretary-General and Chairman of the MSC. The MSC could effectively consist of mission-specific subcommittees comprising the Chiefs of Staff of contributing nations. The Chairman, with a small staff, might help limit a practice which undermines the credibility of UN operations more than any other factor: the stream of undeliverable, incredible and sometimes contradictory resolutions that emerge from the inevitable compromises of the Security Council. A cold, hard douche of military realism, which the MSC was established to provide, could prevent much of this and ensure that mandates issued to SRSGs or Force Commanders really are deliverable.

Inter-operability

The key to successful coordination is inter-operability, which in many ways is also a state of mind. It does not mean that all nations have to buy the same equipment and speak the same language. What it does mean is that there should be a standard list of essential operational procedures and practices – to which all must conform – such as the use of certain radio frequencies and methods of passing information. To achieve this, I would extend the responsibilities of the recently-appointed Assistant Secretary-General for Planning and Support – a German 3-Star general – to those of an Inspector-General, who would have responsibility for overseeing common standards of doctrine, training and equipment amongst assigned forces of all member states. I do not advocate that the UN should set up training establishments or staff colleges of its own, but rather it should invite member nations to run courses on its behalf, for military and civilian staffs, to an agreed syllabus. I commend the recent innovation of such a course for all military and civilian staffs deployed with the Mission to Haiti (UMIH) as an innovative and constructive initiative, as was the joint exercise conducted between the UK Ministry of Defence and the Overseas Development Administration (ODA) in the UK, and the joint training between the US military and US NGOs (PVO) that was introduced in 1994.

Financial and Commercial Control

I hope that the recently appointed, and curiously titled, Under Secretary-General for Internal Oversight Services will also be encouraged to operate as an Inspector-General of commercial activity, eliminating some if not all of the accusations of corruption and malpractice that have not only sullied the name of the UN, but also undermined its efficiency. Already his presence is being felt, and procurement procedures are being tightened up. There is no doubt that improved efficiency, and the adoption of sound commercial practice, will help encourage doubters to support rather than fight shy of the organisation. This appointment has long been needed, and can do nothing but good for the name of the UN in the future.

Public Affairs

Finally, to accomplish these changes, they need to be accompanied by a structured and orchestrated education process. The responsibility for this lies with the Public Affairs Department – greater in numbers than the DPKO. The role and responsibilities of Public Affairs are wide, and should include key operational involvement in each of the three instruments discussed. Public Affairs personnel need to be trained to operate in direct support of an SRSG or Force Commander, who can be deluged with media interest. The operational importance of Public Affairs was amply illustrated when the first item of equipment asked for by the SRSG in Rwanda was a radio station to counter the Hutu propaganda which incited genocide and encouraged the flight of refugees. It is noteworthy that a radio station was a key component of the success of UNTAC.

CONCLUSION

I believe that it is essential that the UN's organisational and operational aspects are re-examined to enhance its capacity to conduct multifunctional humanitarian operations of the type which it is likely to be faced with in the future. The Charter already empowers the UN, at least in outline, to deal with complex humanitarian emergencies, for which it requires the member states to recognise the need and seize the initiative. The NGO community, now essential to fulfilling this work, cannot reasonably be expected to coordinate its actions with an organisation not entirely in harmony with itself and not realising its potential. Every professional and every humanitarian organisation – governments, UN Agencies, civil and military elements, and NGOs – must come to see that coordination is not only desirable but essential, and something for which sacred cows might have to be sacrificed.

Note

1.　See Brian Urquhart and Erskine Childers, *Towards a More Effective United Nations* (Uppsala: Dag Hammarskjöld Foundation, 1991).

10 The ICRC in Complex Emergencies: An Outsider or Part of a Team?

Bruno Doppler

Cooperation and the coordination of humanitarian and military activities in areas of conflict are extremely topical. Meetings, workshops, conferences and symposia gather representatives from governments, international organisations, NGOs and other collectivities interested in 'doing something' to relieve the suffering of innocent people. Everyone wants to be 'humanitarian' and is motivated to contribute his own stone to the building of a more peaceful world – according to personal or institutional ideas, interests and short- or long-term goals. Although the final aim of the endeavour might be clear in the minds of the involved actors, what is often not so clear is the way to reach this noble goal. What is not clear either is what makes the people, organisations and governments act, the drive behind this attractive 'humanitarian screen'. It is now essential to stand beneath the banner of 'human rights' and it is fashionable to be 'humanitarian'. Politicians and governments that want to be admitted to and respected in the international community (and increasingly also in the domestic arena) have to be champions of human rights – at least nominally. But human rights, international humanitarian law, democracy, peace, cooperation, solidarity and other fine principles, values and ideals are used in many different ways and contexts and for so many different purposes. Although peace is what everybody needs, the needs of everybody are not necessarily peaceful.

In this chapter, I should like to shed some light on certain minimum requirements that must be fulfilled if the international community really wants to get to grips with the 'new world disorder'. The following thoughts and ideas do not, of course, pretend to be the key to peace and neither do they necessarily reflect the official position of the ICRC. What I should like to share is the result of my personal experience as an International Humanitarian Law instructor in many countries throughout the world, and the essence of numerous conversations I have had with senior military officers.

THE BACKGROUND

The ICRC is a discreet organisation with a very restrictive information policy, although it works in the midst of the political arena. Its main task is the provision of protection and assistance to people suffering the effects of war or conflict which disrupts normal life conditions – whether as a result of actual fighting or from the threat of the use of armed force. The legal basis on which the ICRC works is quite solid. The international community has defined precisely its mandate through international law (the Geneva Conventions of 1949 and their two additional Protocols of 1977). The mandate is quite clear in the case of international armed conflict, less so in cases of non-international armed conflict, and relatively obscure in what we now call complex humanitarian emergencies. In the latter two circumstances, the ICRC has a right of initiative to offer its services as a neutral and impartial intermediary with the capacity to provide efficient help to those who most urgently need it. These services include the search for displaced people with a view to reuniting dispersed families.

Another set of ICRC activities is labelled 'dissemination'. Dissemination consists of presenting the principles of the ICRC, the Red Cross and international humanitarian law to a variety of publics, amongst which armed forces are a priority. Other publics include Red Cross and Red Crescent societies, schools and universities, the media and the public at large. Dissemination comes in various forms and levels of sophistication but when dealing with the military we prefer to use the term 'IHL training'. We do not so much need to improve the intellectual capacity of the men in uniform nor do we need to make lawyers out of soldiers. What we seek is for those in command to introduce into their military decision-taking process the laws of war, and we want them to train their men in turn so that their behaviour 'accords with the rules'. The better the military are trained and disciplined, the less likely it is that war crimes will occur. It is obvious that individuals can in good faith attach quite differing meanings to such concepts as 'war', 'conflict', 'humanitarian', 'international humanitarian law' and 'complex emergency'. What do these terms really mean? Many of the current misunderstandings stem from the lack of precision of the terms used. However, while the ICRC is willing to help, it must be emphasised that the responsibility to train armed forces in IHL rests entirely with their governments.

The ICRC is a very discreet organisation because governments often find the areas in which it operates extremely sensitive. Sovereignty and the principle of non-intervention are still almost sacrosanct. So when the ICRC approaches a state either to remind it of its responsibilities under international law or to offer the ICRC's services on humanitarian grounds only, governments are sometimes quite reluctant to let the ICRC perform its work. Furthermore, the number of humanitarian actors has increased considerably in recent years and thus also the difficulty of safeguarding an organisation's identity or specifity. If many do the same or similar things, very often the one who shouts the loudest will be heard. Therefore, and because so many claim to be 'humanitarian', governments sometimes put everyone into the same bag labelled 'Human Rights Organisations'. To be 'humanitarian' has become fashionable and is sometimes 'great business'. This is the main reason why a plethora of NGOs, international organisations and even the military strive for 'a place in the sun' when a conflict occurs. You can only collect means if public opinion is supportive. Public opinion arises from a complex communication process between politicians, the media and all those 'actors' who have something to say, or who want to be heard.

This is the heart of the dilemma: the ICRC daily faces a conflict of interests. On one hand, there is the legitimate right of the public to know what happens in the world; on the other, there is the legitimate desire of governments to manage their internal affairs according to their own criteria. In addition, there is the understandable wish of the media to sell their news. We live in an era of communication. The means of communication have become so powerful that information is available almost instantaneously. While the world has virtually shrunk to a market place, it is nevertheless still as multi-faceted as ever in terms of cultures, customs and religions, languages and idiosyncrasies. The world has changed, but have individuals?

In a democracy, and the world is apparently on the march towards democracy, citizens are wont to scrutinise the activities of their elected governments. If citizens are satisfied, governments will be re-elected. Therefore, politicians often feel compelled to tell their citizens what they want to hear. This information might not always be concordant with the truth. For this and other reasons, there is always some measure of manipulation in public pronouncements. However, the ICRC has no right to dilute the truth. The ICRC has a mandate to help people who are threatened when nobody else can intervene on their behalf. As these people are sometimes 'enemies of the State', it is understandable why governments are not always eager to let organisations, be they ever-so 'humanitarian', sniff around their places of detention. But the ICRC is, in most instances, able to visit prisons because governments know the result of the visit will not become public. It will remain confidential and be addressed only to the Authorities in charge.

But the ICRC is no longer the only organisation to be interested in the fate of individuals who are deprived of their liberty because of conflict. There are many very competent organisations that also have the capacity, the experience and the means to perform such humanitarian tasks. The ICRC does not have exclusivity with regard to humanitarianism. But it has a tradition, it has developed a way of doing things that has proved efficient, and it has acquired a humanitarian philosophy. This is very difficult to explain and perhaps even more difficult to understand. The 'secretiveness' of the ICRC is the result of more than 130 years of humanitarian experience in almost all theatres of conflict throughout the world. And as a Spanish saying goes: 'The devil knows more because he is old than because he is devil.' The corporate memory of the ICRC has made it a humanitarian tool which has accrued considerable respect from the principal actors in all types of conflicts, namely governments. The main reason for this is that governments know that they do not have anything to fear from the ICRC which is always neutral, impartial and discreet. As this method of working has proved successful, many other organisations now claim to work on the same principles.

The ICRC is often perceived as arrogant. It says what it does, but it does not say what it sees. And this is precisely what interests the media, because they think that this is what interests the public at large. Despite all this 'secrecy', ICRC delegates are nonetheless people who talk, not only to each other, but also to representatives of other organisations in the field. They attend meetings, for example with UNHCR, or will accept invitations from military commanders to attend briefings; and they will not simply sit in a corner and listen. ICRC delegates will share operational information, details of planned visits to places where people are detained, and schedules and routes of humanitarian convoys. The criterion for the ICRC is always the victim: will the victim benefit from any action or is there a risk that his fate, or that of his family, be worsened?

Undoubtedly there are many conflicts of interest when one takes a closer look at the wide spectrum of humanitarian relief workers – the politicians, the humanitarians, the media, the public – and the victims. Our task here is to find a compromise – a platform to reconcile diverging centres of interest, without creating a 'win–lose' situation.

The ICRC is a victim-oriented organisation. This means the ICRC helps all victims, regardless of the party to which they belong. This humanitarian ubiquity is sometimes difficult for governments to accept as it implies that

ICRC delegates will wish to survey the whole national territory. One can easily see how important this makes confidence-building, confidence-keeping and discretion.

THE FRONT LINE

We have seen that 'transparency', 'neutrality', 'impartiality' – and, we may add – 'non-competition' are essential, if the humanitarian tasks performed by so many different actors in the field are to generate synergy and really benefit those who are most in need of help. And who really cares about the victims? We are all familiar with the transience of televised tragedies. When, suddenly, a conflict disappears and a new one or a warmed-up one is chosen to make the headlines, victims of the earlier conflicts still need help. These 'forgotten victims' are still victims: bombs and bullets still kill nine civilians for each soldier; and mines still take their toll of the innocent. The suffering innocent matter when there is an airlift or an important relief convoy to be publicised. But once the goods have been unloaded (and unloaded does not always mean that they have reached the needy), the victims are in the shadow again. However, there are fortunately some very professional humanitarian organisations who continue to care, who stick to their mandate, and assist in the less newsworthy humanitarian emergencies.

'Samaritan anonymous' is a creature of the past; today we must speak of 'Samaritan Trust incorporated', with its worldwide presence and a great hunger for publicity. We now need coordination because 'business is business' and if you are not effective and efficient, you go out of business. It is as simple as that. What are the consequences of this humanitarian competition, of this struggle for survival by those who work in the market of 'survival'?

THE 'REAL WORLD' OF COMPLEX EMERGENCIES

'Homo homini lupus' said the Romans (Man is a wolf for man – or the other way round . . .). We could extend this saying to the organisations who under the umbrella of humanitarianism want to occupy the world stage. Let us come back to the 'real world' by considering Operation Restore Hope/Solace in Somalia. This contains most of the elements that comprise complex emergencies today: a variety of actors (civilian and military); a political decision to intervene on humanitarian grounds because 'peace' and the 'security' of people and of a region were threatened;

the presence on the ground of humanitarian organisations, of the UN and of representatives of powers with particular interests; the absence or the disintegration of a state structure; the presence of 'clans', war lords, banditry, anarchy and chaos; and the lack of a clear plan to restore 'normal' life conditions.

In this volatile environment, one battalion group was given the mission 'to provide security for the provision of humanitarian assistance within the Baidoa Humanitarian Relief Sector (HRS)'. The battalion commander's concept of operations involved the escort of relief convoys within the HRS, and the domination of the HRS through the use of static security positions, patrolling and on-call quick reaction forces. Another aspect of operations in the Baidoa HRS was the civil–military liaison function. This role was intended to provide an interface between the battalion group and the civilians with whom the group had to deal on a day-to-day basis. The tasks performed in this role included: representing the battalion group at meetings; liaising with NGOs, UN Agencies, and local political groups; providing advice and assistance to NGOs, particularly medical assistance with inoculation programmes and in local hospitals; providing security for NGO funds; providing liaison officers for company in-depth patrolling tasks and for VIP visits; gathering information on key people, banditry and political activity; coordinating the unloading of relief aircraft and the movement of civil and military air passengers and traffic; and the establishment of an auxiliary security force (police, the judiciary and the prison system). Without going deeply into an analysis of these various tasks, it is apparent that the humanitarian tasks of the military component were substantial. But as the battalion commander remarked 'Operation Restore Hope was a near classic example of a modern day military phenomenon – a humanitarian war or intervention. It was a clear case of a humanitarian relief effort leading increasingly to a significant military action'.

The more humanitarian organisations that are involved in an emergency, the more coordination effort is needed but the principal question is 'under whose authority shall we be coordinated?'. Everybody likes the idea of coordination, but few are those who want to be coordinated. The ICRC definitely does not want to be coordinated – not so much because it thinks it could easily do everything by itself (which proved false in Somalia, for example) – but because of the perception which would arise from the association of the ICRC (neutral, independent, humanitarian) with organisations that might not live up to these capital principles of the ICRC.

The President of the ICRC, Mr Cornelio Sommaruga, has agreed that closer cooperation is absolutely necessary in the field:

What can be said at present about the process of strengthening the coordination of humanitarian assistance? First of all, this process remains indispensable, especially in view of the magnitude of existing needs and the growing number of humanitarian players.

However, implementing this closer cooperation among the humanitarian actors in order to avoid the wasting of means, energy and efficiency risks being a lengthy process. What must be avoided at all costs is excessive centralisation and bureaucracy. Mr Sommaruga has commented:

Competition among various agencies and organisations, the tendency of certain states to engage in undisciplined bilateral action, the lack of professionalism shown by some new NGOs – whose goodwill is not in doubt – all these constitute obstacles that must be overcome.

Another factor that is crucial, if humanitarian action is to have long-term effects and not simply protect lives from an immediate threat, is the existence of political will to solve the actual crisis or difficulty. No peace can be imposed by force of arms. In other words, if the military are able to keep an agreed ceasefire, they will be impotent to restore peace if the parties to the conflict have not themselves come to the conclusion that peace is better than war. Peace is a daily political plebiscite. An armed force, provided it has the necessary means to do so, can only preserve peace or defend peace if it is threatened. No crisis can be solved without political action. While the political mechanisms are being set up in order to settle a conflict through diplomatic and political channels, the military can play an important role securing routes for humanitarian convoys, guaranteeing the inviolability of protected or neutralised areas, and monitoring an agreed ceasefire between the parties involved.

It is apparent that complex emergencies require complex cooperation mechanisms; standard solutions for standard problems, innovative solutions for complex situations. For those involved this means training. For all those who are engaged in the humanitarian field, be they civilians or military are in the same disarray; most situations are new. What organisations and personnel have learnt at home is not necessarily valid and useful once they are confronted with the real world of complex humanitarian emergencies.

CONCLUSION

Most of those with recent field experience, be they military or 'humanitarians', state that coordination is not really a problem in the field. The problem arises at headquarters' level because of the need to demonstrate individual identity for domestic political constituencies or the media.

Everybody would benefit from better coordination. For the ICRC, the coordination or, as I have explained 'the operational cooperation' will come through a better understanding of this organisation, its role, its mandate and its criteria for action. This requires a better ICRC information policy, which is currently being put in place. A greater openness and less diplomatic shyness enhanced by a new 'corporate image' will ease the path. Better coordination amongst the ICRC's partners in the field will automatically lead to fewer areas of friction and less loss of time, money, assets and nervous energy.

Personally I think that a trend has been set. Coordination will come. It will have to come. What is needed are adequate mechanisms to allow a proper exchange of information in such a way that every organisation can perform its job in the field it which it is expert. Let the military do the military job, the humanitarian organisations provide the assistance and human rights protection, and the politicians the means to create the conditions that will allow a permanent solution.

To allow 'coordination' or 'operational cooperation' to grow organically, more and better training for all partners involved in complex humanitarian emergencies is essential. Valuable efforts have already been made but must be more widely shared. More research capacity has to be invested to find adequate solutions to an array of problems that have been identified so far. This capacity and the necessary competences exist; I even believe that the will is there.

11 Coordination, Control and Competition: NGOS on the Front Line

Jon Bennett

The international aid community is undergoing one of the most intense periods of reflection and self-doubt in 20 years. The inadequate and confused response to recent complex emergencies has left the image of humanitarianism tarnished. As we watched the ignoble withdrawal of the UN from Somalia in early 1995, we realised that the myth of quick-fix humanitarian relief backed by military muscle could no longer be sustained. These emergencies were born not only of drought, displacement and war but also of long-term endemic social, economic and political turmoil accelerated by the collapse of Cold War certainties. It is no accident that most of today's war-related tragedies take place on the periphery of what used to be the East–West axis. Other than the short-term demands of media-induced concern, they will continue to lie outside spheres of geopolitical interest and thus receive only a modicum of international assistance. In short, the trouble has only just begun.

Notwithstanding pessimism, new ideas abound. The so-called 'relief to development continuum' and a renewed emphasis on conflict prevention and mitigation, not least amongst NGOs who feel that they have a unique entry point at the level of civil society, provide useful starting points. With this, of course, must come a realignment of funding priorities. Keeping the lid on conflict is expensive and requires new skills and new approaches. As NGOs and the UN urgently search for a compromise between the exigencies of relief and the as yet intangible demands of prevention, one thing is certain: effective intervention, whether short- or long-term, requires sustained coordination from donors' offices – right down to the point of delivery. In the highly competitive environment of humanitarian aid (witness the 130 NGOs who descended upon Rwanda in the space of a month in the Autumn of 1994) such coordination can be a daunting task.

Coordination itself is a value-laden concept. For some it has overtones of 'control', while others fear being swamped by interminable layers of bureaucracy. While the principal coordinator should be the host government, foreign NGOs in particular have given scant attention to the

136

requirements of accountability towards that government. Weak and ill-equipped governments emerging out of conflict are particularly vulnerable to 'aid shock' – the arrival and dispersal of hundreds of expatriates with vehicles and equipment, backed by powerful donor interests. Some officials have reacted strongly, imposing regulatory controls unacceptable to donors and aid organisations alike; others have simply relinquished any pretence of control and, perversely, have even established their own quasi-NGOs, often led by a government minister, to attract foreign funds. Meanwhile, the onus of preventing duplication, improving access and rationalising the division of labour among assistance-givers has fallen squarely on the shoulders of either the UN or the NGOs themselves.

The attraction of 'NGOism' – and the accompanying pitfalls – is understandable. Worldwide, NGOs collectively command funds in the region of $8–9 billion annually, reaching some 250 million people living in absolute poverty. International governments increasingly channel resources, especially for emergencies, through their favoured NGOs rather than through the allegedly less accountable governments of the South. In several emergencies of the late 1980s and early 1990s, short-term money available to NGOs – albeit mostly to international NGOs – exceeded even that of the UN. NGOs are now the front line forces of 'neutral' intervention and are more closely linked to the UN, European Commission and donor governments than even before. As the number of crises demanding our attention increases, so too does the number of new NGOs willing to meet that demand. The international safety net of voluntary assistance has never been so buoyant.

However, the phenomenal increase in the number, size and financial status of NGOs in the 1980s and 1990s has to a large extent happened without close inspection of their performance. For all their laudable successes, some NGOs have been guilty of poor practice, wastage and a lack of professionalism which to a large extent has gone unchecked. They have tended to throw a veil of secrecy over importunate practices and actions that would not stand up to public scrutiny. Critics of NGOs have highlighted the lack of accountability, mutual competitiveness and poor coordination as perhaps the three most serious charges levelled at the so-called Third Sector. Alarm has also been expressed about the fact that some NGOs have 'crowded out' governments by offering better resources and salaries and, in some cases, have made little secret of their wish to replace government structures. Another serious charge is that northern NGOs have singularly failed to transfer skills to any significant degree to their southern counterparts.

Some of these issues can be addressed by transferring decision-making to the field – to the recipients as well as to the givers of aid. Much has been said about involving refugees, for example, in the decisions that affect their lives, yet very few lasting structures have been created to ensure that this is not simply rhetorical good sense. Field-based NGO coordination structures are potentially a way forward, for they can be 'owned' not only by the multitude of small local NGOs rarely seen on our television screens but also, with careful nurturing, by at least some of the voiceless majority they serve. The level of genuine participation will depend on how such structures are set up and who controls them. There have been some encouraging examples in Central America and Africa, though local coordination bodies, like their national NGO membership, suffer from lack of resources and the sometimes overwhelming dominance of northern NGOs.

A major obstacle to effective field-based NGO coordination has been the tendency, particularly by large northern NGOs, to perceive coordination only in terms of self-interest. If *ad hoc* meetings with NGO colleagues suffice then why, they argue, should we invest time and money in setting up a coordination structure? The argument rests on the spurious notion that each NGO is at the same level of development and has the same access to donors, governments, the UN and external resources. It neglects the fact that local NGOs in particular are empowered by collective representation and consensus; their working relationship with larger, foreign NGOs is an important component of their institutional development. Moreover, if coordination is decentralised and local participation encouraged, such NGO collectives could become excellent vehicles for promoting conflict resolution and reconciliation. Yet in spite of these potential advantages, proven by field evidence in a number of recent studies,[1] many northern NGOs have failed to highlight coordination as a policy priority, preferring simply to let the issue be decided by already overstretched field directors.

REGULATIONS AND CODES OF CONDUCT

The relative freedom enjoyed by NGOs engaging in cross-border activities of the 1980s has, in many cases, resulted in operational codes of practice that implicitly assume that a host government is an obstacle to, rather than a partner in, the development process. In mid-1994, eight non-governmental humanitarian agencies (NGHAs), including the ICRC, prepared and published a Code of Conduct for their work in disaster relief.[2] Although the 10 codes and three annexes were not binding, and no suggestions were made for monitoring and enforcing them, it was nevertheless a laudable attempt on the part of the major northern NGOs to summarise and reach consensus on a number of operational principles. Notably absent, however, was the recognition of obligations these NGOs/NGHAs have towards host governments. The text declared that:

We [shall] formulate our own policies and implementation strategies and do not seek to implement the policy of any government, except in so far as it coincides with our own independent policy.

In the Annex, five specific recommendations for the behaviour of host governments towards humanitarian organisations were listed, but no reciprocal recommendations were mentioned for NGOs/NGHAs except for a general endeavour 'to co-operate with local government structures where appropriate'.

One can understand, then, why this serious divergence of interest has led in some cases to outright hostility towards NGOs. National governments understandably use regulations and registration as their starting point in efforts to coordinate the NGO sector. As international donors confine their contributions to the observance of good governance – and liberal democratic notions such as the 'rolling back of the state' come to the fore – there is a pressing need to examine the parameters of state intervention in the NGO sector, and the appropriate obligations each has towards the other. Even when autonomous NGO coordination structures are in place, host governments invariably put demands on these structures to provide detailed information about each NGO registered as a member. This can invoke tensions over confidentiality, not least when details of national employees are requested.

In recent years, there has been a discernable shift in favour of channelling funds through southern NGOs. Aside from the implications this has for northern NGOs, there is the implicit assumption that responsibility for social welfare will gradually shift from top-down government structures backed by bilateral aid to that of the smaller, more flexible and cheaper southern indigenous NGOs. Put crudely, aid dependency will become increasingly privatised, with governments acting more in a regulatory than in an implementing capacity. The transition will be fraught with difficulties and will, at least in the interim period, invoke reactive legislation, particularly from new governments keen to invest renewed authority in previously discredited ministries. For example, Rwanda in late 1994 introduced a substantial body of legislation to regulate activities of the plethora of NGOs arriving in the country. Again, in the newly-independent states of the Former Soviet Union, the old state edifice is slowly being replaced by a pluralistic economy and social structure that will have profound effects on social welfare provision. The rapidly growing NGO sector is causing, at best, confusion for governments hitherto unused to dealing with large numbers of relatively autonomous organisations backed increasingly by northern capital.

However, in many recent major complex emergencies, foreign NGOs dominated the humanitarian scene often adding to the confusion and frustration of host governments. Upon arrival, these NGOs expect customs and foreign exchange concessions and other privileges to be provided by the receiving government. Often, these same NGOs are unwilling to be transparent about the sources or amounts of funds and equipment they import into the country, even when the recipient government has good reason to question the ultimate destination of the funds or the quality of the materials. There have, for example, been cases of outdated drugs being imported for distribution, false accounting, exaggerated statistics issued to the press, and a host of other transgressions providing ample excuse for a guarded view of foreign NGOs by host governments.

Registration and protocol arrangements are only one part of a complex web of relationships between host governments and foreign and national NGOs. The nature of this legislation, the manner in which it is monitored, and the political and economic climate in which it is developed, each deserve detailed research if we are to understand more fully the tensions that exist between the imperatives of statehood and the demands of civil society. A rigorous analysis of what is understood by 'freedom of association' and the role of NGOs in expanding the boundaries of civil society would serve as a useful starting point. Human rights NGOs, for example, in challenging the legitimacy of governments, will appeal to a body of transnational agreements which, they claim, override national regulations and restrictions in the event of dispute. Even in a strictly legal sense, little is understood of the legitimate boundaries of NGO work and the extent to which governments, acting nationally or bilaterally, are morally and legally bound to support NGOs in the pursuit of their work.

Although not always reflected in legislation, there is usually a clear distinction between the treatment enjoyed by foreign NGOs and that accorded to indigenous NGOs. The latter are more likely to fall under the various regulations relating to national welfare institutions, cooperatives, trade unions, or the like, some of which might have been on the statutes since pre-independence. Disputed areas of law often reflect the lack of updated regulations. Moreover, indigenous NGOs backed by foreign capital can be suspected of harbouring political dissidents. The suspicion was well founded in the Horn of Africa in the 1980s when the resistance launched by the Eritreans and Tigrayans against Ethiopia's Soviet-backed government was undoubtedly helped by foreign aid inputs. Indeed, it is precisely the reason why the new governments of Ethiopia and Eritrea, no strangers to the world of NGOs, have felt it necessary strictly to regulate NGO activities in the last two years.

The thorny problem of NGO relations with national governments is further illustrated by what happened in Kenya in 1992. The Kenyan government introduced the NGO Coordination Act, which was to regulate and prioritise NGO inputs into the country at large in the wake of the Somali refugee crisis. At field level, UNHCR had already assigned NGO 'lead agencies' as their contractual partner for assistance to refugees, but the government was increasingly concerned about the autonomy enjoyed by the growing number of national and international NGOs setting up offices in the country. The NGO response to the Act was, not surprisingly, one of alarm. Backed by a powerful coterie of government and multilateral donors, they managed to delay – and in some cases cancel – certain provisions of the Act. Where NGO coordination had previously been poor, suddenly NGOs 'under attack' very quickly found a need for coordinated action. Interesting parallels can be drawn with security alerts in Afghanistan, which in the last few years have elicited impressive levels of NGO cooperation through the Agency Coordinating Body for Afghan Relief (ACBAR). A general threat to NGOs is not a prerequisite for coordination, but it certainly helps.

In the rush to support local institutions, donors have not always appreciated local political and economic incentives that can lead to abuse of NGO status. With so many organisations vying for attention, donors and governments need an urgent and rigorous definition of what is and what is not an NGO. While many are competent, there is a danger of opportunism and the emergence of under-skilled or politically-aligned organisations attracting funds. In Afghanistan and South Sudan, where prior to the onset of the humanitarian emergencies there had been few, if any, indigenous NGOs, there are today in excess of 250 in each country. At best, they will become simple delivery agents for donors; at worst they may further erode genuine institutional development by setting themselves up as the only arbiters of change. Moreover, in a phenomenon more frequent than is usually appreciated, government ministers themselves form NGOs to bypass official channels of assistance, using their official status to attract funds and minimise competition from elsewhere.

INSTITUTIONS AND CIVIL SOCIETY

The transference of skills and technology to the South is an issue constantly revisited, not least by those who would wish to involve southern NGOs more fully in the delivery of humanitarian assistance. The focus of activity for many NGOs – particularly those engaged in relief and rehabilitation work – rests on the assumption that the appropriate unit of intervention is the organisation itself, and the 'project' is its vehicle. Yet a central tenet of sustainable development is that the performance of any project – government or private – is critically dependent on the functioning of institutions. An institution is broader than an organisation (although some organisations become institutions) for it implies a stable pattern of behaviour recognised and valued by society. Institutions exert themselves through the rules, norms and values that influence people's lives.[3]

The distinction between an organisation and an institution is not merely convenient semantics. Northern NGOs in particular are more and more engaged in macro policy – a level of action that is often institutional in its nature. By contrast, southern NGOs have little space to evolve a development agenda of their own. In many countries, they lack institutional identity; their role is increasingly as part of an imposed aid system rather than as an autonomous sector within the larger society with a self-determined contribution to make towards national development. Also, as competitors for external aid, they have occasionally felt the brunt of government legislation in an attempt to curtail their activities.

To invest in institutional development, therefore, is to accept the need for a community of viable organisations and a change in the pattern of interactions between the NGO community and other development actors. Such an investment requires more than short-term funds for predetermined projects. It demands an awareness of the distinction between change in social structures – the institutional dimension – and change at an individual organisational level. An institutional development perspective regards NGOs as a sector promoting values associated with self-reliance, social justice, countervailing power and the like – values that need to be protected and extended. Governments, or indeed individual NGOs, cannot by themselves champion such values. At best, governments can provide a conducive political, social and economic environment in which development takes place though a mixture of private and public endeavours. Where freedom of association, participation and empowerment are valued, it is civil society that creates the necessary normative framework.

It is within civil society that we locate the need for collective, coordinated and policy-oriented action by the NGO sector as a whole. This is precisely the unique role that a strong national association, council or collaborative network of NGOs can play. Creating the economic and political 'space' for the development of such structures will require the cooperation and encouragement of the northern aid community. Yet, particularly in disasters, scant attention is paid to the role, potential or real, that existing

institutions play. Northern donors, NGOs and the UN are usually pre-
occupied with logistics – fast and efficient delivery systems backed by
short-term funds. Where local NGOs are promoted, they invariably provide extension services for the larger donors and are rarely given money
even for administration, let alone capacity building.

COORDINATION IN PRACTICE

There have, nevertheless, been some interesting experiments in the last 10
years in attempting to get the NGO house in order. In Lebanon, Ethiopia,
Afghanistan and Mozambique, for example, NGO coordination bodies have
been instrumental in bringing the NGO community into close dialogue
with UN Agencies. They have also developed local codes of conduct
for NGOs, including very specific guidelines for health, agriculture and
food delivery programmes. Most importantly, these organisations have
mapped out where and in what sectors the NGOs work, thus minimising
the duplication of projects.

A coordination body is usually set up in the capital or regional centre
of the country in question. Often a 'lead agency' takes the initiative to gather
NGOs and discuss a common programme of action for a particular problem facing the country. The Committee for Coordination of Services to
Displaced Persons in Thailand, for example, was set up to deal with NGO
inputs into Cambodian refugee settlements in Thailand, although later they
also coordinated NGO responses to Burmese and Vietnamese refugees.
Here, as in other successful endeavours, a small secretariat was paid for
by the members, with supplementary grants from bilateral government
donors, independent foundations and the UN. Usually, a general assembly
of NGO members elects its own executive committee to oversee all aspects of the secretariat's work.

In some cases, however, the coordination body is itself an NGO with
its own field programmes. The danger that a membership agency might
begin to compete with its members for funds was faced by the Christian
Relief and Development Agency (CRDA) in Ethiopia in the mid-1980s;
very soon the members closed CRDA's string of clinics, preferring it to
be restricted to a purely consultative body. Interestingly, the CRDA, now
25 years old, retained a level of power over its members by being the
recipient and allocator of resources from donors.

Traditionally, an NGO coordination body is primarily the centre for
information exchange and the first point of contact for NGOs arriving in
a country. More pro-active organisations will attempt to map out needs in

a particular area, persuade NGOs usefully to assign themselves different tasks and oversee the 'whole picture' of NGO intervention. As such, they have become increasingly important for the UN and others anxious not to have to deal individually with the multitude of NGOs, large and small, that arrive during any emergency. This intermediary role can be instrumental in ensuring that NGOs have a collective voice in formulating policies and priorities at a national level. For example, the LINK NGO Forum in Mozambique now sits on the national Humanitarian Assistance Committee, one of the structures set up to implement the country's peace process. LINK also assists the UN in its allocation of funds channelled through the Trust Fund for Humanitarian Assistance in Mozambique.

Sadly, indigenous NGO coordinating bodies have often been ignored by international NGOs anxious to set up more 'efficient' structures during an emergency. The reaction against northern dominance may, in some cases, involve the setting up of an exclusively indigenous body. In Lebanon, one of the most impressive coordination structures is the Lebanese NGO Forum (LNF), entirely managed by a consortium of 14 Lebanese NGO associations with a collective membership of hundreds of local community-based organisations. Throughout the Lebanese war, this loose coalition provided a counterbalance to the notion that sectarian groups were fundamentally irreconcilable. The LNF comprises Catholic, Muslim, Druze and Orthodox groups with one common agenda: the provision of assistance to a population torn apart by war. The foundations for reconstructing civil society lie precisely in such coordinated initiatives.

In each of these endeavours, it was the day-to-day mechanics of coordination which proved the success or failure of the enterprise. Simply appointing a 'Coordinator' does not ensure success, as has been demonstrated by the UN system. When the UN General Assembly adopted GA Res 46/182 in 1991 and formed a coordinating lead agency, the DHA, institutional jealousies soon followed. Part of the problem has been the extraordinary lack of basic coordination skills demonstrated by DHA (and other UN lead Agency) staff. The notable exceptions – for example, Rwanda in the closing months of 1994 – are due more to individual excellence than to any comprehensive staff training programme.[4] The same criticism can be levelled at NGOs. One would suppose that since aid agency senior staff spend a high percentage of their time in meetings, the basic rubric of conducting such meetings would have been decided long ago, but this is not the case. A poorly designed framework for coordination will simply fan the flames of competing egos. It is often said that everyone wants coordination but few wish to be coordinated. Perhaps this is because too often they leave a meeting without a sense of having achieved anything.

The mechanics of setting up an NGO coordination body and the comparative advantage such an organisation has as a democratic representative of collective NGO views has been explored elsewhere.[5] If NGOs as a community have something unique to offer, then a greater degree of NGO coordination at field level is crucial in realising that potential. The UN's own coordinating role in emergencies will be better served by having a representative NGO umbrella body to which it can relate. Coordination 'owned' by NGOs is not a bureaucratic imposition designed to stifle the independence and imagination of individual NGOs; it is a tool for increasing the effectiveness of a collective endeavour. The challenge is to design a structure conducive to strengthening cooperation without limiting the freedom of any one participant.

Notes

1. J. Bennett, *NGO Coordination at Field Level: A Handbook* (Geneva: ICVA, 1994).
2. Overseas Development Institute, *Code of Conduct for the International Red Cross and Red Crescent Movement and NGOs in Disaster Relief*, Relief and Rehabilitation Network Paper, No. 7 (London, 1994).
3. A. Fowler, *Institutional Development and NGOs in Africa: Policy Perspectives for European Development Agencies* (Oxford: INTRAC, 1992).
4. J. Bennett, 'Reinventing Wheels', *Crosslines*, Vol. 2, Nos 4–5 (October 1994).
5. J. Bennett, *NGO Coordination at Field Level*.

Part IV
Field Coordination of UN Humanitarian Assistance

12 Field Coordination of UN Humanitarian Assistance, Bosnia, 1994

Sir Michael Rose

No language can describe adequately the condition of that large portion of the Balkan peninsula – Serbia, Bosnia, Hercegovina and other provinces – political intrigues, constant rivalries, a total absence of all public spirit . . . hatred of all races, animosities of rival religions and absence of any controlling power . . . nothing short of an army of 50 000 of the best troops would produce anything like order in these parts. (Disraeli, August 1878, in the House of Lords)

When the UN deployed into Bosnia in 1992, its mission was not classic peacekeeping where each party to the conflict invites the UN to act as a mediator – for neither party engaged in the war had demonstrated any intention of bringing about an end to the conflict. Indeed, it could be argued that the worst horrors of the war were still to come. Thus it simply was not possible for the UN Force to carry out the task of peacekeeping in a traditional manner; nor, initially, could it create the necessary confidence-building mechanisms by which the war could be brought to an end. All that would lie in the future. The United Nations Protection Force (UNPROFOR) was therefore deployed purely in order to help UNHCR and other aid agencies alleviate the terrible levels of human suffering which were the inescapable consequence of the ongoing war. This principal role inevitably shaped the entire structure and deployment of the Force. The second role of UNPROFOR, which came later under SCR 743/92, was to try to create those conditions necessary for a peaceful resolution of the conflict. However, under SCRs 824/93 and 836/93, UNPROFOR was required to apply unusually high levels of military force in order to deter attacks against six designated safe areas and to maintain the total exclusion zones for heavy weapons around Sarajevo and Gorazde. Since these enforcement measures were aimed mainly at the Bosnian Serb Army, who controlled much of the key military terrain in Bosnia, it can be seen that the two main roles of UNPROFOR were at variance with each other: humanitarian aid delivery and military enforcement backed by NATO jets do tend to lie uneasily together. Thus, the story of the UN Mission in Bosnia has been one of reconciling these two conflicting roles, and its success in so doing, in the UN's 50th year, has possibly represented one of the most significant advances in the cause of peacekeeping during the past decade.

To face up to the challenges of the new world disorder of the sort which Bosnia represents, the UN has to develop entirely new doctrines and concepts of operation. These were needed partly to create the necessary levels of coordination between the humanitarian assistance organisations and the military elements of the peacekeeping force – particularly in terms of the mission requirement, the integration of command and control, and the rationalisation of logistic effort. Whilst good coordination cannot in itself ensure success, it is quite clear that without the unique and highly successful coordination between UNHCR and UNPROFOR, it simply would not have been possible to have sustained the lives of more than 2.7 million people throughout the midst of this bloody civil war. The outdated theory that the presence of a military peacekeeping force has a negative effect on a humanitarian aid mission has no place in a war-torn country like Bosnia – where aid is regarded as a weapon of war, where the destruction of the country's infrastructure is so great and, where in the absence of law and order only a military force can provide the logistics and security necessary for aid delivery. Since 1992, considerable risks have been taken by those involved in the delivery of aid across the battle lines to those most in need, who invariably tend to be in remote and hazardous locations. Although many lives have sadly been lost during the three-year duration of the Mission, it can justifiably be claimed that the Mission has succeeded to a remarkable degree. Aid targets in 1994 were by and large achieved, and the guns had fallen silent by the end of that year creating the conditions for a just and lasting peace – if the leaders of the different parties to the conflict choose to make use of the opportunities which have been won at such cost on behalf of their peoples. Any failure on their part to do so cannot be blamed on the UN mandate or on the Mission itself. The political leaders will have been seen to be quick to take their people to war and slow to return them to peace. Nevertheless, the lessons that can be derived from an examination of how this remarkable success was achieved are many and will form the basis of this chapter.

The fundamental principle underlying the deployment of the peacekeeping force into Bosnia, and which exclusively allowed it to continue to carry out its tasks, is that it has remained a non-combatant in the eyes of those involved in the war. The clear lesson here is that unless it has the mandate to act like an invading force, a Mission can only operate with the consent of all parties to the conflict. That is, it must remain impartial and neutral in the way that it conducts its business, and that when it is obliged to use force, it does so within the normal rules for the use of force common to any peacekeeping operation: only a minimum level of force is used to achieve a specific aim, warnings are given before the use of force, collateral damage is avoided, and the use of force must always remain relevant, timely, and proportional. Regrettably, a great deal of force, mostly in self-defence, has had to be used in Bosnia since 1992 against all three parties to the conflict. But by consistently adhering to these principles the non-combatant status of UNPROFOR has remained uncompromised – notwithstanding bombing raids by NATO aircraft on at least four occasions. If, on the other hand, military force is used to try to compel one side or the other to change its political position or to alter the balance of force, then what effectively becomes a war-fighting mission will inevitably have gravely adverse effects on the overall status of the peacekeeping mission. In Somalia, it has been well demonstrated that it was the move by the UN Force from peacekeeping to war-fighting which so terminally damaged the prospects of the Mission. The Somalia Mission, as in Bosnia, had the primary purpose of sustaining the population through the delivery of humanitarian aid. Like the River Styx, once crossed it is not possible to retrace one's steps across what has become known as the Mogadishu line.

Bosnia demonstrates that retaining impartiality and neutrality in a civil war situation is no easy matter, as inevitably all sides use humanitarian aid for political ends and to sustain their military forces. Indeed, the delivery of basic foodstuffs or fuel to a besieged population is seen by the besieger as acting against the very purpose of the siege. The fact that aid was delivered to all the enclaves, including Sarajevo, throughout the war (albeit with a number of interruptions) was in itself a great achievement and shows that in the final analysis all parties to the conflict saw the continued presence of UNHCR and the peacekeepers as being in their own strategic interests. The difficulties of maintaining the necessary degree of consent for the delivery of aid in such a hostile environment have been well described elsewhere.[1]

Its commitment to Bosnia brought new challenges to UNHCR, who were invited to become the lead agency for the delivery of humanitarian aid in addition to their customary task of looking after the mass of refugees and people displaced by war. The circumstances facing UNHCR were both extremely hazardous and intimidating. War, ethnic cleansing, persecution of minorities, indiscriminate attacks on civilians, lack of respect for humanitarian principles and deliberate targeting of aid workers continued to threaten daily the work of humanitarian aid workers in Bosnia.

In a note prepared for participants in a meeting on former Yugoslavia convened by the European Union on 22 December 1993, UNHCR wrote:

> Despite repeated commitments by the parties that suggest otherwise, with the conflict continuing, both the Bosnian Croats and Bosnian Serbs see the provision of the necessary humanitarian assistance to the Muslim controlled area as against their miliary interests.[2]

UNHCR was the lead Agency with prime responsibility for logistics and transport, food monitoring, domestic needs, shelter, community services, health, emergency transition activities in agriculture, income generation, and also protection and legal assistance. WFP were responsible for the mobilisation and delivery of basic food to the distribution points outside Bosnia, for the provision of supplementary food, and for the assessment of needs. WHO was the primary Agency for health, whilst UNICEF undertook multi-sectoral assistance for ensuring the provision of survival and development needs of women and children. ICRC were responsible for the release of prisoners of war and other detained people. In addition, there were many governmental and non-governmental organisations active in Bosnia, such as the UK Overseas Development Agency (ODA), the International Rescue Committee (IRC) and Médecins sans Frontières. Not all initially welcomed the deployment of a military peacekeeping force into Bosnia, fearing that this would inhibit their working relations with the parties to the conflict. But, by the end of 1994, it was recognised almost universally, to quote one organisation mentioned above, that 'the task of delivering humanitarian aid could not have been achieved without the direct support of UNPROFOR'. The work of coordinating the activities of the UN humanitarian organisations operating in former Yugoslavia fell to the SRSG in Zagreb and was inevitably more complex than the simple description above implies. To his great credit, the present incumbent, Yasushi Akashi, did not interfere in the detailed workings of UNHCR, whose lines of responsibility went directly to Geneva.

The experience of coordinating the work of so many different and at times seemingly conflicting organisations in such dire circumstances produced a clear second lesson for the future: if such a mission is to succeed, there has to be a common strategy evolved for the entire theatre of operations. In Bosnia, a campaign plan was drawn up for UNPROFOR which clearly described its principal task as assisting UNHCR and other Agencies in the delivery of humanitarian aid; other tasks were to be subordinated to this prime task. UNPROFOR was to be regarded as a supporting arm of the humanitarian aid mission. UNHCR liaison cells were established in all military headquarters and UNHCR representatives attended all military briefings and conferences at each level of command. Battalions on the ground were tasked to establish military liaison with all parties to the conflict for the express purpose of facilitating the passage of aid. Engineer units built roads and bridges, and cleared minefields. Military units escorted aid convoys where it was necessary to ensure safe transit. Secondary aid distribution was monitored by UNPROFOR. Military patrols on the ground were requested to monitor the status and condition of the civilian population, particularly those in areas too dangerous for civilian agencies to reach, and reports regarding the state of essential utilities were made to UNHCR and higher headquarters in Zagreb. Power stations were run by military units, and fuels were transported in military vehicles to places where it was not possible for unarmoured vehicles to proceed. Military helicopters and ambulances were used for the evacuation of civilian casualties. The airport at Sarajevo, through which over 80 per cent of aid for the city was delivered, was run by the French Air Force contingent of UNPROFOR. Although ICRC acted independently as their rules require, they were given assistance by UNPROFOR in arranging security, transport for the release of detained persons, and with the frequent exchanges of bodies or prisoners of war. In sum, the whole spectrum of humanitarian activities, from the delivery of basic food stuffs to civil aid development, became the prime mission of the peacekeeping force and there was no area of the humanitarian aid mission in which UNPROFOR did not play a significant role.

A successfully executed and excellent example of the coordination required between UNHCR and UNPROFOR was the resolution of the problem facing Maglaj. In the spring of 1994, reports were received of increased levels of starvation and death amongst the civilian population of this enclave to the west of Sarajevo. The UNHCR coordinator for the region, Mr Larry Hollingworth, asked UNPROFOR for assistance because for some time all aid convoys had been denied passage across the battle lines. Only one aid convoy had reached Maglaj in eight months and the enclave relied largely on airdrops for its food. However, it was estimated that only about 50 per cent of the food dropped was actually recovered. Furthermore, the hospitals were reported to be jammed with patients and medical supplies were running out. During one heavy shelling incident on the town of Maglaj itself, 1500 shells were reported to have landed in one day. The health centre was hit and five medical personnel were killed. The situation was clearly becoming desperate. In response to the UNHCR request, UNPROFOR deployed liaison teams by military means into the pocket and, as a result of reports that the teams made about changes in the tactical situation on the ground, the first UNHCR convoy since October 1993 entered the town on 20 March 1994. Then, permanent positions were established by UNPROFOR in the area and routes opened to commercial traffic. Utilities were largely restored and life for the people of this remote enclave returned to normal – as far as it is possible in the middle of a war. The initial military operation, the running of the aid convoys, and all the subsequent civil aid development work were coordinated between the UNPROFOR sector headquarters (where an UNHCR officer was based) and Mr Hollingworth's UNHCR regional office in Zenica.

However, not all the progress made in increasing the percentages of aid delivered can be attributed to the improvements achieved in the coordination and integration of the humanitarian and peacekeeping missions. The prevailing security climate clearly will have a major influence on the humanitarian aid delivery mission – for it will obviously be easier to make assessments of needs, deliver aid, rehabilitate health services, and facilitate the work of ICRC in a benign security environment rather than when fierce battles rage. Thus if the peacekeeping mission, through its presence and powers of persuasion, can persuade the parties in the war to cease hostilities or at least reduce the intensity of the fighting to a level where aid can flow freely – and utilities can be restored and life returned to normal – then clearly this will result in improved productivity in terms of the delivery of humanitarian aid. The 9 February 1994 agreement between the Muslim and Serb forces (following the massacres in the market place in Sarajevo) which resulted in the withdrawal of the heavy artillery around Sarajevo and an undertaking not to launch offensive action across the 70 kilometre-long conflict line which surrounds the city, created just such benign conditions. Following the successful implementation of this agreement – which was brokered by UNPROFOR and backed by a NATO ultimatum to which both the Bosnian Government Forces and the Bosnian Serb Army were subject – a second agreement was reached on 17 March 1994 by which aid, and subsequently commercial traffic, could enter Sarajevo via the airport. Consequently, for almost four months, up to 100 commercial lorries per day arrived in a city which had been besieged for nearly two years. As a result of repairs to damaged power lines and transformer stations made possible by the improvement in the security situation, electricity levels, which during the period of siege had hovered at about 12 Megawatts, were increased to 55 Megawatts. This allowed trams to run and other services, such as domestic lighting, to be restored. Gas pressures rose from an average of 0.5 of a bar to 6 bars. Water pipes were repaired, an IRC water pump station and filtration plant were built, and new wells were drilled by ODA. As a result, for the first time in many months, water was delivered directly into homes. The result was a trans-formation of life for the 350 000 citizens of Sarajevo. Stocks of food were built up against future contingencies so that when, as inevitably happened, the situation deteriorated in the late summer and a near-100 per cent blockade was established once again by the Bosnian Serbs around Sarajevo, the effects were not unduly disastrous.

This improvement in quality of life was to be repeated throughout central Bosnia as a result of the Washington Agreement signed between the Croatian Bosnians and the Muslims. This allowed the battle lines in central Bosnia to be eliminated entirely and life once again returned to normal. Nevertheless, it was only UNPROFOR who could provide the machinery necessary for these improvements in the form of regional and district joint commissions, interposition of forces, observation posts, checkpoints, and joint patrols in order to implement the agreement. Much work was also done in rebuilding the shattered infrastructure of the region, and once again it was the close cooperation and liaison between UNPROFOR, UNHCR and the other Agencies involved which proved critical to the successful outcome of the Mission. It is certain that without the presence of UNPROFOR and the security which its presence provided, renewed conflict would have returned to the region and much good work would have been wasted and many lives lost. Indeed, so much progress was made in central Bosnia in turning the war situation into one of peace that humanitarian organisations were able to redefine their objectives and move away from the direct provision of aid. For example, in Tuzla, where in 1993 conditions had been critical, actual food delivery rates in 1994 exceeded target figures, and therefore more emphasis could be placed on looking after and resettling the area's 430 000 displaced and war-affected people.

It is clearly not possible to expect everything to go rationally or smoothly in a country so torn apart by hatred and war – or in a situation which rightly attracts so much attention abroad. Consent for the UN to operate within the country has been patchy at best and at times non-existent. The appalling human rights record of the Bosnian Serbs, and their suspicion that the world is using the UN Mission to pursue the political goal of forcing them to live under a Muslim government, made relationships with the Bosnian Serbs particularly difficult even although some 600 000 Serbs were dependant on UNHCR aid. The Bosnian Government, itself a member of the UN, believes that the world has betrayed it and that because the UN Mission remains technically impartial in terms of the delivery of aid and peacekeeping, it is effectively on the side of the Serbs. The limitations on the use of force by NATO was a particular source of irritation to the Bosnian Government, who continued to hope that NATO would be used as a means of military compulsion. Furthermore, the Bosnian Government's belief that they could recover their lost territory by force of arms resulted in a series of offensive actions being mounted by their Army at the tactical level against the Bosnian Serb Army throughout the summer of 1994. This had conspicuously adverse consequences on the flow of aid – for these offensives so greatly increased the level of conflict in the country and so significantly reduced the relationship of trust that had been painfully built up between both sides that for many weeks during the summer and autumn of 1994 it was not possible to run aid convoys to the enclaves, or to sustain the air bridge to Sarajevo. In addition, virtually all utilities were cut off in that city. In particular, the situation in Bihac was a classic example of the consequences of a foolhardy military adventure by the Bosnian Government Forces being visited on the heads of an already too long-suffering civilian population. Meanwhile the Croats of Bosnia remained deeply suspicious of the Federation, and cooperation in areas such as Mostar continued to be extremely limited especially in terms of freedom of movement and restoration of utilities. This situation provides a good example of political action at governmental level not being heeded on the ground. Elsewhere, during the early winter of 1995, fuel deliveries to schools and hospitals in Bosnian Croatian areas were blocked by the Croatian municipalities on the grounds that they felt they were entitled to more fuel than the technical assessments allowed. In effect, because they no longer saw a chance of personal gain from the resale of surplus fuel, they attempted to blackmail the UN into delivering excess amounts by exposing their own people to further needless suffering.

Possibly the greatest difficulties facing the delivery of humanitarian aid in Bosnia have been caused by the use of force by UNPROFOR. This use of force was necessitated by the need in April 1994 to deter further attacks against the safe area of Gorazde, and by the need in August and September 1994 to maintain the total exclusion zone for heavy weapons around Sarajevo. Subsequently, in November 1994, NATO aircraft acting in self defence engaged Bosnian Serb Army ground-to-air missile systems, and at the same time NATO attacked an airfield from which Serb aircraft had attacked civilian targets in Bihac. Given these circumstances, there had clearly been no alternative open to NATO other than to act, although there were some suspicions that the Bosnian Serbs had engineered these circumstances in order to get themselves attacked, and hence rally Serb public opinion to their cause. On another occasion, Danish tanks quite legitimately returned fire at Bosnian Serb tanks near Tuzla. The effect of all these incidents, none of which was instigated by UNPROFOR, was to reduce to nil the flow of aid through Serb-held areas to the minority Muslim peoples living in the enclaves. Since the Bosnian Serbs had a deliberate policy of preventing the build-up of stocks in the enclaves in order to maintain leverage, the effect of shutting off the flow of aid was that within days people began to run short of food and other items essential for survival. Although the process was slow, UNHCR and UNPROFOR were able to restore aid delivery after each such occasion. This was because UNPROFOR was always able to demonstrate to the Bosnian Serbs that it remained neutral, impartial and a non-combatant, and that it had no mandate to change political positions or the balance of military power by force of arms. Indeed, by August 1994, in spite of the reverses caused by the necessary but minimum use of force, the FAO/WFP assessment of the situation in Bosnia-Hercegovina was already confirming that the overall improvement in the food supply situation, mainly as a result of the opening of the access routes in central Bosnia and the scaling down of the conflict, was having markedly beneficial results on the aid-delivery programme. Cereal production had risen by 15 per cent, and food prices had declined sharply in urban areas. Furthermore, the number of refugees and displaced persons in need of aid had fallen from 2.7 million to 1.4 million.[3]

Thus the central lesson which can be derived from the experience of Bosnia in 1994 is that a careful balance has to be struck between military enforcement measures and the need to continue the principal mission of delivering humanitarian aid to those in need. Although it might have technically been possible to destroy by military means all ground-to-air defence systems threatening NATO aircraft, to have done do so would have run the risk of bringing the aid delivery programme to a halt. Since the presence of NATO aircraft in the skies over Bosnia was to support the UN Mission, it would be a curious logic to allow a military action by such a supporting arm if it had the consequence of disrupting the Mission so completely. Nor is it possible to enforce the passage of convoys by the use of air power. For example, the route for UNPROFOR and UNHCR convoys from central Bosnia to Gorazde transits 55 miles of Bosnian Serb -held territory. It crosses two mountain ranges, and passes through narrow defiles and over 44 bridges. It would therefore be exceedingly simple for a few determined men to deny that route to convoys either by direct fire, indirect fire, mining, destroying bridges, or even by getting the civilian population to block the road. On one occasion in 1994, the latter action did indeed happen when only a few miles from Sarajevo a handful of women held a French convoy hostage for five weeks. No degree of military enforcement, other than that possessed by an invading force which has been given complete authority to take over an entire country, would be able to deliver aid without consent. Since the UN has not been given this mandate, then practical reality must be the key determining factor in developing the best strategy and the most appropriate tactics in any given situation. When convoys are blocked or utilities cut, it is a simple fact that people immediately start to suffer. Posturing has no place in policymaking nor in the feeding of entire populations. Moreover, those courageous countries who have contributed their soldiers to the Mission as peacekeepers have no wish to see them caught up in a war as combatants and returned to their countries in body bags.

Perhaps the greatest failure of the UN Mission in 1994 is that none of these stark lessons have been understood by the international community at large. The public information machinery of the UN is fundamentally unable to cope with the propaganda, lies and distortions that are the daily diet of war-torn Bosnia. Aggravating this problem – and this will invariably be the case – the international media who were present mainly in Sarajevo had a continual tendency to disseminate this propaganda. The explanation for this lies in the fact that the media, many of whom had become emotionally involved in the situation, had a short-term approach to reporting which was furthermore based on morality and idealism rather than with the practical consequences of their suggested policies. Each time the Bosnian Serb Army blocked a route, their immediate and wholly inappropriate call was for a bombing campaign to be mounted against the Serbs – notwithstanding the clear limitations of air power in support of a humanitarian aid mission. The fact that airpower could not preserve the security of the enclaves, prevent Sarajevo from being the daily target of 1200 shells (which was the case at the start of 1994), feed the people or maintain the utilities seems in the minds of the media to be irrelevant. However, peacekeepers and those responsible for humanitarian aid cannot afford such intellectual laxity. Each day, 2000 metric tons of food had to be moved or people would starve. The failure by the UN to get this message across is well recognised and can be attributed to the unaccustomedly hostile environment in which both peacekeepers and humanitarian organisations found themselves. Recruiting people with operational experience of conflict into the UN public information system would give the Mission a more reactive and dynamic image abroad. Such people have the ability to read an operational situation accurately, explain the long-term strategy in the light of short-term difficulties, and debate each issue with a credibility and confidence that was lacking in 1994. It is also important that all elements of the Mission maintain a commonly-agreed position. On a number of occasions in Bosnia the credibility of the UN Mission was undermined by very different slants being put on incidents by spokesmen for different organisations. The lesson of this experience is that the need for full coordination is as great in the world of public information as it is in the operational field (see also Chapter 7).

In conclusion, the circumstances which caused the Security Council to deploy a UN humanitarian mission to Bosnia in order to alleviate human suffering are likely to be repeated in the future. In such circumstances, the clear and simple central lesson is that there must be no confusion of aim. Peacekeeping in these chaotic and violent circumstances must never become confused with war fighting, and the Mission must at all costs retain its non-combatant status in the perceptions of all parties to the conflict. If force does have to be used in pursuit of the peacekeeping mission and its associated tasks, its application should strictly adhere to the traditional peacekeeping principles governing the minimum use of force. Undue use of force will inevitably risk making it impossible for the Mission to continue. Non-combatant status must be preserved at all costs. To keep balance will not always be easy as there will be many influences seeking to hijack the Mission in pursuit of one sectarian interest or another.

The second clear lesson for the coordination of UN humanitarian assistance drawn from the particular experience of Bosnia is that there should be unity of purpose enshrined in a common plan and mission statement for all UN organisations working in the theatre of operations. In order to keep the main effort focused on this mission, there should be reciprocal liaison at all levels of command under the office of the SRSG. The peacekeeping mission of UNPROFOR must always remain complementary to the more urgent task of facilitating the delivery of humanitarian aid. Finally, the public information policy of all organisations deployed in the theatre of operations should coordinate their activities in the same way as the operational structures.

The Mission in Bosnia, as seen at the end of 1994, has demonstrably succeeded in its task of sustaining the lives of people in need, and it has certainly created the necessary opportunities for peace in that country – if the political leaders choose to take advantage of them. New doctrines have been forged, new attitudes developed and new levels of cooperation have been attained between the aid organisations and the peacekeeping forces. The many lives which have been lost by those committed to the UN Mission will not have been wasted when judged against the millions of people whose lives have been sustained by the presence of UNHCR,

UNPROFOR and other aid agencies. It is important that these lessons so painfully gained are not lost to the world, whatever the final outcome of the situation in Bosnia might be.

Notes

1. IISS Strategic Comments, No. 2 (22 February 1995).
2. UNHCR Information Note, No. 1/94.
3. Special Report of FAO/ WFP on Crop and Food Supply Assessment to Bosnia Hercegovina and the UNPAs in Former Yugoslavia (August 1994).

13 The Experience in Angola, February 1992–June 1993

Margaret J. Anstee

INTRODUCTION

Angola is in many ways archetypal of UN post-Cold War peacekeeping operations. It was a civil war, an intra-state conflict with some ethnic overtones, although the ideological roots of the struggle in the Cold War also ran very deep. Another characteristic of the new-mode peacekeeping exercise also developed. It became multi-faceted, encompassing military, police, electoral and humanitarian components, all in some way interlocking.

It did not begin that way, however, but gradually evolved. There have been two phases of the UN operation in Angola so far, with a third about to begin. The first UN Angola Verification Mission (UNAVEM) had the limited but important task of observing and verifying the withdrawal of 50 000 Cuban troops which was part and parcel of the deal with South Africa which led to the independence of Namibia. That was a classic, old-type 'Blue Beret' operation which involved unarmed military observers and was successfully completed, ahead of schedule, in May 1991. UNAVEM II sprang out of the Bicesse Peace Accords, signed in Portugal in May 1991, which dealt specifically with Angola and brought to an end (for 17 months at least) the 16-year-old war between the Government of Angola (constituted by the Popular Movement for the Liberation of Angola (MPLA)) and the National Union for the Total Independence of Angola (UNITA). The peace was brokered by Portugal, the Soviet Union and the USA, with no UN involvement, except for that of a military observer in the last stages of the negotiations.

UNAVEM II's role, to begin with, was also of a classic type. Indeed, it was rather a marginal one, since the onus for the implementation of the Peace Accords was placed squarely on the two sides, and UNAVEM II was merely to verify their compliance with certain aspects of the Accords: the cantonment and demobilisation of the two armies, and the setting-up of a neutral police force. UNAVEM II either had no role, or a very hazy one, in respect of other provisions of the Accords, such as the disarmament of the two sides, the formation of joint Angolan Armed Forces drawn from both, and the extension of the central administration to cover the whole war-ravaged country – all of which were to be completed within an inelastic timetable for the holding of elections between September and November 1992. At the outset, UNAVEM II consisted of only 350 unarmed military observers and 90 police observers, increased in 1992 to 126. Initially, there was no humanitarian or electoral component, and no political or civilian head in the form of an SRSG.

THE EVOLUTION OF UNAVEM II

The decision to broaden the political base of UNAVEM II's mandate, appoint an SRSG and add to its functions the role of observing and verifying the elections (for the organisation of which the main responsibility again fell on the national authorities) was taken in principle at the end of December 1991, but not acted upon immediately. I was not appointed as SRSG until the middle of February 1992, and the Security Council did not formally endorse the addition of the electoral component until March, barely six months before the elections were due to be held.

The terms of reference given me by the Secretary-General were very wide. In addition to representing him I was to be the Head of UNAVEM II, with full responsibility over all aspects of the Mission: military, police, political and civilian. I was also to coordinate 'all humanitarian operations related to the peace process'. This was a more complicated directive to put into practice than it might at first sound. Quite apart from the terrible destruction and suffering caused by 16 years of unremitting war, Angola was, along with other countries of Southern Africa, suffering another humanitarian disaster caused by several years of prolonged drought. A Special Relief Programme to combat the effects of drought in Angola (SRPA I and II), involving a number of Agencies and organisations of the UN system, had been ongoing for some time, coordinated by the UNDP Resident Representative. In addition, organisations such as the WFP and UNICEF had their own 'normal' programmes in Angola, if anything could be called normal in that ill-fated country. Inevitably, there were some grey areas between these programmes and the humanitarian support for the peace process. At the outset, the latter consisted mainly of assistance to some 300 000 refugees returning to Angola after many years of exile abroad, and a further 800 0000 displaced persons now wanting to return to their home regions – both handled by UNHCR, with material support in the form of food and medicines and the like from the WFP and UNICEF. The latter two organisations provided similar assistance to the Assembly Areas scattered the length and breadth of Angola's vast territory where troops from both armies (estimated to total some 200 000 in all) were being held until they were either demobilised or selected for training and incorporation into the new, joint Angolan Armed Forces. This second activity had not been foreseen but had emerged as a necessity to keep the peace process going: the Peace Accords stipulated that the cantonment of troops by both sides was to be completed by 1 August 1991, to be followed immediately by demobilisation, but inordinate delays, which continued to bedevil implementation of key aspects of the Accords right up to the elections in September 1992, not only made this deadline impossible to meet but, more dangerously still, led to a steep decline in the number of assembled troops in October 1991, with no demobilisation programme yet in sight. Troops began to drift away through demoralisation at the length of the process, pay arrears, and lack of food and medical supplies. The situation was particularly desperate in Government Assembly Areas. WFP and UNICEF were therefore brought in to provide the needed basic supplies in the hope of keeping the troops in place. Later still, WFP provided vital food supplies to support the demobilisation and electoral processes. The latter would most certainly have foundered had registration and polling teams, who had to go to remote areas sometimes for weeks at a time because the country's devastated infrastructure made travel extremely difficult, not been provided with basic rations. All these are examples of ad hoc operations that had to be mounted unexpectedly to meet a need. They were also somewhat alien to the conventional concept of humanitarian aid, but they were vital to the success of the peace process.

Field coordination of this plethora of activities proved less complicated than might be imagined. It took place at different levels. At the most senior level, I held regular weekly or bi-weekly meetings (depending on the needs) with the UNDP Resident Representative and the representatives from all the UN Agencies and organisations in Angola. I was always accompanied by my military commander, my civilian deputy in charge of electoral affairs, my Chief Administrative Officer and whoever else might be appropriate. The meetings served several purposes: to brief my colleagues on the latest political developments and on the security situation; to learn from them any difficulties that they might be facing and to try to resolve them; and to discuss long-term operational planning, ironing out any short-term operational difficulties that had occurred and generally ensure that operational dovetailing was functioning properly at all levels.

UNAVEM II was at that point in a very favourable situation to provide overall logistical and other support to humanitarian activities and to act as a pivotal point in ensuring field coordination right down the line to the delivery of aid. Despite our limited size, we had presence in 68 different locations in Angola, including six relatively well-staffed Regional Commands (among them, Luanda). The remaining staff were deployed in smaller teams, such as the five-man teams of military observers stationed in the Assembly Areas, and the two-man teams patrolling 'critical points' on the frontiers. Teams of police observers, and sometimes military observers as well, were stationed in every provincial capital, as were the electoral observers at a later stage. We had an excellent network of radio communications, a regular supply system (mainly by air) to all our main outposts, and an air unit comprising 14 helicopters, two fixed-wing aircraft, and a larger cargo aircraft on call when needed. With all its shortcomings and difficulties, UNAVEM II had a wider coverage of what was going on in Angola than anyone else. WFP also had only one or two aircraft at that time, and UNAVEM II aircraft were often called in to help on the humanitarian side, even though this was not their prime mission. We had an efficient movement control unit (MOVCON) at Luanda airport which planned and dispatched all our flights.

There was also a very free exchange of information. With its far-flung operation, UNAVEM II was probably better placed than anyone else to brief the operational humanitarian agencies on the day-to-day situation on the ground. Added to that, UNDP, WFP, and UNICEF had staff deployed in the same locations as our Regional Commands and that greatly facilitated coordination at the local level.

During the period up to the elections in September 1992, security was not a major problem since Angola was enjoying an unusual interlude of peace. Inevitably, it was interrupted by incidents – some, indeed, serious, but none, as I recall, significantly affecting the delivery of humanitarian assistance. In contrast to our colleagues in Bosnia and Somalia, we were not, in any case, well-equipped to provide protection since all our contingents were unarmed. The main problem was crowds of people surging on to the poorly-controlled provincial airports as the aircraft came in, and trying to seize the goods and make off with them as soon as the hatch was opened for unloading. The rather maverick Canadian officer who headed MOVCON, and who often accompanied the flights, developed a unique way of dealing with this. There were hilarious accounts of his fending off would-be looters in Luena, the capital of Moxico province, by masterful wielding of a baseball bat from the back hatch of our Antonov cargo plane. He never went on a flight without this rather unconventional weapon. I am sure that the UN Rules of Engagement did not foresee a situation like this, but it seems to me that it was a justifiable use of force for defensive purposes in the true spirit of UN peacekeeping. Improvisation in the face of almost overwhelming odds and challenges is also an essential part of that spirit.

Tensions rose as the election approached. Miraculously, the two election days, 29–30 September 1992, passed off in absolute calm, the epitome of civic responsibility, with a turn-out of over 90 per cent of the registered voters. When at last the count was completed and all the alleged irregularities had been investigated, I was able, on 17 October 1992, to declare the elections as having been 'generally free and fair', a view endorsed by all outside observers of the process.

Tragically, however, the situation in the country had deteriorated severely in the meantime. The refusal of the UNITA leader, Dr Jonas Savimbi, to accept the results of the elections (even though there was to be a run-off between him and President José Eduardo dos Santos for the Presidency) and his decision to withdraw former UNITA generals and other officers from the new Angolan Armed Forces (hastily sworn in on the very eve of the voting) led to a series of escalating skirmishes between the Government and UNITA all over the country. These culminated in a major battle in the capital city of Luanda during the weekend of 31 October–1 November 1992.

Thereafter, despite my own efforts and those of the three observer countries (Portugal, Russia, and the USA) to mediate, there was a slow but irrevocable slide into war which, by January 1993, had engulfed the whole country once again – and even more ferociously than before. The grave humanitarian crisis that Angola was already facing, even if peace had continued to be secured, expanded almost overnight to cyclopean proportions.

THE POST-ELECTION HUMANITARIAN DISASTER AND THE UN RESPONSE

The role of UNAVEM II, which had deliberately been marginalised in the Bicesse Accords (mainly because of the Angola Government's sensitivities about sovereignty) had, by the end of 1992, become central, without any change in its formal mandate, and purely by force of circumstances. The process had begun during the run-up to the elections, when the SRSG had been obliged to step in and mobilise the logistical support without which the elections could not have been deemed free and fair because a large proportion of voters would have been *de facto* disenfranchised for lack of access.

With the onset of renewed strife, the UN role became more vital than ever, and it came to rest on two pillars – very different from UNAVEM II's original mandate: mediation and humanitarian disaster relief. My efforts to broker a ceasefire and a return to the peace process, first at a meeting between the two sides in Namibe at the end of November 1992 and then in two sessions in Addis Ababa in January and February 1993, although initially promising, were foiled, first by UNITA's occupation of the towns of Uige and Negage only two or three days after the Namibe meeting, and then by their failure to turn up for the second Addis Ababa session at which, ironically enough, they had wanted to put the subject of corridors for humanitarian aid high on the agenda. By then, the battle for Huambo, the city in the central highlands which UNITA regards as its traditional stronghold, was raging at full tilt with devastating casualties on both sides and among the civilian population trapped there. The battle lasted 56 days, and by the time the city fell to UNITA in March 1993 it was estimated that over 10 000 people had died there, while thousands more fled, many of them perishing on a 200-mile trek to the coast through an inhospitable terrain of mountains, thick forest and torrential rivers.

An even more sanguinary battle was under way for the town of Kuito/Bie; it was to last for 10 months. Not until October 1993 could relief at last be brought to the remaining population: those who had not been killed or wounded by the daily battery of shelling were near to death from starvation and disease. As in Huambo, no one will ever know exactly how many people died there, but estimates range from 25 000 to 35 000, and the surviving 40 000 were in desperate need of help. Only the dogs were well-nourished, feeding from the corpses in the street that could not be buried because of the constant bombardment. The Angolan Foreign Minister, Venâncio de Moura, said many people 'ate human flesh to survive'; certainly they ate rats and roots, and anything that would give them a little sustenance. A member of the first relief flight to reach the town described an 'apocalypse' with people having to drink from the river next to 'dead bodies in the water'. Other provincial capitals, such as Malange, Menongue, Luena and Saurimo, were also under siege for many months, their populations swollen by refugees from other areas of fighting, and access to relief supplies extremely difficult.

I had several times called for a humanitarian truce during my various efforts at mediation, notably during the Addis Ababa meeting, at least for long enough to allow relief supplies to be sent to beleaguered civilian populations, but to no effect. As the situation worsened, I warned the Secretary-General that what I publicly described as 'a disaster of incalculable proportions' was in the making and that the UN must urgently step up its efforts to meet it. An advance team was at once sent out by the Under-Secretary-General for Humanitarian Affairs to look at the situation, and on 25 February 1993, on the eve of the abortive second Addis Ababa meeting, the Secretary-General issued a statement expressing his grave concern and appealing for international support, and for the two sides to cooperate.

Meanwhile, on the ground, we struggled to do our utmost with what we had to hand. In one sense, the problem of coordination was simplified: there were no longer any 'normal' humanitarian or special drought relief programmes. Now, all humanitarian efforts were geared to the peace process or rather, more aptly and tragically, to alleviating the terrible sufferings caused to the civilian population by the renewed onset of war. The Secretary-General asked me to coordinate all of these operations and the Security Council endorsed this role in SCR 811 of 12 March 1993 which, in its operative paragraphs 10 and 11, called on the international community to provide humanitarian relief assistance to Angola and 'encouraged' the Special Representative to coordinate such assistance, adding the customary, and ominous phrase 'with the resources at her disposal'. The Council also called on both parties to the conflict to abide by humanitarian law, including allowing unimpeded access for humanitarian assistance to the civilian population in need.

Apart from the fact that very considerable voluntary donations, in money or kind, would be required from member states to finance the massive aid required, the resources available to me on the ground to support a much larger operation were, ironically, much less than before. By the end of January 1993, I had to evacuate all UNAVEM staff – military, police and civilian – from all the new areas of intensified fighting where, unarmed, they had found themselves caught in cross-fire or under threat (one police observer was killed, other military and police observers were wounded by gunfire or beaten up). The UN Agencies and the NGOs had also had to withdraw their outposted personnel to Luanda. UNAVEM II was now limited to some six locations on the Atlantic seaboard. Our impressive logistic support network was severely truncated and our 'eyes and ears' were no longer available. To make matters worse, in view of the collapse of the peace process and the consequent irrelevance of UNAVEM II's mandate to verify its progress, the Security Council had decided to reduce UNAVEM II substantially. We were soon down to a third or less of our former strength. Thus, no one was in a good position to make a rational assessment of needs, many parts of the country had become inaccessible, and the security risks had multiplied overnight.

Our humanitarian task was now twofold: to do what we could with available resources to meet at least some of the immediate needs, and to prepare for the much larger task now envisaged. With hopes of an early return to peace fading with the collapse of the Addis Ababa talks, I was holding coordination meetings on the humanitarian situation several times a week, and sometimes daily. Although the guns were stilled and Huambo was now in the hands of UNITA, there remained a legacy of terrible suffering and the delivery of aid to the town was a prime objective. Access was still not easy because of the need to be even-handed and get the agreement of both sides. An elaborate three-stage plan to take relief to Huambo by air and by road convoy, due to begin on 29 March 1993, could not be carried out because the Government insisted that parallel assistance be given to the beleaguered town of Kunto/Bie and UNITA refused to give clearance for the latter flights. UNITA then launched a vicious personal attack on myself, accusing me of hypocrisy and impugning my moral character and probity, and made threats against my life. Ten days later I obtained the agreement of President dos Santos to send, jointly with religious representatives and NGOs, an exploratory mission to Huambo to ascertain the number of civilians still there, to assess their needs, and to organise distribution networks to ensure the aid got to the right people. UNITA petulantly turned this down claiming that 'the needs are well known'. Because of the continuing difficulties of this kind, it was not until June 1993 that a first flight to Huambo became possible.

A more successful and well-coordinated operation was carried out in the first days of April 1993 to succour the most vulnerable refugees from Huambo who had descended in their thousands on the small town of Caimbambo, in the foothills, but still some way from the coastal towns of Benguela and Lobito where reception facilities had been set up. These people were now too exhausted from their privations to walk any further. In five days, UNAVEM II carried over 4000 civilians, mostly women, children and old people, in horrendous weather conditions, by helicopter lift from Caimbambo to the west, while WFP and UNICEF provided food and medical supplies.

Even in its depleted state UNAVEM II still had an indispensable role to play: we were the only ones who were still in communication with UNITA, and able to obtain the necessary security clearances for each individual flight, through one of their military commanders in the northern town of Uige. Even that did not always work. On 8 April 1993, a WFP Antonov delivering emergency aid to Uige itself, an area totally dominated by UNITA, came under machine-gun fire as it was landing despite all the clearances having been obtained in advance. One crew member was badly injured in the leg but the aircraft turned around and managed to limp back to Luanda with 45 bullet holes in its fuselage. There were a number of such incidents, some ending in tragedy and almost all, it has to be said, in areas under UNITA control.

I also arranged for one or two UNAVEM II military or police observers to accompany each flight. They were unarmed, but I hoped that at least their uniform and blue berets would provide some symbolic protection and that they could verify that relief supplies were being used for civilians and not for the troops. (The latter was almost inevitable and there was little we could do to stop it without depriving desperately needy civilians as well.)

Angola confirmed my earlier experience that coordination between UN Agencies works much better at the field level than between the various Headquarters, so long as two conditions are met: one, that the situation is really fraught; and two, that there are reasonable personalities on the spot who are genuinely dedicated to helping people in dire straits and who are operationally experienced. In Angola both conditions existed. The only problem encountered was with UNHCR, which is understandably always very particular about its special mandate and status – added to which the local representative had a decided personal predilection for 'going it alone' despite relying on our aircraft and clearance mechanisms, which created problems with other Agencies as well as increasing security risks.

Security in general was a very difficult area of coordination, and not only within the UN system. A considerable effort was made to involve the numerous NGOs in Angola, since they had a special contribution to make, and it was important to ensure the most effective use of the scarce resources available. Predictably, most of them were keen to do their own thing, and to be seen doing it. But they were, in the main, reliant on the UN and UNAVEM II for the air capacity to transport aid and personnel to remote destinations, and totally for clearances and communications. Our general rule of 'safety first' – that no flights or supplies by land could be authorised unless first cleared explicitly by both the Government and UNITA – was not always understood. Often the shots were very hard to call, and these inevitably landed on my desk. One was torn between the overwhelming and urgent needs on the one hand and, on the other, the knowledge that a downed plane, or a mined convoy, and the death of people involved in the operation could, apart from the personal tragedy, place the whole humanitarian effort in jeopardy. If a flight was cancelled for lack of sufficient guarantees, we were sometimes regarded as pusillanimous by Agency or NGO staff bravely ready to risk their lives – a responsibility that I could not undertake for them.

Nor were the difficulties in this regard only operational. On 13 March 1993 the Executive Director of WFP wrote to the UN Under Secretary-General for Humanitarian Affairs, insisting that the latter should obtain the flight security clearances from the Government and UNITA – from New York, and 30 days in advance – to facilitate WFP's planning procedures!

This proposal showed such a lack of understanding of how we were having to operate in a fluctuating situation of all-out war, with clearances often given at the last minute and on the basis of close daily and sometimes hour-to-hour liaison with our Agency counterparts in Luanda, that it left one almost gasping for breath. Thus, while some people on the ground were demanding fewer security precautions, Headquarters wished to have so many that the operation would become unworkable. I eventually won the day on this one but it was unfortunately not the only instance in which scarce time and energy had to be expended in thwarting unrealistic proposals from people in far-away cities who had never had direct experience of handling a disaster-relief operation on the ground, much less in a situation of armed conflict.

While trying to set up these emergency operations, in the midst of much frustration, work was also progressing on the expansion of the humanitarian operation. This involved assessing needs, preparing projects and programmes, launching an international appeal for resources to carry them out, and setting up a strengthened coordination mechanism. An FAO–WFP mission visited Angola and estimated that some 2 million Angolans, one fifth of the total estimated population of 10 million, were suffering severe effects from the war. These comprised those directly affected by the conflict, the displaced, the drought-affected and returned refugees. The assessments, and the resulting food requirements, had to be made on the basis of extrapolation, since access to most of the worst stricken areas was still impossible. UNICEF carried out its own survey of the needs in its own area of competence, reporting a substantial increase in malnutrition and infant mortality. In the second half of April 1993, the DHA sent a mission to Angola which pulled all these strands together and prepared the appeal which it had originally planned to launch in May 1993.

I was no longer in Luanda by then. I had left on 10 April 1993 for Abidjan where I chaired another round of ceasefire and peace negotiations between the Government and UNITA. Originally expected to last two or three weeks, the talks dragged on for six and, having come within a hair's breadth of success, broke up without agreement on 21 May 1993.

Meanwhile the humanitarian emergency effort continued in Angola. One of the main features of the expanded operation was to be a small, central coordinating unit. After a lot of discussion it was decided that this should be headed by a director appointed by the DHA and responsible directly to me as the designated overall coordinator. Even this latter point had seemed implicitly in doubt during a long exchange with UN Headquarters in New York which originally tried to insist that the coordinating unit should be physically located in the already-overcrowded UNDP office and somehow linked to the unit there that had been dealing with the drought disaster. The main objective seemed to be to soothe any sensitivities in UNDP but otherwise the proposal made no sense, and could only lead to confusion on several scores, including the chain of command, so important in disaster relief. This was another example of bureaucratic compromise at Headquarters betraying scant understanding of the requirements for efficient operations on the ground. My own proposal was that the unit should be housed in another downtown building, in which UNAVEM II had offices no longer needed, with a small subsidiary office in the UNAVEM II camp just outside the city where all the communications were centred. This allowed easy access for all the Agencies to the main office, since they too were located downtown. Again, my view eventually prevailed but this was another instance in which the decision should have been left to the senior person on the ground, rather than to second-guessing from a great distance.

The experience over the appointment of a director of the new unit was much happier. The choice fell on Dr Manuel Aranda da Silva, a former Mozambican minister who had been directing the WFP programme in the Sudan in very difficult circumstances. Dr da Silva came through Abidjan en route to Luanda so that I could brief him. I took to him at once and this favourable impression was reinforced by the experience of working with him over the next two or three months, and by everything I have heard since I left Angola. There is no doubt that the appointment of a person so well qualified, both professionally and personally, proved a major element in ensuring successful coordination of the greatly expanded programme that followed. Some of the additional staff needed were eventually seconded to the unit from other Agencies.

During most of April, May and part of June 1993, I had to exercise my own coordinating functions from afar as, once the Abidjan talks had stalled, I was called to New York to report to the Secretary-General and the Security Council. Once Dr da Silva was installed in Luanda, however, we were in daily contact. If that part of the operation went very smoothly, the same was not true of the continuing efforts to get the emergency operation into full swing. Incidents continued to occur. UNITA had scarcely stopped apologising to me in Abidjan for shooting at the WFP plane in Uige on 8 April, and assuring me that it would not happen again, when, on 14 April, another WFP aircraft, bearing UN markings, was hit by UNITA's long-range artillery at Luena airport but managed to limp back to Luanda. On 26 April, tragedy struck with a vengeance: a WFP Antonov 12, with the usual UN markings, was shot down by a UNITA ground-to-air missile when it had just taken off from Luena after delivering emergency supplies.

The crew managed to make an emergency landing and escape from the plane when it burst into flames, but they stepped into a minefield: one died from his wounds and others were seriously injured. The subsequent investigation showed that, apart from the iniquity of UNITA once again firing on a UN plane in cold blood, there had been a problem of communication between our Luanda headquarters and Catumbela, where the Antonov was based: it had not been intended for it to go to Luena that day.

It was clear that, despite all efforts to set up proper clearance procedures, every flight was a gamble with the lives of the UN and NGO people on board, and that no real solutions would be possible without a genuine ceasefire and return to the peace process. When hopes of that lessened as May wore on, we prepared a one-month pilot emergency plan based on 'humanitarian corridors' (four road and ten air) to named destinations, agreed with the two parties, which would be used on selected days of the week for the transport of specified quantities of food and non-food aid. The corollary of this was a one-year plan, from May 1993 to April 1994, which was to provide the basis for the UN's consolidated inter-Agency appeal to the international donor community which, it had now been agreed, I would launch on behalf of the Secretary-General on 3 June 1993. This multi-sectoral plan, the product of a team led by Dr da Silva in cooperation with all the organisations and Agencies involved (UNDP, WFP, UNICEF, FAO and WHO), and covering all their programmes, required external funding in the region of US$226 million. The appeal also included requirements for NGOs, totalling some US$7 million.

On 26 May 1993 I sent personal letters to President dos Santos and to Dr Savimbi requesting their immediate agreement to the proposed one-month emergency plan so that I could make an announcement to this effect at the Geneva meeting. Since many would-be donors were concerned about the safe delivery of aid, this would have improved prospects for a generous international response for funding the one-year plan. Unfortunately, I did not receive the green light in time from either side. The plan, originally due to start on 7 June 1993, had to be postponed. Then, on 16 June, when I was back in Luanda, President dos Santos sent me a formal note of acceptance. We also obtained UNITA's agreement in principle and so rescheduled the operation for 21 June. This was preceded by an initial 'assessment flight' to Huambo on 19 June, the first time we had managed to get to that city after the battle for its capture ended more than three months previously. The initial delivery of food and non-food aid was duly carried out on 21 June – to UNITA-occupied Huambo and to the Government-held towns of Luena and Saurimo. But then it foundered once again because UNITA refused to approve flights to the besieged

Government towns of Kuito, Malange and Menongue for 'techniccal reasons', in riposte to which the Government withdrew its agreement to flights to Huambo. Without common agreement it was impossible to implement the plan and we had to fall back to operating on a sporadic and *ad hoc* basis. My dream of leaving behind a well-organised and smoothly-functioning operation was not be realised. Indeed, the 'stop–go' phenomenon was to continue for many months after my departure. On 15 July a modified plan was put into operation, but soon stalled again. After more firing incidents, it was not until mid-October 1993 that UN aid officials were able to reach Kuito – the first to get there – to find the catastrophe that I described earlier.

As to the appeal for funding for the one-year programme, the initial response was encouraging. At the one-day meeting, which I chaired in Geneva on 3 June 1993, pledges of 'fresh money' came to about US$70 million, just under a third of the required total. By 16 June, the amount had risen to US$92 million. Unfortunately, that momentum – which gave me at least some satisfaction on my final departure from Angola a short time afterwards – was not maintained. Four months after the Geneva meeting only 27 per cent of the pledges made there had been confirmed and a reminder had to be sent out. In February 1994, an updated appeal reported that confirmed pledges had still only reached US$103 million, less than 50 per cent of the target. By then, the estimated number in need of emergency assistance had risen to a staggering 3.3 million (that is, one in every three Angolans) and the amount needed for the six-month period February to July 1994 was US$179 million. Food aid had proved most popular with donors; other important areas such as agriculture, health and education inspired less interest. As always, there was reluctance to provide 'core funding' for the very modest coordination unit set up under Dr da Silva.

The disappointing and waning response to the Angolan appeal was no doubt in part due to the clamour of other appeals for help in dealing with disasters elsewhere. But another key factor was the lack of media interest in the sufferings of Angola, apart from brief flurries of attention – such as when the tragedy of Kuito/Bie became accessible to the outside world – in stark contrast to the intense coverage given to Bosnia. When, in my opening speech to launch the appeal in Geneva, I stated that the UN estimated that at least 1000 people a day were dying in Angola as a result of direct or indirect effects of the conflict – more than in any other conflict in the world at that time – an audible gasp went round the Conference Room. Comparisons are never more odious than when they relate to human suffering, but everyone was shocked to realise that the toll in Angola was far greater than in Bosnia, and hard-pressed to believe it simply because the media had chosen to ignore the story and so it had gone unremarked by the rest of the world. In fact, it very soon became evident the figure of 1000 deaths per day was a considerable under-estimate.

In the 20 months that have elapsed since I completed my Angolan mission, the prospects for peace, though still alarmingly fragile, have improved with the signing of the Lusaka Protocol on 20 November 1994, and the UN humanitarian operation has grown steadily in strength and effectiveness. A new appeal was launched for January–December 1995 amounting to US$212.7 million, and comprising a three-pronged programme of humanitarian assistance for civilian populations, mine clearance, and support for the demobilisation of former combatants and their re-integration into society. UN Agencies and NGOs have developed one of the largest relief operations in the world, providing emergency assistance to some 3 million people in every province of the country – a task greatly facilitated in recent months by the decline in fighting. If the peace process is consolidated, responsibility for coordination will be gradually handed over by the UN Humanitarian Assistance Coordination Unit (UCAH), headed by Dr da Silva, to Angolan institutions, and humanitarian emergency assistance will eventually be phased into rehabilitation and reconstruction. A good logistics capacity serving all Agencies has been developed by WFP, while a communications network, also used by all, has been built up and is to be extended to all provinces. Arrangements for coordination with the 102 national and international NGOs working in Angola have been put on a more systematic basis.

THE LESSONS OF THE UN HUMANITARIAN OPERATION IN ANGOLA

By any standards of measurement, the UN humanitarian operation in Angola must be rated a success, albeit one that has remained unsung and largely unnoticed by the world at large. Coordination at the field level might not have been trouble-free, but on the whole has been very successful. In considering such matters anywhere, it is important to bear one or two basic principles in mind.

First, coordination – an ill-defined concept at the best of times – should not be allowed to become an end in itself, otherwise the situation will worsen, with layers of coordinators coordinating one another.

Second, there can be no universal blueprint for ensuring impeccable coordination in every international disaster relief operation; there are certainly general and proven principles that should be applied but it must never be forgotten that each situation is different, has its own characteristics, and that there will therefore inevitably be a certain amount of 'ad-hocism', improvisation and innovation in every instance, and of adaptation of proven practices.

Third, the delivery and coordination of humanitarian aid will always be exceedingly difficult, and less than optimally effective, in situations of open war unless there is genuine cooperation from both sides of the conflict. More often than not, as was the case in Angola, both sides try to use humanitarian aid for political or military ends.

Critics of the UN frequently, and conveniently, overlook these three realities. With these caveats, the following precepts may be derived from the Angolan operation:

- Coordination should be decentralised as far as possible from headquarters to field and thence, if feasible, to the local level, with clear-cut definitions of responsibilities and limitations of authority at each level. There should be no second-guessing, especially of the field by headquarters in matters which should be the responsibility of the senior person on the ground – in whom full confidence should be placed. For this to happen, only people with the right professional capacity, personal attributes, and proven field experience should be appointed. These qualities are more important than considerations of nationality, and certainly of politics.

- By the same token, all middle-level and senior posts in the Headquarters of UN organisations and Agencies dealing with humanitarian and disaster relief should be filled only by people who have direct experience of field work (and by this is meant working on the ground for significant periods of time, and not simply taking part in short-term visiting missions).

- Field coordination units are most effective when the director comes from an impartial source, normally the DHA, and is responsible directly to the SRSG (where one exists) as the highest political authority on the spot. Giving this responsibility to one of the operational Agencies, as has been done in other instance (e.g. UNHCR in various cases, including Bosnia) is usually less effective because it often causes sensitivities among the other Agencies, as well as difficulties to the selected Agency itself in distinguishing between its coordinating function and its role as one of the operating organisations.

- Field coordination works best when it is not intrusive but supportive, combining a centralised humanitarian aid policy with decentralised activities: negotiating clearance and security guarantees; spearheading

team assessments of needs and multi-sectoral, consolidated appeals to
the donor community for funds; and providing, under the SRSG, a 'political shield'; while at the same time maintaining respect for the independence of the UN Agencies, NGOs, and the ICRC in implementing
humanitarian activities in which they have particular competence and
mandate.

- Coordination should extend to NGOs and, where possible, to bilateral
  programmes in the sense of providing an 'umbrella', under which all
  can operate within a framework which ensures optimum and complementary use of resources in response to the total needs. This concept
  was first developed, and applied with great success, in the Bangladesh
  disaster relief operation in the early 1970s.
- Coordinated logistics support and communications networks are vital
  and should preferably be provided on behalf of all by the Agency best
  equipped to do so in each case. Coordination of information, leading
  to a common assessment of needs, and reflected in consolidated inter-
  Agency appeals for resources is also indispensable, especially to win
  donor confidence and generous funding.
- A coordinated public information strategy and consistent statements to
  the media are likewise important. In Angola, there were unfortunately
  a few instances in which Agency spokesmen said different things, or
  tried to score off one another – a situation which is grist to any journalist's mill but not conducive to harmony or effective teamwork. More
  importantly still, all major humanitarian relief operations should have
  a solid public information unit to ensure that the world is kept informed,
  in a balanced and regular way, of the extent of the disaster and what
  is being done about it. This was lacking in Angola, as it often is in
  other cases, because of shortage of funds. Donors usually object to
  funds being used for this purpose but it is in fact essential to effectiveness in the media-conscious world of today.
- Donors must also realise that no humanitarian relief operation can be
  effective, nor can the best coordination in the world succeed, unless
  sufficient and timely funding is provided in response to consolidated
  inter-Agency appeals, and that this must include financing modest field
  coordinating units since no regular budget funds exist for this purpose.
- Coordination by the UN must gradually phase into coordination by
  national authorities, as and when more peaceful conditions permit, and,
  to that end, capacity-building must be emphasised.

I would like to add a final word on coordination between humanitarian
components and the military and police components in a complex UN

peacekeeping operation such as that in Angola, and in some other places as well. Humanitarian organisations are often wary of too close an association with military operations, even those of a peacekeeping nature under the aegis and flag of the UN. The issue arose several times in the initial stages of expanding the humanitarian operation in Angola in 1993 and was the subject of many exchanges, and sometimes arguments, between myself and the DHA in New York.

There is no doubt in my mind that, had I not involved the military part of UNAVEM in 1993, we would never have been able to deliver as much emergency aid as we did during those first fraught months. At that stage, only they had the logistical capacity, the communications, and the contacts (particularly with UNITA) to provide the support and obtain the clearances needed. Security was also a priority concern, and I regarded the presence of military or police observers on the flights, even though they were unarmed, as providing some moral protection. Others contend that their presence, on the contrary, could serve as a provocation to attack, but this is surely not a tenable argument – nor should it be accepted by the UN – when a UN peacekeeping operation has been agreed to by both parties to a conflict. In some cases, indeed, as in Somalia and Bosnia, the UN military presence – at least initially – was intended solely to provide security to massive humanitarian relief operations. That was not the case in Angola where, as I have recounted, the humanitarian component was at first only a support to the peace process, coming into pre-eminence only after the collapse of the latter and the return to open hostilities.

After the frustration of my third attempt at negotiating a ceasefire and a return to the peace process in Abidjan in May 1993, UNAVEM II's mandate had to change. There were only two main roles possible: continued mediation efforts and massive humanitarian aid until such time as calmer counsels prevailed and the two combatants came to terms in favour of peace and reconciliation. I strongly recommended that a small contingent of 'Blue Helmets' – armed troops – should be sent in to provide security for the flights and road convoys that we were then trying to organise to carry aid to all regions of the country. I did so, not only because of the difficulties and attacks which we were encountering but also because I was convinced – and still am – that such a move could also have hastened a return to peace by demonstrating a sense of purpose on the part of the international community and meeting UNITA's condition – on which the Abidjan talks broke down – that at least a symbolic presence of UN 'Blue Helmets' should be in the country before they withdrew their troops from the locations they had occupied since the elections.

However one likes to look at it, in present-day conflict situations where

UN peacekeeping forces are called in, military and humanitarian activities go hand in hand and it is necessary to promote and gain comprehension for the new role of the military, in contrast to their traditional image. Apart from anything else, this is the only way in which one will obtain the maximum use of resources in support of effective humanitarian aid, which must surely be the leitmotif of successful field coordination.

14 The Humanitarian Response in Cambodia: The Imperative for a Strategic Alliance
John M. Sanderson

INTRODUCTION

Most would agree that we are living in a period of great change. But while the recent strategic shifts have relieved the threat of global nuclear war, they have also removed pressures which, since the end of the Second World War, had contained many of those deep ethnic, religious and cultural tensions of an historical nature. These tensions have now been released to emerge anew, straining contemporary international conflict resolution machinery which was developed for very different circumstances. Around us, we see brutality and suffering on a scale unprecedented since the major conflicts of this century. The cost in lives and infrastructure, along with the diversion of finances to arms and military capabilities, continues to detract from prosperity and the social progress needed to alleviate the causes of conflict. Our common humanity demands that we find an escape from this vicious cycle of violence. The international community is divided on how to proceed, or how to focus the collective will to achieve this end. A cohesive response which can efficiently and effectively end the suffering seems to be lost in the confusion of interests.

The humanitarian purpose of conflict resolution is clear. Where operations have had as their objective a political outcome which meets the aspirations of a majority of the population, the UN has experienced a measure of enduring success. Perhaps this serves to underscore the fundamental political nature of UN intervention. Ultimately, it is only through processes which franchise the people that a leadership can claim a legitimate mandate. While the military can only be a part of this sort of outcome, operations of this type are an enormous step forward from the interposition or observer missions traditionally associated with peacekeeping.

But it seems that the UN and other international agencies have not fully grasped the magnitude and complexity of the task these missions pose and the need for a coordinated response which they demand.

THE CAMBODIAN OPERATION

Amongst attempts in recent years to resolve conflicts, the UN Transitional Authority in Cambodia (UNTAC) from March 1992 to September 1993 stands out as a notable international achievement. In Cambodia, 16 000 troops from 34 different nations, 3600 UN civilian police and over 2000 UN civilians successfully implemented the UN mandate in the face of dire predictions of failure and much pessimism from many observers.

Many dimensions of the UNTAC mandate had their origins in other UN Missions, but the totality of objectives was staggering in its unprecedented scale. UNTAC was to: verify the withdrawal of all foreign forces from Cambodia; verify the cessation of outside military assistance to the Cambodian factions; regroup some 200 000 armed forces of the Cambodian Parties into cantonments, disarm them, and demobilise at least 70 per cent of them; disarm 200 000 local militia; repatriate 370 000 refugees; commence reconstruction; resolve the problem of mines scattered throughout various parts of the country; supervise the administrations of the four Cambodian factions to ensure a neutral political environment; and conduct an election for a constituent assembly. The Cambodian operation has been the most complex and intrusive UN Mission to date in the category of modern peacekeeping which seeks to rebuild states out of the residue of colonialism and/or the Cold War. The smaller operations in Namibia, Nicaragua and Mozambique are examples of this category. At some time in the future, it might be possible for shattered countries such as Rwanda, and eventually perhaps Angola, to join this list.

In Cambodia, the aim was to settle the differences between the tripartite Coalition Government of Democratic Kampuchea (CGDK) and the Vietnamese-installed State of Cambodia (SoC) regime, through the support of an internationally-sponsored settlement. The CGDK included the Royalists (FUNCINPEC), the remnants of the United States-backed Lon Nol regime (KPNLF) which overthrew the Royalists in 1970, and the Party of Democratic Kampuchea (PDK, the Khmer Rouge), which in turn defeated the Lon Nol regime in 1975. To achieve a settlement, it was also necessary to nullify the international dimension of the conflict through the disengagement of the parties' regional and strategic backers.

The UN mandate was the product of a process which began almost from the time of the Vietnamese invasion in 1979. Much of this diplomatic activity was conducted by the ASEAN countries, led by Indonesia. The end of the Cold War and the Soviet Union's capacity to pursue a global strategy led to the withdrawal of Vietnamese forces in 1989, removing a major impediment to a settlement by diluting the Sino–Soviet dimension. But an agreement between the Cambodian Parties depended on their interests, and those of their sponsors, being protected. The process had to allow their sponsors, first, to disengage from the impasse, and secondly, to re-engage in the context of a new framework.

The mechanism to achieve this was the Paris Agreements, signed on 23 October 1991 by the four Cambodian Parties and 18 interested countries, including the five Permanent Members of the Security Council. The Agreements were the result of many years of diplomatic effort and they clearly specified the role of the UN in the process. They form a highly credible objective document, which warrants close study. The central element, the basic process on which all were prepared to agree, was the UN-sponsored election. The election would establish the benchmark for the legitimacy of the Cambodian authority which was to emerge from the process.

Making an agreement is one thing; gaining the compliance of the leadership of the parties in conflict is quite another. There has to be some element of coercion in this. The only way to generate and maintain consensus on the path to a peaceful resolution of the conflict is for everyone to have something at stake. The benefit of complying with an agreement has to be seen to exceed the consequences of not complying. In this process, it is essential that leaders are forced into considering the needs of their followers. The humanitarian and human rights dimensions are critical in this respect.

HUMANITARIAN RELIEF IN CONTEXT

Humanitarian objectives cannot be separated from the issue of conflict resolution. Relief can help end a conflict, or it can help prolong it. If delivered in a timely, targeted way, it can help prevent crises from emerging in the first place, or at least diminish their gravity. If a strategic view is taken, it becomes clear that large groups of people who are disadvantaged by circumstances, or consider themselves to be disadvantaged, are highly exploitable. Often, they see no choice but to lend what weight they have to the support of a party to a conflict. This is often seen as a matter of survival. Alleviating the cause of these grievances may be considered only possible with the intervention of outside agencies. This is where the partnership between the UN and humanitarian agencies comes into play.

Humanitarian relief is not strategically neutral unless it is made to be so. In the same way that peacekeepers who maintain the strictest impartiality will nevertheless find difficulty implementing a mandate which lacks strategic objectivity, humanitarian relief has the capacity to advantage or disadvantage one side or another. Relief does not operate in a political vacuum and should not seek to do so. Humanitarian relief can also create its own dependency by drawing refugees and displaced persons to areas where support from the agricultural infrastructure is limited or impossible, leaving relief as the only means of support. This in turn can generate its own political dynamics, with control over the humanitarian relief sowing the seeds of further conflict.

HUMANITARIAN RELIEF AND PEACEKEEPING

Given the passion surrounding these issues, peacekeeping forces can easily be drawn into conflict situations from what appear to be the purest humanitarian intentions. The fact is, that while the presence of military units can provide useful assistance to negotiations and technical support, caution needs to be exercised in how they are engaged. International military forces can become a factor in the conflict, whether they are intended to or not. This is not to suggest that there is no role for force in humanitarian action, but it must be recognised that it is potentially disastrous for military forces to be caught up in a conflict in which they have no clear and achievable objectives. This is not peacekeeping.

It is important to understand that if peacekeepers are deployed, then the peacekeeping ethos must be strictly adhered to. This means that weapons are provided only for self-defence and the forces are not structured or equipped for war-fighting, or even for the maintenance of law and order.

Operations are conducted with the consent of the parties to the conflict. In the case of humanitarian relief, the agreement of both formal and informal groups might be required. This might be forthcoming only at a price. If agreement cannot be reached, or if the price is too high, then serious consideration might have to be given to whether the humanitarian objectives are achievable. Any attempt to 'fight the aid through' would probably mean conflict and could create its own dynamic of violence. If the international community is not ready to confront this with forces equipped with the full array of resources necessary for war-fighting, then it is probably better for all concerned – military, humanitarian agencies, donors and recipients alike – if military forces are not deployed in the first place.

A difficulty is also created when the presence of peacekeepers, who have been deployed to achieve limited humanitarian objectives, raises unrealistic expectations among observers and commentators over the resolution of a range of other problems in the area – including violations of human rights, crime and corruption, as well as the underlying causes of the crisis. This is not to say that these should not be addressed, but simply that if the international consensus does not or cannot clearly articulate the goals it wishes to achieve, then they might prove unachievable. And if the international community does not support these goals with additional resources, then they can only be pursued at the expense of humanitarian relief. Moreover, international action requires legitimacy. If the goals cannot be achieved within a recognisable legal framework, they risk undermining international support for the relief programme.

AN ALLIANCE WITH THE PEOPLE

Realisation of the aspirations of the people is a means for generating both legitimacy and the international support necessary for crisis resolution. The legitimacy of the Cambodia operation was established in the Paris Agreements whereby the UN would act as the transitional authority in the country. There is no question that the conduct and verification of the election was the focal point of the Mission and was the aim to which all could aspire. As long as everybody, Cambodian and international alike, believed that it was possible to conduct the election, the Mission retained its legitimacy. Little appreciated is the fact that the Mission came close to failure on this single issue.

The Agreements also established the conditions under which the factions would continue to have any form of international legality (and therefore support from their sponsors who were signatories to the Agreements). Essentially, these conditions amounted to compliance with the specified steps to bring Cambodians back together into a unified state. The problem in the Paris Agreements lay with what was not written – the hidden understandings, or ambitions about using the new dynamics generated by the Agreements to create opportunities to bypass obligations. Every faction, and some nations, engaged in this to some extent. And, of course, non-compliance by one faction automatically precluded full compliance by others. What was clear was that the Cambodian people desperately wanted peace. The essential task was to forge an alliance between UNTAC and the Cambodian people which would overcome the distortions created by the power struggles between and within the faction leaderships.

The first requirement was an information programme undistorted by faction propaganda, and every component of UNTAC participated in this programme. Initially, there was great difficulty in convincing the UN that UNTAC needed its own radio station. This meant that Radio UNTAC did not commence operation until more than a year after the signing of the Agreements. In the end, there was clear evidence that Radio UNTAC was instrumental in bringing many of the Khmer Rouge rank and file into the Cambodian mainstream. This alone would have justified its use. But, more generally, it convinced the Cambodian people that they were in a period of national transformation, manifested by the huge international presence of peacekeepers, UN civilians, humanitarian agencies and NGOs.

A key need was for UNTAC to be present everywhere in a way which generated confidence in its intention to deal equitably with all the people. The security situation made this a primary role for the military component which had to provide security not only for civilians and military alike, but also a logistic support structure which penetrated to district level. The 16 000 troops of UNTAC were therefore deployed to some 270 locations throughout Cambodia.

The Khmer Rouge, realising that they had a highly plausible competitor for the hearts and minds of the people, staged a series of intimidatory hostage situations designed to establish control over the way UNTAC interfaced with the people in the countryside. With great courage, UNTAC troops continued to push out into the villages despite the deep concerns by some that the risks were too high. In this process the military component defined the safe extent of international action. Of greater concern was the SoC propaganda which sought to erode respect for UNTAC by asserting that it lacked the commitment to face up to the Khmer Rouge. This was a cry taken up by many NGOs and some journalists. Clearly, the SoC would have preferred a solution where the UN was pressured into an enforcement alliance with them against the Khmer Rouge, rather than having the election.

But peacekeepers can only use their weapons for self-defence. In UNTAC, self-defence meant defence of anyone going about their legitimate business under the Paris Agreements, nothing more. So other neutral ways of gaining respect among the people in the countryside had to be found. Civic action programmes which bring immediate improvements to conditions of life are an obvious way. Unfortunately, the UN contention was that this sort of activity was the responsibility of UN Agencies and NGOs – not the business of the military component. This missed the point. The military had a much deeper presence and was often the only means the UN had to build confidence in its intentions; 'hearts and minds' activities always formed an essential part of the military component's method of operation. In the event, the UNTAC military component was able to establish a reasonable programme through the generosity of voluntary donations from individual countries and by close cooperation with UN Agencies and NGOs, as well as by making effective use of the nation-building and other skills that many of the UN soldiers brought to Cambodia.

Ultimately, UNTAC scored a significant victory when the Cambodian people came forward to vote on the day, despite the threats and pessimistic predictions. Achieving this through gaining the people's confidence was the challenge UNTAC faced and to do this, UNTAC needed to be united in its purpose.

A STRATEGIC ALLIANCE

Unity and impartiality are closely linked, and are issues which pervade all recent peacekeeping missions. Both these factors represent the true strength of a peacekeeping force. The key requirement is unity of purpose, unity of command and unity of understanding. Without this, the Force fractures very quickly and can no longer truly represent the will of the international community. From that point on, its ability to retain its neutrality is doubtful.

There were definite attempts to break the unity of the Force in Cambodia. Very early in the Mission the Khmer Rouge began classifying some units as 'good UNTAC', and others as 'bad UNTAC'. Unquestionably, some units were directed by national interests to take positions which were not in harmony with the overall mission objectives as reflected in the policy of the Force Commander. Fortunately, these difficulties could be overcome in the main by involving everyone in the planning process, by continuous briefings, and by clear directives and orders. It was necessary to go to great lengths to prove to everyone, both internal and external, that UNTAC was doing everything it could to implement the Paris Agreements – the only source of its authority and jurisdiction.

It is important to add here that UNTAC's full and free access to the Parties' areas was included in the Agreements, which the Khmer Rouge leadership had signed. But the Khmer Rouge refused UNTAC personnel access to the areas under their control. At the same time, humanitarian agencies prepared to provide assistance to them were permitted access to some Khmer Rouge areas. The situation might have proved different if clear political sanction had resulted from non-compliance. Although the Khmer Rouge's attempts to split UNTAC largely failed, the overall international effort in Cambodia was divided in this case.

Greater service could have been rendered to the Cambodian people by harmonising operations in accordance with the political objective. Regrettably, there was no integrated strategic planning within the UNTAC Mission, which could have supported unity from the outset. From the very beginning, each component conducted a separate survey mission and prepared a plan (of sorts) separately. Humanitarian agencies initially planned and conducted operations in isolation from the UNTAC Mission. The operation as a whole, including the overall humanitarian commitment, was uncoordinated and piecemeal. This planning shortfall was never corrected in Cambodia, except in the case of the military and electoral components, and by the Information and Education Division, which forged the necessary planning and control alliance to see the election through. This lack of strategic coordination was overcome in part by senior staffs networking as problems arose, and by the military component simply assuming the detailed planning role, pulling the other components along in the wake of military operations.

It was clear that many people were selected for UNTAC and elevated to positions for which they were not equipped by either training or experience to fulfil their duties in an integrated environment. In the past, the UN has tended to rely on the international amateur rather than the trained professional. To run a conflict-ridden country, members of the UN are either going to have to make people of the right quality available, or be honest about the inability of the organisation to fulfil responsibilities of the magnitude in the Paris Agreements.

This lack of integrated planning reflects a number of serious deficiencies in the ability of the UN Secretariat to plan and conduct operations. There were no integrated planning staffs, and the few experienced staff had difficulty adjusting to changes in the nature and size of operations. Similarly, too many members of the humanitarian agencies and NGO community in Cambodia focused their gaze narrowly, failing to comprehend the extent of the objectives the UN had set. As a result, their concerns over more immediate issues tended to distort priorities. They became easy prey for outside commentators with an interest in sensational reports, or in supporting long-established prejudices which were opposed to the broader process of reconciliation contained in the Agreements. With an integrated approach, the short-term objectives of NGOs, UN Agencies and, indeed, other UNTAC components, which often became factors working against the primary purpose of implementing the mandate, could also have been given their proper perspective.

While it is in the nature of many NGOs to spring from a base of uncoordinated compassion, too many of them end up in direct competition.

The fact that so many have very limited resources often makes this lack of coordination destructive. Humanitarian and peacekeeping objectives should not be in opposition; rather they are different instruments of the same purpose. The humanitarian effort should be the subject of properly constructed plans which form part of an overall integrated plan working towards the common objective.

One particularly adverse effect of the lack of an integrated approach in Cambodia was that there was great difficulty in ensuring that all UN personnel and other influential expatriates knew why UNTAC was there. There were many confused messages from members of the international community in Cambodia, some of whom actually succumbed to faction propaganda. On a number of occasions, in response to atrocities, the military component was called on by people both within and outside the UN to use the peacekeeping force for the conduct of operations against the Khmer Rouge. These would have been offensive operations – no one could draw any other interpretation. What was most astonishing was the passion with which the use of force was espoused. Often, the most fervent advocates of violence were those who would otherwise declare their total opposition to war!

It is true that UNTAC suffered severe impediments as the result of a delayed start, which had sacrificed the hard-won opportunities provided by the Paris Agreements. But enforcement action by UN peacekeepers was never an option. Enforcement would have required a force several times larger, one structured and equipped for a protracted conflict, and at a significantly greater cost. Such a mission would have spelt doom for the Cambodian peace process, even if it had been given wide international support, and the many years of diplomatic effort and a huge expenditure of international funds would have been wasted.

Had an integrated approach been used from the outset and maintained throughout the UNTAC operation, many of the problems which endure in Cambodia could have been more contained. A central lesson to emerge from the UNTAC operation is the need for a strategic alliance between peacekeeping forces, humanitarian agencies and those NGOs which feel that they have a role to play in pursuing common goals. This would have enhanced, rather than diffused, the moral authority of the international effort.

FOCUSING DIPLOMACY

The success of UNTAC had to be political. To be successful, the diplomatic strength of the international community needed to be mustered.

Success could not have been achieved if there had not been unity in the Security Council, and between it and UNTAC. Fortunately, a diplomatic body had been set up in Phnom Penh when the Paris Agreements were signed. Dubbed the Expanded Permanent Five (EP5), it consisted of the Ambassadors of the five Permanent Members of the Security Council, and those of Australia, Germany, Indonesia, Japan and Thailand (India and Malaysia joined subsequently). The EP5 served to remind the Cambodian Parties of their obligations under the Paris Agreements during the five months between the signing and the establishment of UNTAC, and continued to support UNTAC throughout the mandate. The EP5's relationship with the SRSG and the Force Commander was a corporate one. They met regularly and the EP5 were briefed about developments and our projected operations.

The EP5 mirrored a grouping in New York known as the Core Group. Contact between the two groups ensured coordination between the decisions in New York and Phnom Penh, through the policy processes in the capitals of the nations concerned. This meant that SCRs on Cambodia, drafted in the face of major obstacles as the Mission progressed, were achievable and reflected the realities on the ground. Through this process, consistency of operations with the agreed political purpose was ensured and UNTAC could then proceed to implement its mandated responsibilities, confident of both its jurisdiction and support. The diplomatic structures were essential to unify and focus the diplomatic support. At the same time, UNTAC needed structures to concentrate its efforts on its important task of defining and fine-tuning a policy framework for the implementation of the mandate.

COORDINATING HUMANITARIAN ASSISTANCE

The military doctrine of most countries identifies three levels of command: strategic, operational and tactical. Different names might be used but, in effect, they all describe the same things. Understanding the different levels is critical if confusion is to be avoided. If one of these levels is absent or deficient, or their roles become merged, the capacity of the others to function is effectively curtailed.

The strategic level cannot afford to become involved with tactics if it is to maintain its broad perspective. At the same time, actions at the tactical level impact on the strategic objectives and must therefore be conducted within a strategic framework. Without such a framework, actions at the tactical level will become directionless. The operational level binds the other two together. For the UN's operation in Cambodia during 1992 and 1993:

- The strategic level was the Security Council in New York, supported by the UN Secretariat and the state structures of Security Council members, with their links to the national capitals of interested states and the highest level headquarters of UN Agencies and NGOs;
- The operational level was the UN Headquarters in Phnom Penh, with its links to the leadership of the Cambodian Parties and the most senior authorities of the humanitarian organisations in-country which allied themselves to the UNTAC operation;
- The tactical level was the military units, civilian groups and elements in the field, coordinated by regional headquarters normally located in provincial capitals.

The success achieved in Cambodia was due to the operational level of command being able to achieve harmony between all levels and, to maintain it up to the end of the mandate. The key issue is that the three levels have separate roles, while they are at the same time complementary elements which form an effective whole. If humanitarian assistance is to be effectively coordinated, it must be brought under or into a relationship with this framework in a way which brings all relevant agencies into harmonisation. If structures to this end do not exist, then they need to be created, as they were in Cambodia. But rather than the *ad hoc* arrangements in UNTAC, it would have been better if formalised structures had been in place at the outset, and staff selected who were trained to use them.

Some organisations will find these suggestions at odds with their ethos. Bodies such as the ICRC have a long-established tradition of independence which warrants respect (see also Chapter 10). However, this does not rule out cooperation in a range of activities. For the most part, the creation of cooperative mechanisms will draw the capacities of relevant organisations to them.

GRASS ROOTS COORDINATION

The need for cooperative mechanisms established at grass roots level is illustrated by the experience of the Cambodian Mine Action Centre (CMAC). The issue of mines was understandably a matter of deep concern to many, but in particular to the UNTAC Repatriation Component which clearly did not wish to settle people on unsafe land. Although there was much goodwill and aid available to assist with this problem, the mineclearing resources of UNTAC were very limited; the military component being tasked under the Paris Agreements only with 'assisting with clearing mines and undertaking training programs in mine clearance and a mine-awareness programme among the Cambodian people'. The intention of the Agreements was clearly that the task would mainly be the work of other agencies; but if these were uncoordinated, they would have been unlikely to achieve maximum effectiveness.

The magnitude of the problem quickly became clear. There could be no quick solutions as in Kuwait in 1991; only a long-term coordinated approach would work. CMAC was designed to continue well beyond the UNTAC mandate with the fundamental objectives of: acting as a focal point for mine information; coordinating the training of Cambodian mine-clearers (10 000 was the plan); and coordinating the funding for mine clearance and the long-term programme.

In this last respect, the CMAC process was also designed to gain the commitment and coordinate the efforts of those humanitarian organisations who sought a role in resolving the mine problem. Unfortunately, the demands of the repatriation programme and the appeals of NGOs concerned with the mine problem eventually required the diversion of training resources to mine clearing. Given the terrible debilitating effect of mines, it is easy to have sympathy for this short-term approach. But the resources available were never enough to have a meaningful impact unless they were dedicated to training a significant Cambodian mine-clearing force. The effect was the opposite to that intended and slowed progress in generating an extensive Cambodian capacity to clear mines from the countryside.

Of course, if an integrated approach had been adopted from the outset, the repatriation scheme, which formed an important part of the UNTAC plan, could have avoided incorrect assumptions and included all the relevant security and mine-related factors. Due to these and other difficulties associated with developments in the peace process, CMAC did not achieve the goals set for it during the life of UNTAC; but taken overall, CMAC still proved successful. Before the end of the mandate, CMAC was established under Cambodian law as a statutory authority. At the time of writing, it is still functioning in accordance with its original objective.

Despite the problems CMAC faced, the CMAC model demonstrates the effectiveness and efficiencies which can be generated through the establishment of coordinating agencies within a legitimate framework. The CMAC model needs to be extended to other areas of endeavour which contribute to nation-building, including social and economic development, public security, law and order, and justice.

The cooperative structures should draw in the parties to the conflict.

The aim should be to build confidence and further the cause of peaceful resolution. This does not involve partisanship; rather it forces the parties to demonstrate their political commitment to conflict resolution. Non-involvement would be their choice but it would send clear political signals, and should carry political penalties. Ideally, a range of cooperative mechanisms covering the functional areas dictated by the circumstances of the crisis would be formed. As the UN is the recognised authority representing the will of the international community, it would seem to have a central role in the identification of those functional areas and establishment of the mechanisms, as well as overall coordination.

JUSTICE

It seems appropriate to add something on the issue of 'justice packages' as part of peace-building. The idea has been suggested by Australian Foreign Minister, Senator Gareth Evans, in his book, *Cooperating for Peace*.[1] The approach should be to promote an indigenous process which will uphold human rights and which can be left behind after the international community has completed its task. This was an objective of the UN mandate in Cambodia.

In the absence of a satisfactory indigenous process, a justice system might need to be imposed, but the implications of this should be well understood. A tribunal imposed on a society from outside is a provocative act. In some cases, the perpetrators of criminal acts might be political or military leaders with significant forces at their disposal. They might also be signatories to an internationally recognised agreement aimed at achieving a peaceful settlement. Attempts to try to punish them or their followers could be perceived as a lack of impartiality, and could lead to further conflict. Furthermore, the physical protection of the overall process, the police, judiciary, witnesses, and prisons, could prove extremely demanding of resources. It might even be necessary to be prepared to conduct internal security operations in their defence. Operations of this nature would have to be planned for in detail; they cannot be approached in an *ad hoc*, haphazard manner. They also require a strong, united and enduring international commitment. This process itself might create a dependency which goes well beyond the intention of the participating nations.

Importantly, the neutral political environment for a free and fair election cannot be achieved if perpetrators of political terror cannot be brought to justice. This was and remains a complex issue in Cambodia – and elsewhere. The horror of the past has created a high degree of tolerance for acts of violence but increased the resilience of the Cambodian people. This fact might have made a profound contribution to the success of UNTAC. But if the people are going to share in the commercial benefits of their new conditions, there has to be a legal climate of justice which fosters both opportunity and investment.

Short-term objectives might need to be balanced against the longer-term objective of establishing a respect for human rights within the society. The critical element is to understand that it is only through influencing the values of the society that a human rights culture of any substance will be inculcated. Along with issues of peace, reconciliation and sovereignty, those of human rights and justice form an important element in conflict resolution. Again, the critical issue is that a holistic approach is required.

CONCLUSION

It is difficult to draw comparisons between UNTAC and other UN Missions since every operation is unique. For example, the operation in Somalia did not have clear operational objectives extending from an agreement, as was the case in Cambodia. This is often the problem of humanitarian military missions where the stated aim is to support relief operations and provide technical assistance. In the initial stages, at least, they often do not have a clear-cut objective aimed at resolution of the conflict. The military can only identify very limited tactical objectives in these circumstances. But nearly all UN Commanders come under pressure to use their peacekeepers for tasks in excess of their mandated responsibilities. When confronted with these issues, a Force Commander must consider most carefully his aim, his legal jurisdiction and the unity of his force, since the potential for disunity and loss of neutrality is high.

This urge to become involved in conflict situations must be tempered by these longer-term considerations. The many smaller conflicts which have emerged in the post-Cold War global flux have seized the attention of the international media and the humanitarian movement. The sense of urgency generated by the resulting refugee flows and abuses of human rights has led to some responses which might be viewed as ill-considered and ill-prepared and, when tested against the UN Charter, might not be clearly established within its framework. It is perhaps for this reason that we see a diminished capacity of the UN to build sustainable coalitions in the shorter term.

The international community lends its weight to the resolution of conflict through the structures of the UN. Results are achieved through the allocation of resources – diplomatic, financial, human and material – which come from many sources, both government and NGOs. The critical issue is for these to function in a structured way which aims at the identification and achievement of common purpose for the maximum benefit of those who suffer. The role of the UN is central to this. It can provide the framework for leadership upon which the muscle and sinews of the humanitarian response can be built.

To most observers, UNTAC stands out as an important UN success and is an example of the possibilities of rehabilitation and reconciliation which exist in the post-Cold War climate. If Cambodia can be set on a remedial path, there is hope for all fractured nations, those whose inhabitants appear despairingly in nightly scenes of misery on television screens. Such operations remain a source of some optimism for the future, where the UN, by its presence, lends its moral authority to a majority who want peace and reconciliation. How to give that majority a voice is a key issue. Too often, UN peacekeeping has been seen as an end in itself, as if a peace settlement will materialise from the UN presence alone. The reality is that peace-keeping is a means to an end. It must be linked to and coordinated with other conflict resolution elements, including the humanitarian effort.

Note

1.   G. Evans, *Cooperating for Peace: The Global Agenda* for *the 1990s and beyond* (Sydney: Allen & Unwin, 1993).

15 The Coordination of Humanitarian Assistance in Mozambique in the Context of ONUMOZ

Aldo Romano Ajello

THE ESTABLISHMENT OF UNOHAC

On 4 October 1992 in Rome, under the Chairmanship of the Italian Government, Joachim Alberto Chissano, President of Mozambique, and Afonso Macacho Marceta Dhlakama, leader of Resistençia Nacional Mozambicana (RENAMO), signed a peace agreement and put an end to 16 years of devastating war. The Agreement consisted of various protocols covering four main sectors: political, military, electoral and humanitarian. The composition of the subsequent UN peacekeeping operation in Mozambique (ONUMOZ) reflected the structure foreseen in the Peace Agreement.

On the political side, the engine moving the peace process forward was the Supervision and Monitoring Commission (CSC), composed of the two Mozambican parties, the representatives of the countries most directly involved in the peace process (which had been accepted by the parties), the OAU, and the UN which acted as chair. In the implementation of its task, the CSC was assisted by three subsidiary bodies: the Cease Fire Commission (CFC), the Commission for Reintegration of the Demobilized Soldiers (CORE) and the Commission for the Formation of the Mozambican Defence Force (CCFADM). All these commissions were also chaired by the UN. Monitoring of Police, Intelligence Services and unification of Public Administration was conducted by three other commissions composed exclusively of Mozambican members: COMPOL, COMINFO and the Commission for Territorial Administration.

The military side of the Mission consisted of 350 UN military observers, who were to investigate any alleged violations of the cease fire and supervise the assembly and demobilisation process, and an armed force of five infantry battalions to protect the main roads and corridors. These units provided logistic and technical support to the entire peacekeeping

194

operation, even in areas not covered by their mandate, such as the formation of the new Mozambican Defence Force.

On the electoral side, the major role was played by the National Election Commission and its provincial branches, which were composed entirely of Mozambican members representing all the political parties. In the implementation of their tasks, the electoral commissions were supported by a technical team from UNDP. The electoral division of ONUMOZ was in charge of monitoring the electoral process and observing its various phases: registration, the electoral campaign and the voting process.

As with other components of ONUMOZ, the mandate of the humanitarian assistance element was spelled out in the General Peace Agreement. Immediately after it was signed, the two Mozambican parties as well as the international mediator and the observer countries asked the Secretary-General to dispatch to Maputo an *ad hoc* Mission to design the humanitarian component of the peacekeeping operation. The Mission's terms of reference were:

> to assess existing United Nations operations in this area and to devise a more effective United Nations response to the intended expansion of humanitarian activities, with emphasis on the development of an appropriate coordination mechanism.

Based on the Mission's report, the Secretary-General recommended to the Security Council that a UN Office for the Coordination of Humanitarian Assistance (UNOHAC) be established as an integrated component of the peacekeeping mission, under the overall authority of the SRSG. It was to be located in Maputo at the ONUMOZ HQ, with sub-offices at the regional and provincial levels. To ensure the proper provision and delivery of relief assistance to an expanded beneficiary population in Mozambique, UNOHAC was given the task of coordinating the humanitarian assistance programmes managed by UN Agencies, and, to the extent possible, those conducted by the NGO community. Both UN Agencies and NGOs were therefore to be invited to designate representatives who could participate actively in UNOHAC's work.

Through SCR 792 (16 December 1992), the Security Council approved the Secretary-General's recommendations, and immediately thereafter UNOHAC was formally established. At that time it was estimated that, as a result of both the war and the drought, there were 3–4 million displaced people inside Mozambique, in addition to some 1.4–1.8 million Mozambican refugees dispersed in neighbouring countries. All of these people had to be resettled.

THE CONTEXT OF HUMANITARIAN AID COORDINATION IN MOZAMBIQUE

The establishment of UNOHAC was not the first UN effort to coordinate the humanitarian aid activities of the numerous organisations in Mozambique. Shortly after the death of President Samora Machel in late 1986, at a time of drought and political destabilisation, the British NGO Oxfam launched an emergency appeal for Mozambique, warning that the country was on the brink of an Ethiopia-scale famine. The UN Secretary-General strongly supported this appeal, organised a special donors' conference and, in February 1987, appointed the UNDP resident representative in Maputo as UN Special Coordinator for Emergency Relief Operations (UNSCERO). This appointment was modelled on the very successful emergency operations in Ethiopia during the period 1984–6, when a high-level special coordinator, at the prestigious level of Assistant Secretary-General, had effectively harnessed the joint forces of the UN Agencies in the fight against famine.

However, the UN Agencies strongly opposed the idea of again having someone who would outrank all their representatives in the country placed in charge of emergency relief, thus threatening their relative autonomy. To avoid potential dissent, the Secretary-General decided to appoint the UNSCERO as the *primus inter pares* of the UN system in Maputo, rather than appointing an outsider. While this decision diffused the tensions surrounding the appointment, it did not provide the tools for strong leadership. The UNSCERO had to rely on the voluntary cooperation of his peers.

The problem of coordination was compounded by the many coordination mechanisms within the Government. While UNDP, as well as most bilateral donors, dealt mainly with the Ministry of Cooperation and with the Comissão Executiv a Nacional de Emergencia (CENE), the World Bank's key contacts were in the Ministry of Finance, while WFP supported the Ministry of Commerce. UNICEF, meanwhile, worked mainly through the Department for the Prevention and Combat of Natural Disasters. At the same time, many NGOs bypassed existing central Government coordination mechanisms altogether, and worked directly with local authorities or with local NGOs.

All this added up to a somewhat fluid and amorphous situation, and this was a major consideration when, in the planning of the Peacekeeping Mission, the humanitarian implications were being considered. Thus, the decision was taken to abolish UNSCERO's office, and to transfer its functions to UNOHAC, a high-level operation under the overall guidance of the SRSG, who reported directly to the Secretary-General himself.

UNOHAC'S DESIGN AND STRATEGIC PLAN

On 15 October 1992, when the first team of UNMOs and I, as the SRSG, arrived in Maputo, the drought was still severe and its effects were devastating. It was immediately evident that the timely and effective delivery of humanitarian assistance had to be given priority to create the basic conditions for the implementation of the peace agreement.

Four target groups had been identified. In addition to the refugees and the displaced people, assistance had to be provided to those soldiers who were in the process of demobilisation and/or already demobilised, and to the local population in need, especially in the areas most severely affected by the drought. These four groups all had to receive the same level of assistance simultaneously. Any disparity of treatment could have produced tensions among the different groups, and put in jeopardy the entire peace process.

The first priority was to assure free circulation of the humanitarian assistance coming into the country, and especially the food aid. The main task assigned to the five infantry battalions authorised by the Security Council as the UN Peacekeeping Force in Mozambique was to protect the main roads and corridors in order to assure the timely and effective delivery of this humanitarian assistance. While this was the first priority, the mandate of UNOHAC was much wider. According to the General Peace Agreement, humanitarian assistance was also to serve as an instrument of national reconciliation by opening up channels of communication with communities residing in RENAMO-controlled areas and restoring basic community services for displaced persons and refugees returning to their homes.

Upon its establishment, UNOHAC worked out a Consolidated Humanitarian Assistance Programme, covering a large spectrum of activities: repatriation of refugees and resettlement of displaced persons; demobilisation of the armed forces; emergency relief; restoration of essential services; multi-sectoral support for re-integration; balance of payments and budget support; and institutional support. The requirement for restoration of essential services was specifically foreseen in the following sub-sectors: agriculture, health, water supply and sanitation, education and social welfare, road maintenance and mine clearance.

The very concept of an *ad hoc* Office for Humanitarian Assistance in the context of a peacekeeping operation was an innovation. Equally innovative was the appointment of a high-ranking officer, a former Assistant Administrator of UNDP, as Director of this Office reporting directly to the SRSG. The main reason for these innovations was the magnitude of the task, which required of the coordinator, competence, experience and an undivided commitment. It was also considered that only a high-ranking officer of repute would have the necessary prestige and authority to be accepted as coordinator by the Mozambican parties, by the various UN Agencies and by the NGO community.

The concept of coordination developed by UNOHAC was also innovative: the Office was supposed to provide services and not just give instructions. The intention was to make UNOHAC a valuable support unit for its partners: to provide them with a full, updated picture of the general situation; to keep them informed on the progress in the political and military areas; and to help them to solve the problems they would encounter with the government and with RENAMO in the implementation of their specific mandates.

ACHIEVEMENTS AND SHORTCOMINGS

Was UNOHAC able to support the UN Agencies and the international NGO community adequately, and did it fulfil its ambitious goals? The results achieved were quite remarkable: between October 1992 and December 1994 approximately 3 million displaced persons and 1 million refugees had returned to their villages of origin and been resettled. At the end of 1994, it was expected that a further 680 000 displaced persons and 300 000 refugees would be resettled during the following year. Tribute must be paid to all the UN Agencies, to the bilateral aid organisations and to the NGO community for their often exemplary concerted efforts. The collaboration between such diverse entities as UNHCR, UNICEF, WFP, IOM, ICRC, USAID and NORAD was truly impressive.

As refugees spontaneously began to return to Mozambique, UNHCR established a three-year programme, funded with some $200 million and implemented mainly through NGOs, to restore basic services and assist these refugees in their efforts to resettle. Simultaneously, more than 30 NGOs participated in programmes to re-integrate internally-displaced people and demobilised soldiers. UNICEF, meanwhile, was leading international efforts to provide drinking water in order to redress the effects of the drought and to facilitate resettlement.

Donors channelled their relief food aid through the WFP and NGOs, and UNOHAC closely monitored deliveries to the areas controlled by both the government and RENAMO to ensure equity. As roads were opened and mines were cleared, deliveries to RENAMO-held areas steadily increased: between October 1992 and May 1994, UNOHAC recorded that 74 000 tons of food were distributed. All across the country, the availability of food increased dramatically, thanks to the peaceful conditions, the increased access to food aid, and the return of the rains.

A major achievement of UNOHAC was the successful demobilisation of some 77 000 soldiers – 20 000 more than originally foreseen, as 14 000 soldiers were included who were demobilised before the Peace Agreement was signed. The soldiers were provided with 18 months of re-integration subsidy payments, financed by the donor community, and six months' severance pay from the government. They were also given access to a country-wide information and referral service, an occupational skills development programme, and a fund to promote their involvement in community activities. Their transportation home, often under difficult conditions, was organised by the IOM.

At the beginning of its activities, UNOHAC enjoyed the full support and the approval of the government, RENAMO and of the donor community. Subsequently, while the relationship between ONUMOZ and the Mozambican parties, especially the government, remained positive and constructive, the cooperation with the UN Agencies and the NGOs in the area of humanitarian aid became more difficult, and the love affair with the donor community came to an end. Increasingly, criticism was raised against UNOHAC's excessively bureaucratic rules and procedures, its tendency to build overly heavy structures at central and provincial levels, and its inclination to be involved in medium- and long-term programmes, where it had no mandate. The donor community began to question the very concept of an *ad hoc* Office for Humanitarian Assistance Coordination within ONUMOZ. It was suggested that a peacekeeping mission should not have a humanitarian component under its responsibility, and that humanitarian assistance should be the responsibility of those UN Agencies which had a permanent presence in the country.

LESSONS LEARNED

Some of these criticisms and suggestions were valid, and they must be analysed carefully to take corrective measures for the future; others were wrong – in particular, the hasty dismissal of the concept of an *ad hoc* Office for Humanitarian Assistance was short-sighted. The coordination of humanitarian assistance should be an essential component of any peace-keeping operation. After all, the first priority for a peacekeeping mission is to consolidate an often fragile peace, and to remove all possible sources of tensions which could put the peace process in jeopardy.

To identify the consolidation of peace as the first priority is not without consequences in terms of the daily decisions that must be taken. Sometimes these decisions can appear unfair, and they often are; for example, the provision of food to the assembly areas for soldiers in the process of demobilisation should be considered a priority even when other vulnerable groups are more needy than the soldiers. To keep soldiers content during the demobilisation process is a precondition for peace to hold. To give another example: demobilised officers and non-commissioned officers can represent a serious risk to peace and stability if they are unemployed. Moreover, in societies where they are the bulk of the middle class, they should be, or should become, the central pillar of a democratic system. Demoting these key groups both economically and socially would be a political mistake. If consolidation of peace is the *sine qua non*, programmes for the re-integration of demobilised officers and NCOs should be given more attention and resources than the programmes for other, more vulnerable, groups which under normal circumstances would have priority.

In less complex circumstances, humanitarian assistance is a task in itself with its own dynamics. In a peacekeeping operation, the coordination of humanitarian assistance is, above all, an essential instrument in the implementation of the peace agreement. In the case of Mozambique, the establishment of an Office for Humanitarian Assistance under the overall authority of the SRSG was the correct decision. Equally correct was the concept of coordination linked to the provision of valuable services. The fact that in Mozambique the implementation of these services was not entirely satisfactory does not mean that the concept was wrong.

Coordination of the operational activities of the UN system at the country level has always been a very difficult problem. It becomes even more difficult when the NGO community is involved. If the various organisations providing humanitarian assistance perceive the coordination as an imposition, they will resist it and they will make the job of the coordinator impossible. On the other hand, if the coordination brings them a valuable support structure, they will be keen to participate. This seems the most constructive approach for the UN at present, where the coordinator, regardless of rank, has neither a line of authority over the many partners inside or outside the UN system, nor control of their financial resources.

INTERNAL INCONSISTENCIES: A CONFRONTATION OF TWO CULTURES

The criticism levelled at UNOHAC (and in a sense at the UN itself) that it was burdened by an excess of bureaucratic rules and procedures was correct. This is a major failing which should be addressed systematically.

The first problem is the complexity of the UN's operational rules and procedures, which focus far more on transparency and accountability than on efficiency and timely delivery. However, in a peacekeeping mission, time can mean lives as well as money, and timeliness can make the difference between success and failure. Often, to save a little money, big money is wasted. In addition, a delay in delivery can mean the loss of momentum, with negative consequences for the political aspects of the operation. This was evident, for example, in the implementation of the mine-clearance plan. Conscious of the importance and the urgency of the issue, on 31 December 1992 the CSC approved a list of roads that should be cleared of mines as soon as possible to facilitate the delivery of humanitarian aid and the return of refugees. UNOHAC was requested to identify a suitable de-mining company and begin operations immediately. But it took UNOHAC until July 1994 to receive all the necessary clearances and approvals from Maputo and New York in order to have the contract signed and to begin the actual mine clearance.

All the rules and procedures were followed carefully and transparency and accountability were assured, but the mine-clearing project was labelled as a bad failure by both the parties to the conflict and by the international community; it was considered to be the most unsuccessful project of the entire peacekeeping operation. Fortunately, some bilateral donors, instead of using the UN as a channel, directly contracted private companies and began clearing roads long before UNOHAC could have its own project approved and implemented. This donor community initiative also reduced the negative political impact of the UN's failure on the peace process but nothing could reduce the negative impact that it had on the UN's image. Even although corrective measures were eventually taken and the project was completed more rapidly than originally foreseen, this negative impact persisted.

The second problem is the variety and inconsistency of rules and procedures adopted by the UN and its various programmes and Agencies. Finally, the third and most serious problem is the conflict between 'the culture of development' and 'the culture of peacekeeping'. UN staff members for peacekeeping missions are usually recruited from the Secretariat or the UN development organisations. Since no specific training is provided for them, they carry with them the culture of their organisation of origin.

What I call the culture of development is clearly reflected by the well-known story of the fish and the fishing pole: 'if people are starving do not give them fish; give them a fishing pole and teach them how to catch a fish'. What matters in this approach is how to do the job, not how long it will take for the job to be done. Although the culture of UN peacekeeping was never defined, it is self-evident that in a peacekeeping operation time is an essential and very expensive factor, especially when large numbers of military observers and armed troops are involved. In a peacekeeping operation, therefore, the development approach is just not applicable. UN peacekeepers do not have time to follow that approach. They must ensure that things move as fast as possible and, thus, they must undertake many of the tasks which under normal circumstances would by carried out by the government or the local people.

A clear example of this cultural conflict was the preparation of the assembly areas in Mozambique. The problem was how to organise and equip the 49 assembly areas where the soldiers of the government and RENAMO had to be concentrated in order to be demobilised or integrated in the new Mozambican Army. In accordance with the culture of development, a decision was made that the UN Technical Unit would provide the soldiers with tools and raw materials and that they should build their own African cabanas in the shape of the traditional peasant houses. This decision proved to be ill-conceived and it caused very serious problems. The soldiers were extremely disappointed; in some cases they had marched for many days through the bush to reach the camp, and they were not prepared to start building houses. In addition, they were offended to be treated like peasants. In general, they felt that the UN was an unreliable and ineffective organisation. As a result of these frustrations, and on the assumption that they would spend only a few weeks in the assembly areas, the soldiers built very basic shelters.

Unfortunately, for political reasons, the soldiers were forced to remain in the assembly areas not for a few weeks but for many months, and life in the camps became a nightmare. In many cases, riots and mutinies were the result of the bad accommodation. It was evident that prior to the arrival of the soldiers, the camps should have been prepared by UN personnel and provided with tents, at least for the first group of soldiers. A timely preparation of suitable accommodation would have impressed the soldiers and would have commanded respect for the UN and its staff members. The discipline in the camps would have been better and the demobilisation process would have been smoother.

There was another criticism which I consider to be basically correct: UNOHAC was too involved in the elaboration and planning of medium- and long-term programmes. An analysis of the Consolidated Humanitarian Assistance Plan shows that it covered areas which went beyond the scope one might consider appropriate, given the UNOHAC's mandate and in the context of the time-bound plans for implementation of the peace accord. UNOHAC should have limited its actions to the short-term and should have worked out, together with the relevant ministries, UN Agencies and

NGOs, an appropriate plan to bridge this short-term plan with the long and medium-term planning of the government and the development agencies. Once again, the conflict between the culture of development and the culture of peacekeeping was clearly apparent.

UNOHAC's staff were mainly development people and they acted according to their culture. They immediately perceived the importance of long-term and medium-term planning, and acted accordingly. Their perception was correct: there was a need to plan for the long haul, and to make these plans consistent with the short-term goals at the beginning of the operation. But it was not their job; at least it was not their primary job. The obvious question to be addressed is 'who should assure the harmonisation of the short-term projects with the long- and medium-term programme'? Is the UN Resident Coordinator that person? How should that official interact with an *ad hoc* structure such as UNOHAC? Should the Resident Coordinator have been in charge of UNOHAC? Finally, how can the conflict between the culture of development and the culture of peacekeeping be addressed?

THE FUTURE, WITH PERFECT HINDSIGHT

Many of these questions were present in the minds of the people who had to decide how to provide timely and efficient humanitarian assistance in support of the peace process in Mozambique. I stand fully behind the decision finally taken, after much deliberation, to set up UNOHAC within the peacekeeping operation and not outside of it. This decision was the correct one. There was, however, a lack of analysis and clarity about the mandate, the functions of the Office, and about the way in which short-term humanitarian assistance, coordinated by the Office in the context of the peace process, should have been linked to the medium-term and long-term development programmes to be implemented after the completion of the peace process. As happens in every innovative operation, lack of experience played its part.

One of the secrets of the success of ONUMOZ was its political flexibility. Rules and procedures were adapted to the reality in the field and appropriate decisions taken on the spot. The same freedom was not given to UNOHAC. In the implementation of our mission, we often had a tall man to cover and a short blanket available. On the political side, every time that we were faced with a similar situation, we managed to change the blanket; on the humanitarian side, we had to cut the man because we did not have the authority to do otherwise.

When designing future peacekeeping operations, all of these questions should be addressed at the outset. To abandon the idea of humanitarian assistance coordination as an integral part of peacekeeping is not the solution to the problem. It would make the management of a peacekeeping operation even more difficult. What needs to be done to address the problem is to change the cultural approach: to reform the rules and procedures and make them consistent with the reality in the field; to increase the delegation of authority to the SRSG and to the Director of the Office for Humanitarian Assistance Coordination; to define clearly what should be done in the short-term and what should be done in the medium-term and long-term, to decide how the two operations should be harmonised; and to determine who should do what.

Administrative decisions taken by the UN Secretariat will not be sufficient to bring about the fundamental and complex reforms required. To achieve change, we will need nothing less than the full concurrence of the member states, and their active support in all the bodies where decisions of this nature must be taken.

16 The Changing Role of UN Peacekeeping Forces: The Relationship between UN Peacekeepers and NGOS in Rwanda

Roméo A. Dallaire

There are several factors which help explain the re-emergence of the UN and NGOs as prominent actors in the international arena. There was the change in attitude among the permanent members of the Security Council which transformed Council proceedings from ideological sparring to unprecedented consensus. The Council also began addressing a variety of intra-state as well as inter-state concerns including 'non-military sources of instability in the economic, social, humanitarian and ecological fields'.[1] At the same time, members of the Security Council, and indeed many citizens of the world, recognised the expanding scope of security: that international security is as much threatened today by the possibility of collapse of the economic system, the scourge of international terrorism, drug trafficking or by ethnic and social unrest as by inter-state armed conflict.[2]

Another factor which has had an effect on NGOs as well as the UN is the changing nature of warfare. The twentieth century, and more specifically the post-Second World War era, has been marked by an exponential increase in the number of civilian casualties of war. Nine out of every 10 war casualties are now civilians.[3] If one also adds the number of displaced persons and refugees to this figure, the effect of war on civilians becomes a crucial factor in the strategy of war-making. This situation is now compounded by what has been called the 'CNN phenomenon' whereby images of innocent victims, suffering from all of the horrors traditionally associated with war, are beamed into everyone's home.[4] While these images do not guarantee a response by the international community, they rarely leave viewers indifferent. This effect has been enhanced since Cold War tensions no longer polarise societies. The point that must be stressed here is that any attempt to manage or restrict conflict must resolve the overall issue of civilian victims, and the resolution of this element of human abuse must be addressed in tandem with security concerns.

UN PEACE SUPPORT OPERATIONS

The UN is trying to adapt to this new reality by undertaking several new roles. This has made the classic UN peace support triad of the consent of the parties, the impartiality of the UN and the peacekeeping force, and the use of force only in self-defence much more complex.[5] The former UN Under Secretary-General for Peacekeeping Operations, Mr Marrack Goulding, outlined the characteristics of the emerging form of peace support operations as including: a large civilian component; often, the organisation and conduct of elections; a substantial public affairs unit; a police contingent and a human rights dimension, possibly intruding into the judicial and penal system of the country in question; constraints on duration; and, more often than not, dealing with internal conflicts.[6]

Needless to say, this new paradigm requires UN peacekeepers to be armed with, amongst other things, a new willingness to understand:

the complexities of hate, of passionate, aggressive self-assertion, of the long and painful memories of those who refuse to forget, and the quickened, curt character of those who refuse to remember.[7]

Or to put it differently, 'Without dialogue, communication and integration with other elements of human society, separating warring parties is simply a war waiting to happen'.[8] Therefore, successful UN peace support operations must now operate with great sensitivity, high moral standards, compassion and generosity and well-practised social exchange skills, particularly of brokerage and diplomacy – albeit in concert with the potential use of military force. This is in stark contrast to traditional peacekeeping in which peace was often equated with simply separating the warring parties.

NON-GOVERNMENTAL ORGANISATIONS

In today's post-Cold War international community, the US has become the *de facto* world superpower and, by the same token, it has become the only nation capable of projecting its military force anywhere in the world.[9] Yet, in part for this very reason, many countries in the UN General Assembly are now enthusiastic about furthering the UN's role in conflict management and the maintenance of intra-state as well as inter-state peace based on international law rather than great power cooperation. In the eyes of the developing countries, the UN is regarded as more transparent and possessed of greater moral authority and political legitimacy than any single state or coalition. Ironically, as a general rule, NGOs tend to have considerable difficulty with the implications of this view.

Overall, NGOs do not, by their very nature, represent any national or international self-interest. In fact, NGOs:

> in the simplest of terms, attempt to direct the goodwill of professionals and ordinary people, and attempt to do good things with it. Goodwill is both [their] calling card and [their] product.[10]

As a result, many NGOs have been hesitant about working with UN peace support operations and particularly with those employing uniformed soldiers, in spite of the UN's moral legitimacy. They fear that they might be co-opted into a new Cold War strategy whereby the national interests of a dominant power define the operations of the day – meaning that NGOs could become a non-military extension of a new structure for great power interests working beside or through the UN.[11] In operational terms, some NGOs fear that the use of armed forces to protect relief supplies and personnel might, in fact, have the opposite result: that is, it could turn the humanitarian facilities and staff into perceived antagonists and, therefore, targets.

RWANDA: INTERACTION BETWEEN THE UN AND NGOS

All of these complexities came into play in Rwanda during my time as Force Commander of UNAMIR from its inception to 19 August 1994. It was the impressive number of Canadian NGOs in Rwanda in the first place which helped to make the crisis in Rwanda a Canadian concern. Rwanda had long been a recipient of Canadian aid and money for development projects. Canadian, more specifically French Canadian, religious orders were also quite active throughout the country. To my surprise, I discovered that, next to the Belgian flag, the most common flag was Canadian.[12] Canada therefore had a strong interest in supporting UN initiatives in Rwanda.

Unfortunately, neither the strong Canadian support for the UN's involvement in Rwanda nor the presence of Canadian NGOs guaranteed that this UN peace support operation would be any different from most other UN missions. UNAMIR suffered several important shortcomings from the very beginning. This was due, at least in part, to a conscious decision by the Security Council seemingly to classify the crisis in Rwanda as a low priority. In addition, there were no formal links (through Security Council resolutions) between UNAMIR and various UN humanitarian assistance Agencies, such as UNHCR. One consequence of this apparent low priority was that the specialised civilian staffs in legal affairs, human rights and humanitarian activities coordination were still not deployed six months after the publication of the Mission mandate. This left enormous gaps in the Mission's ability to be more pro-active which, in turn, affected its overall credibility.

The low priority accorded to Rwanda also meant that many of the inexperienced civilian staff assigned to UNAMIR were overtasked. For example, the UNDP permanent representative was acting as a coordinator for humanitarian affairs, as the representative for the re-integration of demobilised soldiers, and as the representative for national reconstruction. To make matters worse, there were tensions between the UN civilian hierarchy in-country, the major funding Agencies and countries, and some NGOs. Separate solutions and priorities of effort – towards the refugees, displaced persons, re-integration projects – and the level of funding afforded to each, plagued the creation of any operational or theatre-level coordinated plan.

The lack of foresight, harmonisation and experience of the various UN staffs and Agencies played a role in weakening the Mission's overall effectiveness in mediating and reconciling the contentious issues between the belligerents, and did not help advance the peace process signed at Arusha. The UN's inability to orchestrate the contributing nations and the inherent weakness of the UN administration and management methodologies to provide the necessary stores and equipment for UNAMIR precluded any semblance of possible sustainment, even for a few weeks, despite the fact that the Force was on the ground in late 1993. Battalions were without crew-weapons and/or vehicles; the small armoured personnel carrier fleet had neither spare parts nor mechanics.

The UN Mission, and those Rwandans it was intended to secure, fell victim to an inflated optimism to which I contributed, thereby creating expectations that the UN did not have the capacity to fulfil.[13] This classic peacekeeping mission was itself a victim of the larger resumption of the conflict, following political decapitation and the subsequent descent into the maelstrom of genocide (with nearly a million Rwandans slaughtered in only a few months and in excess of 3 million displaced persons and refugees). Even today, the evil aims of some power-hungry elements are raising tensions and preparing for a second round of massacres. Against this background, it was very difficult to have any systemic relationship between NGOs and UNAMIR. It was not until after 6 April 1994, when Rwandan President Juvénal Habyarimana died in a plane crash under mysterious circumstances, that a rapprochement and working arrangements developed between UNAMIR and the NGO community.

THE CIVIL WAR

From the start of the civil war, the Presidential Guard embarked on a series of reprisal killings of Tutsis and Hutu moderates which was quickly imitated by local members of the Hutu militias. This situation soon developed into a downward spiral of lawlessness, violence and mass murders throughout most of the country, which continued for many weeks. Paralleling this rise in violence, huge numbers of displaced persons and refugees, often injured either by the reprisals or the war itself, took flight in all directions. During this period, they were also subjected to harassment and attack by the militias and some military forces under covert direction from the new interim government of Rwanda. Throughout most of this carnage, UNAMIR's hands essentially remained tied.

Since the UN has no power akin to that of a sovereign state, it can only act on the wishes expressed by the international community through the auspices of the Security Council. So long as this body of sovereign states procrastinated and bickered amongst themselves and, in some cases, pursued what appeared to be their own insular national interests within this body, the UN, and consequently UNAMIR, remained relatively powerless. This was exacerbated further by the fact that only days after the start of the civil war the Belgian Government unilaterally withdrew its soldiers and most of its equipment and weapons. This evacuation followed the slaughter of 10 Belgian soldiers and the deliberate targeting of the Belgian contingent by the RGF because of their colonial past. This contingent, the best-equipped in UNAMIR and with significant operational experience from Somalia, could have become an effective deterrent force had we been given the appropriate mandate and backing. Although one might argue that the UNAMIR forces on the ground should have been more pro-active regarding the terrible murders of innocent civilians, in most instances they did not have the mandate from their national capitals to conduct any deterrent operation other than that prescribed under the 'routine' UN peace assistance mission, nor did they possess the means to do so. Therefore, the Force consolidated in a few reasonably defendable sites and opened its doors to those who could reach the sites and who sought protection. The Force also continued to negotiate cease fires and truces, and ultimately kept a UN and international community presence throughout this storm of destruction in order not totally to abandon innocent Rwandans to their fate.

By this time, it had also become clear that the UNAMIR contingent would have to be reduced from 2100 to approximately 450. The reason for this reduction was that UNAMIR had little or no ammunition, only a few days of food and water left, no medical stores and no means of evacuation except for sporadic flights by a Canadian C-130 aircraft.[14] To make matters worse, there was no resupply of any description expected in the immediate future. Still, in spite of the reduction in UNAMIR's size, a complete withdrawal from Rwanda was out of the question because this would have been perceived by the belligerents as sanctioning an even more intolerable escalation of hostilities and would have endangered Mission personnel as well as large numbers of the populace. The possibility of having to fight our way out by hand was also very real.

UNAMIR continued to broker truces to assist in the evacuation of expatriates and injured civilians from the ICRC field hospital in Kigali. The Mission also maintained dialogue between the RPF, the Interim Government (RGF) and former Rwandan Government moderates and their military leadership in an attempt to end the fighting, the massacres and the displacement of still more civilians.

It should also be noted that, unlike most of the other international organisations and foreign nationals, a small UN civilian humanitarian cell and the magnificent and courageous ICRC stayed in Rwanda. The remainder of the NGOs re-formed and operated from Nairobi, with advance stations in either Bujumbura and/or Kabale, Uganda. The problem with these moves, and with Nairobi in particular, was that the coordinating staffs were too distant and too limited in experience (with the exception of some distinguished individuals) to be able to coordinate all of the NGOs and UN Agencies in any coherent planning process. The staff attempted valiantly to deal with the on-going crisis in Rwanda and the problems that would arise once the fighting stopped, but their impact was often blunted by aggressive, strong, unilateral and autonomous actions by Agencies and NGOs.

It has been argued that even if there had been sufficient numbers of experienced people to organise such an effort from the start, the NGOs would have tended, as a general rule, neither to coordinate fully nor wholly cooperate with the UN leadership in and around Rwanda. In fact, they often claimed to have enough experience in dangerous situations that they did not need the UN's help or protection. So despite herculean efforts by UNREO advance staff at my Kigali HQ and in Nairobi, they were not, as a rule, fully supported by all interested players or NGOs. Representatives were sent to meetings but the results were often questionable at best. Willingness to listen, to follow a plan, and to fully integrate all of their efforts were not always evident.

In a number of cases, NGOs flatly refused (and even resented the suggestion) to follow any procedures that UNAMIR and UNREO proposed either to ensure their own protection or to maximise the humanitarian relief efforts being deployed throughout Rwanda and its periphery. Likewise, some NGOs even refused to allow UNAMIR to support their efforts or needs, and thus permit them to be able to deliver the supplies to Rwandan civilians as opposed, in certain cases, to the fighting forces – who took all of the credit for distributing some of the food supplies and hoarded the rest for their war effort. To make matters worse, there was sufficient aid to the RPF-controlled areas while nothing was being distributed behind RGF lines, where the bulk of the suffering clientele was situated. This inequitable distribution of humanitarian assistance, due in part to the significant security risks behind RGF lines, only heightened the tension and UNAMIR's difficulties in negotiating any truces or cease fires between the belligerents. Indeed, at one point, UNAMIR was accused of supporting the RGF war effort because of this undisciplined humanitarian effort.

The overall humanitarian assistance effort essentially proved to be a crisis response mechanism instead of a theatre-planned capability. This is not to suggest that help was not provided to Rwandan refugees. Indeed, those refugees that fled to Tanzania in the first months of the war were quickly and expertly taken care of. Goma, however, may have been an example of 'over-aid', quite aside from the fact that no effort was being made to establish security in the camps by separating the RGF and militias from the general civilian population. As a result, RGF elements took control of the camps and put at risk not only innocent Rwandan civilians but also the relief personnel. Furthermore, no one was willing to listen to UNREO or to address the larger issues: how to encourage the Rwandans to return home by building up humanitarian assistance and security inside the country, and how to prevent aid saturation in some areas outside the country while thousands upon thousands of displaced persons in Rwanda were without food, water, medical support or shelter.

While UNAMIR was struggling to balance moral concerns with these practical considerations, the international community finally began to respond to the crisis. UN resolutions in early and mid-June 1994 finally intimated a more pro-active humanitarian protection and support mandate, in addition to increasing the Force to 5500 personnel. The mandate included the establishment of secure humanitarian areas for refugees and displaced persons, the provision of support and security for the distribution of humanitarian relief supplies, and the establishment of an arms embargo against Rwanda. UNREO was reaffirmed under the authority of DHA and was to continue to be directed by the new UNDP Resident Representative for Rwanda, with some US$349 000 in funding from USAID. UNREO's main purpose was to enhance the coordination of UN organisations providing comprehensive relief response in Rwanda and to integrate the efforts of the relief Agencies and NGOs.

At this point, the interaction between those involved with humanitarian assistance and security became much more symbiotic. After all, the problems incurred when maintaining an army in theatre are quite similar to the logistical problems associated with assisting large numbers of displaced persons and refugees. UNREO had provided UNAMIR's Kigali Headquarters with a small advance team in order to take the security situation on the ground into account in its planning efforts. UNAMIR established a humanitarian cell, commanded by a colonel and with a staff of 6–8 officers, which worked with UNREO on humanitarian relief and transportation matters, and made plans for refugees to cross the belligerents' lines.

This military–civilian integration permitted the humanitarian effort to be a single-source activity, including NGOs, with direct access to senior decision makers and up-to-date information. The team was supported by liaison officers at all UNREO HQs, from Bujumbura to Kabale to Nairobi. However, it should also be pointed out that, at first, efforts were wasted because the UNREO advance team, although integrated into the UNAMIR HQ, received advice from sources distant from the field which conflicted with the reality on the ground. On several other occasions, the actual decision-maker for the NGOs and Agencies lived on a different continent. It was only after the decision-makers began to move command and coordination posts to Kabale and Bujumbura, or to Rwanda itself, that they began to understand the actual situation with which UNAMIR was dealing.

While this rapprochement and integrated humanitarian effort was evolving, the crisis in Goma gave a new sense of urgency to all of the parties concerned. Dozens upon dozens of exemplary organisations had done rather well over the first two months or so in the reasonably safe areas of Rwanda. Yet the continued advance to the west by the RPF, the ongoing killings by the militia, and the massive movement of displaced persons both into the southwest and towards the northwest of the country, created significant disruption to the various humanitarian efforts. Specifically, there was the Goma crisis itself and the Operation Turquoise Humanitarian Protective Zone (HPZ) to name but two. The Goma crisis was perhaps the lowest point in the cooperation between the Mission and the various NGOs and Agencies. There is no doubt that the media coverage of Goma stimulated the NGOs, various humanitarian Agencies and foreign states wishing to help, but the haste to aid the Rwandans living in Goma indirectly contributed to a dearth of assistance in the southern region of Rwanda. An increase in tension had led to another crisis in the southwest; indeed, the southwestern region of Rwanda was suffering immeasurably from the Goma 'over-aid'. The ICRC and elements from such NGOs as CARE tried to help the $1\frac{1}{2}$ million displaced persons in the region but they simply did not have the necessary resources, the security, or the media coverage to ensure sufficient attention from the rest of the world. As a result, this second human tidal wave was left to its own devices to survive.

This situation in the southern region continued until Operation Turquoise began; even then, many displaced persons remained stranded without any hope of relief. Many displaced persons in this zone were distraught over the option of having to move to Bukavu through the forest, because they feared attacks by the RPF. They also sensed that only if they became refugees, or if they created a horrific catastrophe like Goma, would they get attention and relief for their families. The HPZ provided an atmosphere of security and humanitarian coordination in an extremely demanding area of the country, and went a long way in preventing a second Goma. However, limited aid entered the HPZ as most of the effort was going to Goma. There seemed to be little left for, or highly prioritised to, the HPZ. This slow start and the less than adequate effort was most troubling. The potential for a second Goma was very real but this did not seem significantly to influence the overall aid effort.

Herein lies the dilemma. On the one hand, NGOs depend heavily on media interest so as to generate public or official support for their work. Some NGOs exist solely to disseminate information on impending crises in order to put pressure on various governments and have them change their foreign policies; others use information to combine their humanitarian assistance with fund raising. On the other hand, too much coverage may – as was the case in Goma – lead to 'over-aid'. The international community may have been shamed into helping to address the crisis in Goma and other refugee camps but, ironically, the help provided served also to rejuvenate the defeated RGF elements located in these camps. Moreover, this abundance of aid encouraged refugees and armed groups to stay outside Rwanda, providing the RGF and militias with a pool of people with whom they could rebuild their forces and maintain insecurity in the region.

That the herculean, rapid, and sustained effort in Goma did stabilise the situation for over 1 million Rwandans is an undisputed fact, but it did concentrate much of the humanitarian effort in only one of the two major crisis areas in Rwanda. It precluded any effort or support to the UNAMIR humanitarian coordination mandate for the whole Rwandan crisis, even though the SRSG was the overall authority for humanitarian efforts for Rwanda. His tasks were to help stabilise the zones where the fighting had stopped, to build up stocks, and to implement a strategic or operational-level plan for all Rwanda in order to get the refugees and displaced persons home as safely and as rapidly as possible.

By late July 1994, UNREO was fully deployed in Kigali but was still not getting the total support and attention of NGOs and Agencies, or even the national contingents, to solve the larger problem. There was disagreement between UNAMIR and UNHCR concerning the Goma effort, and seemingly endless bickering over the security mandate for UNAMIR to enter refugee camps to separate those suspected of the mass killings from the innocent. Such a mandate would have permitted tens of thousands of souls to return to Rwanda instead of remaining as displaced persons in camps, which eventually came under RGF coercion. Open conflicts between UN Agencies and NGOs on how to handle the former government forces and their families created much confusion. This confusion, in turn, played into the hands of the same extremists who had participated in the slaughter of hundreds of thousands of Tutsis and Hutu moderates.

Most Agencies and NGOs did not seem to grasp that the aim of the UNAMIR operation was to stabilise and secure Rwanda, and to begin a process of return by using stocks of stores, camps, and transportation inside the country to encourage the Rwandans to return home. The concept called for Kigali to be a magnet with towns such as Ruhengeri, Butare and Byumba acting as major protection centres – all interconnected by way-stations and temporary sites under UNAMIR protection. They also did not seem to understand that there was a need to emphasise the temporary nature of the refugee camps. Here again, the lack of cooperation between humanitarian assistance organisations and the military precluded any co-ordinated plan to re-integrate Rwandan refugees, even when UNAMIR forces were becoming more available in late July and early August.

Yet it must also be said that UNAMIR as a whole learned much from the various Agencies and NGOs. These providers of humanitarian assistance tended to have unmatched access to refugees and displaced persons, and some had long-standing relationships with the local people and a thorough knowledge of the local culture, including the local language – Kinyarwanda. They also helped UNAMIR understand the movement of internally-displaced persons, land-mine risks, local areas of potential conflict and provided reports of human rights' abuses. This knowledge was crucial to supplement the process of political reconciliation, not to mention saving lives. It is no exaggeration to say that cooperation on relief efforts did give rise to negotiation which quickly moved beyond relief efforts to issues of conflict resolution. Consequently, it was appropriate that Agencies and NGOs be briefed by HQ staff, engineers and signal staff on current security issues more often than I had originally planned. In turn, they reciprocated by briefing my Force on security risks in specific localities. As a rule, I felt that it was important that NGOs be allowed to voice their concerns to me and this brought considerable returns. I also believe that military responses to their calls for assistance were usually prompt.

One small drawback was that a number of NGOs became dependent on UNAMIR support assets – including Canadian, British, Australian and, finally, American military assets such as hospitals, emergency communications, water supply, transportation and the opening of the Kigali airport – which caused some funding complications, but we felt these were an effective means of enabling assistance efforts in the more remote but devastated areas of the country. This contribution of assets did not reduce the NGOs' ability to move and act freely. On the other hand, an argument could be made that, while NGOs generally appreciated the support they were given by UNAMIR, they feared, and I believe they continue to fear, that their commitment to neutrality had sometimes been compromised through this association. One example occurred during the time when RGF broadcasts were regularly attacking both the UNAMIR operation as a whole and certain of its senior officials. These broadcasts not only alienated UN personnel from the large Hutu population, thereby hindering the mediation process, but also put numerous NGOs in a difficult situation.

RECOMMENDATIONS

The first task is to make the spectrum of UN humanitarian organisations a more pro-active force with a staff of dynamic people akin to many of those found among the NGO field staffs. Acting in concert, the UN humanitarian organisations must play a central role in planning, organising, directing, coordinating and controlling the implementation of the humanitarian assistance plan in conjunction with the military security plan. There must be an effective forum for all UN Agencies at UN HQ where agreement can be achieved on aid coordination. These Agencies must then support UN efforts for coordination in theatre by mandating a senior liaison officer to the UN Force Commander.

Further to this proposal, there is much promise in the current DHA project on Military and Civil Disasters Assistance (MCDA). The participants in MCDA are working to develop appropriate arrangements with interested governments, and inter-governmental and non-governmental organisations. This would ensure expeditious access, when necessary, to their emergency relief capacities, including food reserves, emergency stockpiles, personnel and logistic support.[15] Although this project favours major natural and technical disasters usually short of war, since June 1994 the use of military assets in a humanitarian context has become part of its remit. Once completed, the knowledge from the study could be used as the basis for discussion, consultation and negotiation between the NGOs and UN Agencies involved in humanitarian assistance.

Secondly, and perhaps the more relevant issue in the short term, I believe that the UN needs a multi-disciplinary team of senior crisis managers. The resolution of any conflict or human catastrophe requires a team to develop and execute an integrated and mutually supporting plan of action. For too long these elements in the UN itself have operated in isolation and the result has been political theory with no capability, military operations with no political aim, humanitarian missions without the necessary means, and logistical systems that are not responsive to the Commander in the field – who himself cannot find the resources to mount and sustain the operation. To rectify this, there should be regular meetings between the UN and NGOs to create standard operating procedures and Rules of Engagement for UN peace support and humanitarian missions.

I recognise that these recommendations might be a little utopian at the present time, given the fears that many NGOs have expressed with respect to UN Missions and their military component. Nevertheless, it should still be studied. The creation of an interdisciplinary, UN-led, crisis management and humanitarian assistance centre would be of great benefit. It could bring discipline, standard operating procedures, confidence, loyalty and transparency between the various UN Agencies, which would in turn help to provide the UN with a united team vis-à-vis the NGOs – thereby maximising the chances of providing the most help with rather limited resources.

Any UN peacekeeping operation, if it is to enjoy long-term success, must continue to increase the level of coordination and consultation between national governments, grassroots organisations, other UN Agencies and front-line humanitarian NGOs. A successful UN operation will reduce long-term tensions and bring a sense of confidence and wellbeing to the peoples concerned. This will not be achieved only by having foreign troops on national soil. It is the work of long-term, sustainable, community development supported by the international NGO community. Whether it starts as a so-called security problem or as a humanitarian problem, we are intertwined by the very nature of the crisis. A concerted effort is needed, and I therefore predict that in the not-so-distant future there will be an even greater level of harmonisation between UN operations and NGOs in spite of some of the shortcomings mentioned earlier. Clearly, peacekeeping can not be an end in itself – it only buys time. In its goals and its design, it must always be a part of the larger continuum of peacemaking, that is to say, conflict avoidance, resolution, rehabilitation and development.

Notes

1. UN Security Council, *Annual Summit Declaration*, 31 January 1993, pp. 1–5.
2. According to one comparative study, 79 per cent of wars between 1900 and 1941 were between states. In contrast, from 1946 to 1969, some 85 per cent were internal civil wars. I. Kende, 'Twenty-Five Years of Local Wars', as quoted in H. Wiseman, 'Peacekeeping in the International Context', in I. Jit Rikhye, *The United Nations and Peacekeeping* (London: Macmillan, 1990) p. 37.
3. Between 1988 and 1989, for example, this has meant the deaths of some 4.4 million non-combatants. Rene de Grace, 'Peacekeeping: Norms, Policy and Process', *1993 Peacekeeping Symposium* (Toronto: York University) p. 98.
4. Jeff Sallot, 'Opening Remarks: Defence and Public Opinion' (Ottawa: Conference of Defence Associations Institute, 1994) pp. 1–8.
5. D. Cox, '*An Agenda for Peace* and the Future of UN Peacekeeping', in *A Report of the Mohonk Mountain House Workshop* (Ottawa: Canadian Centre for Global Security, 1993) p. 3.
6. Proceedings of the Standing Senate Committee on Foreign Affairs, 'First Proceedings on the Study of Peacekeeping' (Ottawa: Senate of Canada, 24 February 1993) Issue 16, p. 16B43.
7. James Orbinski, 'Panel on Non-Governmental Organizations', in *Peacekeeping: Norms, Policy and Process*, Peacekeeping Symposium (May) (Toronto: York University, 1993) p. 104.
8. Ibid, p. 106.
9. The recent deployment of French troops to Rwanda under Operation Turquoise proved to be so costly to the French Government that it is unlikely that they will embark on any similar venture in the near future.
10. Orbinski, 'Panel', p. 105.
11. Orbinski, 'Panel', p. 107.
12. Canadian NGOs included: Médecins sans Frontières (Canada), CARE Canada, Canadian Catholic Organization for Development and Peace, Canadian Lutheran World Relief, Canadian Physicians for Aid and Relief, Urgence secours Rwanda/Centre canadien d'études et de coopération internationale, Urgence secours Rwanda/Oxfam-Québec, Urgence secours Rwanda/Proveda,

World Vision Canada, World Relief Canada, Collaboration santé internationale, Proveda (Avions sans Frontières) and Sherbrooke University. International organisations supported by Canada included: ICRC, International Federation of the Red Cross and Red Crescent Societies, UNHCR, UNICEF and WFP. Together, they were given some $21 280 000 from the Canadian International Development Agency (CIDA), in addition to any private donations they might have received.

13. By the terms of UN SCR 872 (1993), UNAMIR was assigned particular duties, including 'to assist in the coordination of humanitarian assistance activities in conjunction with relief operations'.

14. There were considerable joint efforts between UNHCR and UNAMIR to ensure the operation of Kigali airport and UNHCR's relief airlift mission – with varying degrees of success.

15. *MCDA Project/Executive Overview* (Geneva: MCDA Project Secretariat, 1 December 1994).

17 The Role of the Humanitarian Coordinator

Mark Walsh

One of the biggest challenges facing humanitarian coordinators in multi-dimensional peace operations is striking the proper balance between cooperation and independence among the different members of the humanitarian community responding to the crisis. This chapter will focus on this balance and examine solutions to the organisational conflicts which arise during and within an international humanitarian response. To illustrate and reinforce the discussion, insights are offered based upon personal experience directing UN operations in the southern zone of UNOSOM.

The first tool in the coordinator's kitbag to deal with the many and diverse organisations he must coordinate is a clear understanding of their roles, missions, and operational methods. The nature of the crisis will be a major factor in determining the make-up of the partnership responding to the problem. In recent international interventions, Missions have included military forces to provide stability and meet security requirements and, in the absence of local civil law and order institutions, a civil police training and advisory element. Political initiatives, including cease fires and disarmament, as well as national and local reconciliation, are undertaken by the UN Mission, usually under the direction of an SRSG. Humanitarian assistance in the food and health areas is usually the responsibility of one or more UN Agencies and other international organisations such as the ICRC and a host of international, national and local NGOs. Longer-term economic rehabilitation is the responsibility of international financial institutions, UNDP, regional development organisations, interested nations through bilateral aid programmes, development NGOs, and the host government to the extent that it can assist. Providing for refugees and displaced persons falls to UN Agencies such as UNHCR, the DHA, and the IOM. Additionally, human rights' issues come under the purview of the UN and, in some instances, human rights' organisations. It should be apparent that there are many actors with interlocking, overlapping and at times conflicting interests. To be effective, a humanitarian coordinator in the field must have a clear understanding of these factors, and exercise an intense and continuous influence to balance the diverse capabilities and remits of these actors against the humanitarian requirement.

What is very important to the field manager, in this constant effort to bring coherence to the humanitarian response, is the necessity to determine what is acceptable among and between organisations regarding shared goals, plans, and operations. In southern Somalia, military forces were to be employed in conventional security operations; food and health agencies in feeding, nutrition, and health clinic activities; and ICRC and UNHCR in refugee and displaced persons programmes. An underlying need affecting all of their missions, however, was reconciliation in the region. This became the zone director's first priority. Once the various organisations were informed of the broader strategy, encouraged to participate in its execution, and persuaded where possible to focus organisational efforts to support this goal, a sense of teamwork and common purpose began to take hold and the overall Mission accomplishment was enhanced.

In trying to determine the relief community's boundaries of acceptable operation, the humanitarian coordinator should strive for early, selective, and purposeful collective planning and decision-making. Capitalising on the threatening environment in which risks and sacrifices are by and large shared, efforts should be directed at daily coordination meetings, with a constantly changing venue and leader. If handled properly, no single member of the team will be perceived to 'be in charge'. It is imperative that bones of contention among actors, usually between the military and the rest of the team, be removed as soon as they appear. A sense of shared purpose and the constant emphasis on the collective benefits to all players through cooperation have to be stressed continually. Military outposts in remote areas of the southern zone in Somalia were better received by the local communities when they saw humanitarian relief routinely appearing with a military escort. The benefits to the military of this were real even if, at times, escorting such convoys interfered with other military operations.

The changeover of personnel and the occasional arrival of a new relief organisation into the coordinator's area had to be disseminated to all members of the team. Similarly, if relief agencies shifted geographic emphasis which, in turn, brought those agencies into contact with other parts of the team that had no prior experience of them, such shifts had to be anticipated and the information publicised to prevent unintentional upsets. Major decisions by an organisation that have potentially profound effects on the team have to be discussed, coordinated and collectively implemented. In the Somalia southern zone, the ICRC decided that its feeding programmes had effectively dealt with the region's malnourished, that the food crisis had passed, and that it should relocate to other areas in need of its services.

The decision made, the ICRC abruptly left the zone, and a large number of local nationals were confused and upset at the consequences. At very short notice, the rest of the relief community had to scramble to put together a programme to gradually wean the local communities away from the international feeding programme and adjust the sources and distribution of food. Early coordination would have done a lot to reduce anxiety on the part of local Somalis and the international community trying to assist them.

Central to all coordination of the range of activities characteristic of these interventions is the need for large measures of flexibility and creativity. Generally speaking, these ingredients for successful operations are more abundant in the non-military components of the team. Once the civilian agencies acquire confidence in each other and in the broad strategy, they are capable of considerable initiative and resourcefulness in coming together for a common end. Paradoxically, the military, while having much to offer the collective enterprise, require more time and deliberate effort to join the somewhat less structured NGO approach to resolving day-to-day obstacles. In the case of the southern zone reconciliation effort, establishing a conference over two months with daily meetings by 200 local delegates proved to be a major burden for the zone's UN military forces. Repeated discussion and persuasion between the humanitarian coordinator and the local force commander, and between the coordinator and the UNOSOM leadership, was necessary to retain the military's support of the reconciliation process. Relief agencies were quicker to get behind the initiative in a variety of ways providing food, administrative material, blankets upon which to sit and so on, which in some instances went beyond the normal operational charter of the donors.

Absolute cooperation by all members of the team will never be achieved. In some cases, events will exist or unfold that will drive an organisation to more independent operations. It is essential that the coordinator respect such decisions and not interfere with members of the community that feel compelled to function without coordination or collaboration. Such decisions may be the result of headquarters' directives, or NGO heads might change, with the new leader less receptive to adapting constraining organisational guides to suit the operational environment; or forces unknown to the coordinator might impact on an NGO's operations and decision-making that result in more independent activities. In southern Somalia, local threats to humanitarian workers received varying responses. In some cases, organisations decided to deal with these threats without involving other members of the relief community, and took decisions that led the organisation on a path that separated it from the cooperative effort.

Consistency by the coordinator when making decisions can reap many dividends towards achieving respect by, and usefulness to, the relief community. While outcomes of deliberations might, for some organisations be difficult to accept, once decisions are made, a less than totally resolute stance can injure team cohesiveness and seriously hinder accomplishing mission objectives. Fairness in all dealings with the relief community and with local nationals is the foundation upon which sound relations are based. Weakening that foundation by a selective application of loyalty and acceptable values risks losing the communities' confidence and support. During times of heightened threat, often all that the coordinator can bring to bear on the problem is integrity and respect. In the aftermath of a major armed attack in the southern zone of Somalia, appeals to the relief organisations to persevere and to continue to implement their programmes in the face of increased danger were made; the strength of this appeal was based largely upon a perception of mutual trust and confidence in the field manager's actions, decisions, and judgements regarding the most advantageous course of action for them to follow.

The prospect of ever-increasing difficulties and hazards in conducting the range of military, political, and humanitarian operations necessary for the successful resolution of current complex emergencies can be relieved through attention to learning how to cope with the hardships on the ground. At times, the tasks and challenges the coordinator faces might appear insurmountable. Often, conditions are such that it is easy to lose sight of the relief programme's direction. This uncertainty can result from the intensity of the daily routine as much as from the routine's unpredictability. What remains critical throughout these periods of tension and ambiguity is the requirement to keep in mind the Mission's strategy, and, in the prevailing circumstances, what is a reasonable course of action to pursue. Having some sense of the next step is crucial, to avoid missing opportunities that are sure to arise. A significant missed opportunity was the single most important failure of the UNOSOM II reconciliation effort in the southern zone. In pursuing that reconciliation, essentially without an overall plan, when the prospect of a successful outcome to the mediation was at hand, the rewards for the local community, in the form of an economic recovery plan, were not ready. The result was unfulfilled expectations and withdrawal of confidence in the international community.

What is of equal significance to the humanitarian strategic plan is that courses of action have to accommodate the goals of all the participating organisations and, as the situation changes, there is a continuous need to reconcile conflicting objectives and operational methods. Given the stressful and demanding nature of his post, the coordinator can easily lose sight of the many external factors that can have a devastating impact on the Mission's programme. In the southern Somalia case, the attitude and behaviour of international donors to the country's economic recovery were driven by events in the nation's capital. Hence, as the situation in Mogadishu deteriorated, donor enthusiasm waned not only for the capital region but for the country as a whole. The prospects for meaningful economic relief for the southern zone diminished appreciably long before the coordinator was aware of the implications for the zone of the conflict in the central region of the country.

When considering the humanitarian objectives, it is essential that the coordinator takes into account the aims of the Mission as a whole. It is often necessary for all the different elements of the Mission to undertake multiple and parallel initiatives simultaneously in order to achieve the Mission's overall aim. In southern Somalia, diverse local institutions (such as the clergy, women's groups and young business leaders) required varying degrees of empowerment to sustain the region's social, political and economic reconstruction. However, such empowerment placed these institutions in conflict with militia or political factions which interpreted the coordinator's actions as a threat to the latter's authority. Other efforts, specifically directed toward militia and political faction leaders, were necessary to diminish this perceived threat and to persuade them that, given the degree of destruction and destitution in the region, power-sharing was in everyone's best interests.

The essential points are that the humanitarian coordinator must maintain perspective, understanding, and coordination both vertically and horizontally; and that immediate events must not be allowed to distract the coordinator from the strategic overview. Indeed, excess attention paid to current crises, at the expense of monitoring the broader horizon, can have crippling consequences. The coordinator cannot neglect the former, obviously, but effective lines of communication for reporting activities and receiving guidance is paramount to success in these complex operational environments. The lack of quality, dependable and timely communications with the SRSG in Somalia was a major contributor to the southern zone's operational failure. Moreover, had such communication been available, other serious deficiencies noted above – such as missed economic development opportunities and a less than complete appreciation of the deteriorating events in the capital – would have been more apparent.

Institutional friction is inevitable in diverse organisational enterprises such as complex humanitarian emergencies where charged goals and objectives exist in extremely volatile environments. However, the coordinator must seek to respond constructively to this reality and seek to minimise organisational conflicts. First, the coordinator must remain cognisant that his objectives are part of a broader initiative. He must uncover the sources of any conflict or dissent amongst the humanitarian community and evaluate their impact on the goals of the humanitarian mission. Is the problem one of individual or organisational fatigue? Is it a resource or operational process shortfall? Is the local environment changing or reacting to events in an unforeseen manner that presents confusing, unclear, and unacceptable options for future courses of action? The list is endless, but clear analysis is essential, particularly if the coordinator is to discern what aspects of problems he needs to address, what he can reasonably influence, likely sources of assistance, and what aspects are beyond immediate solutions and need to be recognised as unsolvable but perhaps ameliorated with careful attention.

Second, when confronted with team members at cross-purposes, it is important that differences be addressed and solutions found at the lowest, most informal level of relations between the opposing individuals or organisation. The in-country humanitarian community is usually small, well-connected for information, and sensitive to personal or organisational hiccups. The coordinator needs to avoid exacerbating the problem by a public airing of unnecessary detail which risks inviting other actors into the debate, thereby precluding a simple, straightforward solution to the difficulty.

A more important reason to limit the circle of knowledge regarding internal problems is the damage done to the humanitarian community and its mission if the issue becomes known to the local populace. This is an extremely important consideration but a difficult situation to prevent. It is virtually impossible to prevent 'family quarrels' becoming public and once they become known to local nationals, considerable caution has to be exercised to avoid local efforts to drive wedges between the humanitarian organisations. Local factions that oppose the international effort will not waste time in capitalising on fractures in team cohesiveness to the detriment of all. The failure of the humanitarian community in southern Somalia to standardise local labour wages for offloading relief ships proved almost disastrous when the local labour committee pitted one organisation against another when negotiating wages. The head of one NGO was threatened because he resisted paying higher wages that another NGO had been coerced into paying.

In summary, the job of humanitarian field coordination requires considerable managerial skill to balance the many demands of multi-dimensional peace operations. First, the balance between cooperation and independence among organisations responding to international crises is not something that can be pre-determined or dictated, but must be continually negotiated. Since this involves achieving consensus on coordinating goals, plans, and operations, as well as cooperative planning and decision-making and accommodating diverse organisations' goals and operational methods, the value of flexibility and creativity need hardly be re-emphasised. The second factor is the skill and experience required to respond constructively to organisational conflicts. The concepts of Mission clarity, early and low-level resolution of problems, the danger of local factions exploiting difficulties and the subordination of organisational differences to broader Mission interests are not difficult to grasp, but in practice often require a mixture of force and tact that cannot be prescribed. These points of managerial focus for field coordinating staff undertaking international Missions are by no means exhaustive: pre-mission preparation, impartiality, cultural awareness, and operational control are among other essential management tools that will not in themselves guarantee success, but can contribute immeasurably in improving the ability of the humanitarian field coordinator to overcome the daunting challenges faced in resolving complex emergencies.

18 Peacekeepers, Humanitarian Aid and Civil Conflicts

Cedric Thornberry[1]

Many of the UN peace support operations that have been created since 1989 are complex international conglomerates. Humanitarian organisations, governmental and non-governmental, often work alongside them. Despite the long field experience of bodies such as UNHCR and the ICRC, cooperating with peacekeepers is opening new perspectives. At times, there is no peace to keep. Especially in civil war situations, the parties usually do not fully accept that humanitarian assistance has any special status. This new environment is having a major impact, not only on the UN, but also upon some of the aid organisations. There are not, yet, many maps, and the process of discovery continues.

Most of the UN's 16 peacekeeping operations which had been established prior to UNTAG in Namibia in 1989–90 did not have mandates which expressly conferred humanitarian tasks.[2] ONUC (the United Nations Mission in the Congo, 1960–4) had major humanitarian roles pressed upon it as disintegration and violence spread in the former colony. UNFICYP has had some such tasks in respect of dwindling minority populations on either side of the Green Line since the large population movements consequent upon the Turkish invasion in 1974. These have been exercised by a small (30–40) group of UN policemen, working alongside the rest of UNFICYP, UNHCR and ICRC. In a 'diplomatic adviser' role, UNFICYP has participated in the painful activities of the Committee on Missing Persons which is chaired by the ICRC. Since 1948, when the UN's first peacekeeping mission, UNTSO, was created, other subsidiary humanitarian tasks, expressly mandated, or just inevitably arising and having to be fulfilled by a large, disciplined, logistically-competent force, have recurred. The underlying purpose of many of these missions was, of course, humanitarian – to further conditions of peace and security for the local population, often through the supervision of a cease fire while a more permanent peace settlement was sought. Humanitarian aid was also often dispensed by the UN military in order to win hearts and minds. Many battalions arrived in theatre with a substantial capability, including medical facilities, and, traditionally, any spare capacity was shared with the inhabitants. Thus, for example, the UNIFIL field hospital at Naqoura, in southern Lebanon has, for nearly a generation, given medical help to the often-deprived population of the region. And, as one saw in the Krajina region of Croatia, even battalions that themselves come impoverished and under-equipped into the field have frequently shared their limited resources with the war-ravaged villages which they protect and where they live. In many armies there is an old tradition of local support and solidarity.

With the arrival of the multi-task, multi-component peace support operations of recent years, the UN has found itself with a wide range of responsibilities which are designated 'political', 'civil' or 'humanitarian', as well as military. Beginning in Namibia, and continuing in Iraq, Cambodia, former Yugoslavia, Somalia, Angola, Mozambique, Rwanda, Georgia and Zaïre, vast repatriation and/or relief operations have been carried out, or are planned, in conjunction with UN peace support operations, on the part of UNHCR, ICRC, WFP and other inter-governmental and non-governmental organisations. In recent years, virtually all armed conflicts have been primarily internal, with the parties' objectives also including targeting the local population. UNHCR has assumed the new function of providing for the displaced and other victims of conflict in their own countries (alongside its traditional role of dealing with refugees outside their home states). It has also suddenly found itself working on the front lines. And it has doubled in size since 1990.

Meanwhile, a senior ICRC official has recently noted that starvation and terror have become:

> a predominant method of warfare ... no quarter is given during armed confrontation ... Neutral and humanitarian organisations are denied the basic conditions, laid down in international humanitarian law, which are indispensable for carrying out their activities.

Pressure on all involved with peacekeeping is increased by the growing political role of the media – satellite television brings, fresh and devastating, the savagery of war into millions of homes. Reactions and funds are generated, often in response to such publicity, impelling governments and NGOs to '*do* something'. Pressures build on those in the field to tend to the victims, stop the mayhem, and somehow banish the awfulness. But the humanitarian organisations have often found that their mandates run directly counter to the objectives of the contending parties. UN peace operations, for their part, are frequently (especially in former Yugoslavia) knee-deep in mandates promulgated by a Security Council which, in 1992–3, lost contact with reality in regard to Yugoslavia and perhaps also elsewhere.

Some missions had not even a fraction of the resources required to implement crucial tasks, nor was there the political will to see them fulfilled. Adding to the complexity of the new peacekeeping/humanitarian cooperation, while UN bodies and some NGOs are organically committed to impartiality, other NGOs are partisan, and make no pretence about it. They nevertheless often expect full assistance – including, at times, protection – from the UN. And, not infrequently, they bring their equally *engagé* media with them.

Thus, on several continents, new types of relationships between humanitarian organisations and peacekeeping soldiers have had to be developed, often under stressful conditions, in the eye of the camera lens, and with no instruction leaflets.

Rarely do the internationals' *objectives* conflict. Peacekeeping operations fully endorse humanitarian goals, and aid workers usually believe that the peacekeepers should try to keep whatever peace there might be. Where problems arise, they do so over *means*, not *ends*. A public international mission in the field, whether political, humanitarian or military, carries out the mandate conferred on it by its executive authority, whether that be the Security Council, General Assembly or other inter-governmental body. This is, in principle, also the position of non-governmental humanitarian bodies, although with them, in practice, the degree of headquarters' control might be more varied. There is unlikely to be conflict between the mandates of UN political and UN humanitarian and aid agencies; there is not much chance that the Security Council will direct a peacekeeping operation to contravene humanitarian principles, and there can be few instances in which humanitarian agencies might be mandated to take action incompatible with a peacekeeping mandate.

It is not proposed here to discuss Chapter VII enforcement situations, wherein the coercive weight of the international community is brought to bear. In such situations there is, indeed, the real possibility of a clash of mandates, whether coercion takes the form of economic or military sanctions. In the case of economic, communications and transport sanctions, responsibility is often placed upon the overseeing Sanctions Committee of the Security Council to ensure that appropriate exemptions are expeditiously made in circumstances of humanitarian need (for example, casualty evacuations or a hospital's urgent need for particular drugs).

In a peace support, Chapter VI, situation, whatever problems arise tend to do so during implementation. As regards NGOs, while some are quite eager to coordinate their activities with UN bodies, and are also able to do so in practice, it might prove impossible to achieve much in the way of cooperation with many others. Some may have mandates which are very narrow, or are openly partisan, and thus incompatible with the impartiality of UN bodies; other NGOs, such as the ICRC, have a firm tradition of autonomy, and do not ordinarily seek coordinated arrangements with the UN (though there may in appropriate situations be close cooperation between them and the peacekeeping force and its UN humanitarian companion body).

A UN peacekeeping mission and a UN humanitarian body that share the same theatre of operations will, in today's scheme of things, have multiple points of interface; while their mandates will, though interlocking, in principle remain distinct and non-overlapping. It is self-evident that both military and civilian components of the peacekeeping mission seek the same objectives, and also share them with the major aid organisations. Yet while cooperation in some countries has been immaculate and, as it should be, mutually supportive, in others, most notably Somalia and, at some points, Bosnia, there have been problems. In recent months, both UNHCR and ICRC have been making commendable efforts to learn from their experiences. They have concentrated on the range of problems that has emerged from this new cooperation, by holding civil–military seminars and by producing training modules designed to explain each to the other.[3] This is an absolute necessity, exacerbated by the fact that *in situ* there is a frequent rotation of key personnel. The learning process has therefore to be virtually continuous. Learning the elementary features of one another's *modus operandi* in theatre is not very efficient and both humanitarian officers and the military need this training as an integral part of their basic instruction and orientation process, with regular refresher courses thereafter. For it seems likely that combined humanitarian–security operations will become a regular feature of international action, whatever future routes UN peacekeeping may follow.

In general terms, the problems that exist between humanitarian workers and the military stem from a lack of familiarity with one another, and with the new kind of tasks they are having to undertake, jointly and severally. As already indicated, some agencies such as UNHCR have suddenly found themselves in largely uncharted territory, having to learn new operational tasks which must often be undertaken in more exacting circumstances than has usually been the case. Moreover, because of the rapid expansion of UNHCR's duties, it has had to recruit a large number of personnel 'from the street'. These new staff, however willing, able and courageous, may have little experience of international operations of any kind. Indeed, this is a problem besetting the whole of peacekeeping, to the extent that the last major operation which could largely be staffed by the UN from its own personnel was Namibia in 1989. In Yugoslavia, for example, only about 10 per cent of UNPROFOR's political personnel had previously been UN staff members. There is no rotation system in the UN Secretariat (there is in UNHCR) and Missions are staffed with those volunteers who can be extracted from their headquarters offices.

One can probably also blame a two-way lack of familiarity for the attitudinal abyss which frequently separates aid workers from the military. Aid workers are often suspicious of the military, and the feeling is reciprocated. Especially in recent missions, aid workers tend to be much younger than their military counterparts, and this can reinforce perceived differences of approach. One example comes vividly to mind. A senior general, veteran of many campaigns, had a key operational role in his first UN Mission. His initial meeting took place with his humanitarian opposite number. This officer turned out to be female and, however field-experienced, in her late twenties. It did not go well. Afterwards, the general was near-incoherent. 'She lectured me', he spluttered, 'just like my wacko teenage Peacecorps daughter'. (It might be added, first, that he proved an effective operator, and was rated 'very supportive' by aid workers. Second, there is no record of what the aid coordinator said after the meeting.) Analogous stories abound on both sides of the military–humanitarian fence.

The second problem that exists, and can be cured if there is a full awareness of it and a determination that it be overcome, is lack of information about what each element is supposed to be doing (and is actually doing) in that particular Mission. As in a high proportion of the multitude of managerial problems that arise in peacekeeping, the key is coordination. Yet ensuring even moderate standards of coordination may require much determination at senior levels on all sides. Failure might bring about confusion and mutual hostility; these can create serious dangers for all concerned, and will certainly undermine the Mission's viability. The effectiveness of some recent UN Missions has been seriously affected by management's failure to focus on coordination, or through allowing established mechanisms to disintegrate.

In summary, lack of coordination (including lack of clarity over tasks and command and reporting lines), mutual unfamiliarity, and attitudinal divergence are the principal sources of stress between peacekeepers and aid workers. Nevertheless, Chapter VI mandates rarely give rise to difficulty over the reconciliation of objectives.

However, another issue has arisen with regard to some recent operations. It centres on the application of the principle that aid is provided on the basis of need only, and that it is provided impartially and neutrally. The principle is unexceptionable, and would be fully endorsed by all representatives of the international community. The trouble is, that in its application to the kinds of conflict which have arisen, especially in Bosnia and Croatia, what the humanitarian bodies excoriate as 'linkage' has appeared in various forms. For this, they tend to hold peacekeepers responsible.

'LINKAGE'

In UNHCR's recent training handbook *Working with the Military*, the problem is described thus:

Linkage occurs when the parties to a conflict condition humanitarian activities upon other humanitarian actions or the progress of political or military events. The acceptance of linkages by humanitarian or military actors violates the principles of humanity, impartiality and neutrality. From a practical point of view, acceptance of linkages creates operational gridlock, because linkages tie the continuity of humanitarian programmes to matters beyond the control of the operation's participants. The insistence on linkages by the parties to a conflict also suggests a vitiation of consent.

The military, more accustomed to autonomy, may find it difficult to apply this principle, as to them it may appear to prevent the achievement of reasonable objectives. An escort commander who is told at a checkpoint that passage of his humanitarian aid convoy is conditional upon sharing some of the aid with needy locals, for example, may not immediately appreciate the implications if he has not been briefed about the problem of linkages and the fact that each linkage however apparently reasonable may become a precedent for obviously unreasonable demands.

Further,

each of the political, humanitarian and military elements must exercise caution and sensitivity in order to avoid interference with the other's pursuits. In practice, this requires restraint and strict limitation of negotiations and mediation to each party's respective sphere of competence. The alternative is the nightmare of linkage, which inevitably leads to operational paralysis.[4]

In UNHCR's parallel *Handbook for the Military*, it is stated that:

allowing humanitarian objectives to become linked to military or political events can cause paralysis in Missions, where extraneous issues are allowed to cloud the primary principle of *humanity*.[5]

Some of these issues, and others, were analysed from the ICRC's stand-point at a 1994 symposium on *Humanitarian Action and Peacekeeping Operations* by its Director of Operations, Jean de Courten. He expressed ICRC's acute concern over:

> the subordination of humanitarian action to political objectives during recent UN operations . . . Such situations have given rise to confusion which in turn has had an adverse effect on the acceptability and thus the security of independent and neutral humanitarian action. Mandates, tasks, means and objectives have all been affected by this confusion.

De Courten emphasised that states have a duty to respect international humanitarian law, and that this also compels them to agree to humanitarian action – which depends upon consent. But he noted that in Bosnia political bargaining had developed, and the politicisation of humanitarian action – calling into question even so pivotal a principle as that of non-reciprocity. He said that similar issues had recently arisen in Angola and Liberia. During the ensuing discussion on the pressures which require peacekeepers to adapt principles to immediate humanitarian concerns, he added that the ICRC had faced similar dilemmas to those confronting the UN in Bosnia-Herzegovina; for instance, unable to prevent 'ethnic cleansing', the ICRC helped to move some of its victims to save their lives.[6]

THE 'POLITICISATION OF HUMANITARIAN ACTION': A CLASSIC DILEMMA

The preceding paragraphs identify a number of issues: one is that everybody should stay within their own terms of reference; another relates to the need, under compelling circumstances, to adjust humanitarian goals to what overwhelming circumstances demand; another is about using aid as a means of pressure or reward; a further issue refers to parties' conditioning their agreement to do what humanitarian law requires them to do upon reciprocal action by their foes. All in fact relate to the same underlying issue: what are international peace or humanitarian personnel to do in the absence of the parties' consent, or in an environment of qualified consent? UNHCR and ICRC have at various times indicated that force is not the answer; one cannot achieve humanitarian goals by fighting one's way through. If withdrawal, also, is not an alternative, how does one function on the dangerous shifting sands in the middle? (Neither flight, nor paralysed rumination, being acceptable options.)

Described below are some examples of humanitarian problems that have arisen in former Yugoslavia. Each has required a practical and defensible solution so as to advance humanitarian objectives in hostile environments. Each was answered at the time. But were they the correct answers? How does one define 'correct'? Does an imperfect means destroy a good objective? What would the potential or actual victims think? What is one to make of our pondering Hamlet if, meanwhile, the victims are themselves annihilated?

The Bihac Blockade

A simple example of the problem, albeit involving an aid agency only, without the involvement of any UN political entity, arose in March 1995 over the blockade by the 'Krajina Serbs' of UNHCR aid convoys to mainly Moslem areas of the Bihac pocket in Bosnia. The UN Secretary-General's spokesman announced that, on 8 March 1995, UNHCR had written to Mr Milan Martic, the Krajina leader, informing him that because his followers were obstructing the delivery of aid to their adversaries in the Bihac pocket, humanitarian assistance in the Krajina (which the Serbs were, obviously, not obstructing) would be suspended. Under questioning the spokesman said that this 'was not at all a political, but a technical, decision'. He emphasised that it was not a cancellation, but a 'temporary suspension' of deliveries.[7] It is indisputable that vulnerable groups in both population groups were in need and it would appear that the 'temporary suspension' of aid delivery by UNHCR was a means to seek a humanitarian objective, namely, the restoration of a transit right for aid convoys to Bihac, and, paradoxically, in order not to continue providing aid to one side only.

Such a decision is, perhaps, more readily understandable by those living with the problem and having to resolve it, than by those at a distance. The justification might be that it was a last resort taken to cut through an issue which imminently threatened human life. On the other hand, *prima facie*, UNHCR decided that it must impose humanitarian pressure to achieve a humanitarian objective, and this raises a basic issue. Without having personal knowledge of the situation, it may be inferred that the UNHCR theatre representative decided that the desperation of the humanitarian situation in Bihac was so much worse than that in the Krajina that a value judgement had to be made between two conflicting moral imperatives. The representative would then have obtained the support of his or her head office in Geneva and taken the relevant decision, no doubt after coordination with UNPROFOR in Zagreb.

It has been nowhere suggested that extraneous political factors entered into the equation – that, for instance, the Bihac Moslems tend to have more sympathetic press coverage in the principal donor countries and more diplomatic support in UNHCR's governing body than the Serbs of Krajina; or that, in the crisis situation over the Croatian president's proclaimed intention to 'discontinue the mandate of UNPROFOR', certain pressures will have existed in respect of the Bosnian Moslems with whom the Croatian government then had an alliance. While, as stated, no public reference to such interpretations is known to the writer, it is certain, given local conditions, that these (and others) will be widely discussed in the region. Whether the act of 'temporary suspension' will affect the reputation for impartiality of UNHCR in the area, and therefore its humanitarian competence, is likewise a matter for judgement; this too will have been considered by those taking the decision.

'Ethnic Cleansing' in Croatia

One midnight in May 1992 in the Serb-controlled Sector East in Croatia, a patrol of UNPROFOR's Russian battalion intercepted an instance of 'ethnic cleansing' – a remaining minority of Croats were being forced from their village, Tovarnik, by local Serbs. The Croats – old people, mothers and children, who had lived in Tovarnik all their lives – were given sanctuary by the Russian soldiers. UNPROFOR personnel came to meet with them there, listened to their story and their concerns, discussed their options with them, and offered them full 24-hour protection. But they were too afraid to return to Tovarnik (that night's events had been the culmination of pressures and, they said, the local authorities themselves were involved) and asked, instead, that they be taken to Osijek, in Croat-controlled Croatia. UNPROFOR gave them 48 hours to think over their decision, but their minds were made up. Accordingly, UNPROFOR provided transport and security when they left the Russian sanctuary and crossed to Croat-controlled territory. UNCIVPOL conducted a full criminal investigation and established a 'prosecution dossier' of witness statements which it provided to the Serb authorities in Erdut and Belgrade[8] and, ultimately, to the newly-established international tribunal in The Hague.

Was UNPROFOR participating, as an accessory, in the barbarism of ethnic cleansing (as the Croat media immediately trumpeted) or was it exercising the only form of protection that, in the circumstances, was going to be effective? This was the first of many similar dilemmas faced by UNPROFOR, UNHCR, and the ICRC in former Yugoslavia.

Once, UNPROFOR refused to accept the collective decision of the whole population of a village, Podlapac, to leave Sector South and go to Croat-controlled Croatia. It declined to do so despite intimidation and murders which implicated members of the local Serb authorities. It was the last mainly Croat village in the Serb-controlled sector – all others had been abandoned in flight long before. However, UNPROFOR perceived there to be special factors, and the peacekeeping body was able to deploy a significant presence in the area. Two years later the situation is holding, but all involved in the decision knew that they would share a heavy responsibility if other atrocities were to take place.

In both Tovarnik and Podlapac difficult decisions – practical, humanitarian, political, moral – had to be taken on the facts. In peacekeeping, such decisions cannot be avoided. In former Yugoslavia, only rarely did senior officials have the luxury of choosing between viable 'legitimate' alternatives. All too often, the choice was between what one or more of the parties, for political reasons, would certainly portray as indefensible behaviour by the UN, and what negotiators knew was impossible. Soon, whatever was least immediately bad (from the humanitarian standpoint) began to be the normal favoured course of action. Better no bloodshed today; tomorrow might never come.

Reciprocal Releases of Serb and Moslem Hostages

From about May 1992 onwards, UNPROFOR frequently negotiated the release of civilian prisoners, non-combatants held as hostages by Bosnian government or Bosnian Serb forces; often – when it had representation in the area – in conjunction with the ICRC. Habitually, neither side was prepared to release prisoners unless a specified number was released by the other side. Each threatened to kill their prisoners – threats which, from experience, one knew to take seriously. Taking of hostages is illegal. Linked releases not only may, but probably did, encourage more prisoners/hostages to be taken. Having failed to secure their release on a unilateral basis, UNPROFOR nevertheless participated in the negotiated release. Had it not been involved, perhaps the practice would have diminished (though history lent little encouragement to that hope). Alternatively, more hostages might have been killed. Faced with these alternatives, UNPROFOR negotiated reciprocal release.

Reciprocal Repair of Sarajevo's Utilities

From Autumn 1992 onwards, UNPROFOR military personnel, often at great personal risk, repaired water and electrical lines in parts of Sarajevo. Each side had disrupted basic utilities in order to make the lives of its opponent's civilian population even more awful than before. This was in breach of international humanitarian law. As usual, UNPROFOR told the parties that they were behaving unlawfully and asked them to stop. When, also as usual, they paid no heed, UNPROFOR negotiated with each side, then conducted repairs (the parties, despite their prior consent, often opening fire upon the UN military when they began repair work). Gradually, some aspects of the inhuman conditions under which Sarajevans lived were thereby moderated until, in some fresh paroxysm, the parties redynamited power pylons or fired tank rounds into pumping stations. Was UNPROFOR, by going beyond a demand that unlawful and inhumane practices cease, and permitting reciprocity where there should have been moral and legal absolutes, encouraging illegality? Was this 'politicising humanitarian action'? From the outsider's standpoint, undoubtedly. In the view of the parties, probably not. Utilities, in civil war situations, are seen by them as rather political to start with.

The Sarajevo Airport Agreement

Sarajevo airport is now seen throughout the world as a symbol of a city's survival and of an international determination to provide aid to its people. Each day – except when the war makes flying plainly suicidal – a dozen or more huge planes dip suddenly below the rim of surrounding hills (which bristle with weapons), drop precipitously onto the runway, and quickly unload a hundred or more tons of aid from all over the world. 29 March 1995 marked 1000 days of the airlift. During that time, according to UNHCR, more than 150 000 tons of aid have been carried in more than 12 000 sorties. The airlift has provided around 95 per cent of the assistance received in Sarajevo. It has also enabled more than 1000 medical evacuations to be conducted.

Since 1992, many have died at the airport, many more in delivering or protecting the aid that arrives there. Fighting between government and Serb forces which, from their ruins, face one anther across the runway, did not cease with the airport's handover by the Serbs to UNPROFOR in June 1992. One cannot but be aware, when emerging from behind the protective sandbags and earthworks, that one might have slipped into the rifle-sights of a sniper belonging to one or the other side – or, now crazy, perhaps no longer to any. The humanitarian airlift is the most extensive the world has ever seen. It is run with great efficiency. A plane may be unloaded and back on the runway five minutes after touching down. Though some would have wished the international community to have adopted a more forcibly interventionist policy, this joint operation between UNPROFOR and UNHCR has enabled the city's people to survive a three-year siege.

By June 1992, the airport had been captured by the Serbs. Their siege and shelling of the city had begun two months earlier and they had seized it after prolonged and bloody battles with Bosnian Government forces. It was useful to them not so much as an airport – for each side can easily destroy any aircraft planning to use it – but because of the strategic importance of the site. Without it, a major Serb base, Lukavica, could easily be separated from their main population centre, Ilica. The UN had to have the airport if the Security Council's demand that the people of Sarajevo be provided with humanitarian aid were to be realised, and if a link to the outside world were to be maintained. The Bosnian Government side wanted it because they could thereby acquire a major strategic advantage. But they also supported the idea of the UN having it. While, for geographical reasons, the Serb side was not so dependent on humanitarian aid being brought in, they needed to be seen to have their due share; it would have been politically unthinkable for them to have appeared to have given the airport to the UN for the support of their adversaries.

The Serb decision to hand over the airport to UNPROFOR was a most unexpected outcome to several days' intensive and difficult negotiations. The Serb negotiators were Dr Radovan Karadzic, Mrs Biljana Plavsic and General Ratko Mladic. Mladic was strongly opposed to the UN demand. All three were clearly nervous of having to explain to their own people any decision to give to the UN what many Serbs had died to conquer. The UN team explained that it had a Security Council mandate whose terms were not negotiable, though the idea of barter was explored for some time by the Serbs. The UN insisted that there could be no trade-off. This led to an apparent breakdown in the discussions. But, in the end, a regime was established for the delivery of humanitarian aid which would enable the Serbs to check everything being imported at the airport; and to have an at least mathematically appropriate share of incoming supplies, even though it was clear that, in terms of need, such share would probably be disproportionate. Various other provisions were included in related agreements to enable the Serb side to justify its actions to its own constituency, and the Bosnian Government endorsed the deal.

It might be appealing and 'politically correct' to pretend that the UN imposed the airport agreement on the parties; but this would be false. Even two months into the war, and with the UN's standing still high with both sides, marginal undertakings (from the UN standpoint) had to be given to satisfy Serb concerns, especially from the standpoints of security and public relations – because it was imperative that the UN had the airport. It was of such importance that negotiators might have had to show even more flexibility than their initial authority afforded. (They did not foresee early

Serb agreement, or the significance the airport would have over such a long period.) As one can now see, it was perhaps one of the most important humanitarian negotiations in the region, and was relatively 'tidy' in terms of avoiding 'linkage'.

East Mostar, 1993

Considerably less 'tidy' was the series of interlinked negotiations in August–September 1993 in and around the Croat–Moslem city of Mostar; West Mostar was mainly Croat and East Mostar mainly Moslem. The city was divided, nearly down the middle, by the River Neretva whose once graceful and historic bridges had by then been reduced to savage parodies, a major killing-ground. Mostar had been bombarded for months in 1992 by the Serbs. What was left on the Moslem side was then pulverised by Bosnian Croat (and allegedly Croatian) artillery. The condition of East Mostar, overall, was a good deal worse than that of Sarajevo. Croats controlled all access, except for a track across the mountains, impassable by vehicles. To all intents and purposes, East Mostar was cut off from the world, though the Bosnian army had a rudimentary radio capability. There was no international presence; it had either been expelled or had withdrawn because of conditions there. Negotiations by the UN to end this state of affairs continually broke down because one or the other side would not agree part of a package deal whose first provisions dealt with humanitarian access and a permanent international presence on both sides of the Neretva; and also because the city had become so dangerous for UNPROFOR, (especially its Spanish battalion) which had lost several personnel there.

The long deadlock showed some sign of yielding when Croatian Foreign Minister Mate Granic became involved, together with senior UNPROFOR officials, and a complex and unfolding agreement was achieved in outline, in consultation with all concerned (many participating elements had to be co-opted to make sure the agreement stuck). The Croats largely controlled the situation, but had become much concerned over the international image of what they were doing in Herzegovina. In its first stage, therefore, there would be an UNPROFOR military–UNHCR humanitarian convoy to Croat Mostar, media-covered talks with the Bosnian Croat leadership there, and a visit to the heavily-damaged hospital. The international media would be encouraged to accompany this visit and, the Croats said, they would also facilitate their coverage. They did not, initially, agree to a visit to East Mostar. As a result of this first step, the media carried images, worldwide, of the makeshift hospital arrangements, the dedication of medical personnel there, the UN–Croat consultations, and the Bosnian Croat version of the story. The Croats, stressed by the rebounding publicity which they themselves had chosen to generate, were then politically compelled to permit a parallel visit, two days later, to Moslem East Mostar. Despite the daily images of death and destruction from Sarajevo, the condition of this part of Mostar, with its ancient elegance reduced to a fretwork shell, and the humanitarian horror which existed there after months of bombardment and siege, shocked international opinion. The Croatian Government in Zagreb leapt into further action, and more pressure was imposed on the Bosnian Croats. Further negotiations at Medjugorje, in the presence of Croatia's Foreign Minister, brought about a Bosnian Croat agreement, in principle, for a cease fire and an initial convoy of food and medical aid. Getting this convoy into East Mostar proved very difficult and, in the end, was brought about by a series of complex and unattractive collateral agreements. They included one whose main features were that a small proportion of the aid was to go to the west side of Mostar (though it was hard to see any objective humanitarian need for this – it was, instead, part of a face-saving device for the Bosnian Croats); a second was that there would be a subsequent visit by senior UN officials to a Bosnian Croat hospital near Vitez (Nova Bila); and a third, that specified numbers of bodies of former military personnel, buried or otherwise in the possession of the opposite side, would be carried by the convoy and exchanged as it crossed the lines. Other provisions in a deal which was intended to break the long humanitarian logjam over Mostar related to the re-establishment of the UNPROFOR presence on both sides of the Neretva – with a civil affairs office, UNCIVPOL, military observers and a company of the Spanish battalion – and a 'permanent' cease fire. The initial relief convoy into Mostar did not proceed without incident – with Croat demonstrators, blockades, surrounding firefights and other problems. It took 12 hours to cover 25 miles. It culminated in the convoy (which had reached East Mostar with its 200 tons of aid in the middle of the night and immediately been unloaded) being blockaded – in effect held hostage – this time by the Bosnian Moslems who wished to draw still more world attention to East Mostar conditions. They held it for two days. Other parts of the agreement were implemented over the next week or so, together with new agreements, which also had to be negotiated on a reciprocal basis, as each side's active support was necessary, for access by international medical personnel to the main hospitals in the region of the Moslem–Croat conflict, the regular provision of medical and food aid and – perhaps most difficult of all – the evacuation of gravely sick and wounded personnel including many civilians, especially young children and mothers. Many humanitarian objectives, blocked for months, were attained and some element of movement, from peacekeeping, humanitarian and political standpoints, was inserted into a savagely-contested region, at last beginning to open it up to external influence.

However, the agreement became controversial within sections of the aid community during the dangers incurred by the convoy while it was blockaded into Mostar. During these days, fighting, including bombardment and intensive sniping, broke out again, and some international elements, which had tagged onto the convoy somewhat unnecessarily, experienced the less euphoric side of peacekeeping and rued their decision. In the end, the whole convoy safely extricated itself. But soon the initiative came to be criticised because it was said not to be a 'clean' agreement. The amount of 'linkage' and, indeed, unequivocal political leverage, that had been used to break the immobilism, and insert some momentum into the deteriorating Herzegovinan situation, made it retrospectively unacceptable, even reprehensible, to some. And yet, for better or worse, it was probably one of the most effective examples of linked agreements during the Bosnian operation. Lives were saved and the belligerents had to begin a dialogue, at least on humanitarian matters. Even to the most hardened, conditions in East Mostar were traumatic, over and beyond the 'regular' awfulness of war. It was hard to explain, much less justify, the lack of effective attention that had been given to Mostar over the previous 18 months, while the media had focused on Sarajevo and the so-called 'safe areas'. While, for months following, the Mostar situation was far from happy, it has never again descended to the Inferno depths of late August 1993.

THE PARTIES' PERCEPTION OF HUMANITARIAN AID

With UNPROFOR, UNHCR has done excellent humanitarian work in Bosnia. WHO surveys and analyses confirm how effective its aid programme has been.[9] It is all the more remarkable because each side has principally been making war on the other's civilian population. Destruction of the people's morale has been the main objective. Mortar-bomb attacks on population centres; the destruction of utilities; blockades to induce near-starvation conditions; sniping, preferably to maim rather than kill, children often being the targets of choice; anti-personnel devices in population centres; the use of quasi-concentration camps and of hostages as 'human shields' during infantry advances; maintaining maximum pressure on hospitals (often reducing them to near-medieval working conditions) and siting weapons adjacent to them; limiting the evacuation possibilities of the gravely wounded – whether adults or children; the destruction of cultural institutions – dynamiting churches and bulldozing graveyards; these, and more, have been used by all or some of the parties as characteristic features and tactics of the war in Bosnia and Croatia. While much savagery has been wanton, a great deal has been calculated; often showing meticulous logistical and operational planning and, in some cases, almost certainly commanded at very high official levels.

Humanitarian assistance has been seen by the parties as providing not only materiel aid but also as helping to uphold the morale of beleaguered communities. Each humanitarian convoy passing through the lines of a besieging force diminishes its power and capacity for terror. Humanitarian supplies may be destined especially for the vulnerable groups – children, mothers, the sick and wounded, the elderly. However, secondary delivery from warehouses is essentially for the local community to arrange. Monitoring may be carried out by the international agency concerned but, at best, it cannot be wholly effective. In many cases (air-drops, for instance) control may be almost impossible; without doubt, much aid is not going to vulnerable groups. It has become a commodity, a means of wealth and power; and it has certainly been augmenting the rations of the fighters. All the humanitarian agencies know these things. By blunting the impact of belligerent action, and in the absence of negotiated settlements (which have been the business, at the macro-level, of the International Contact Group), humanitarian relief has probably prolonged the war (which is not to say that it should not be provided). When the parties yield to the international community's demands that relief be permitted to pass, they do so with a clear understanding of what they are doing. They perceive it as a concession with its price. That price may be exacted on the spot – 10 per cent, perhaps, of the convoy's content; or 50 per cent of its fuel supplies. Or, it might be permitted to pass on some other condition – that, say, all persons of its cultural background should be evacuated from an adjacent town (whether they wanted this or not); or that they would be given safe passage to evacuate wounded through opposing lines to a major medical facility; or some other *quid pro quo*. This is not to say that aid did not reach vulnerable groups at all. It generally did, in some degree, else the mortality and nourishment statistics would be much worse than they have been. But it reached more than sick babies and nursing mothers.

All who served in former Yugoslavia and had to negotiate with the parties doubtless explained to them their obligations under international humanitarian law, and may have emphasised its commonsense, practical, and humane foundations. The effect has been minimal. At best, belligerents might concede that what was said was just, but, they would add, 'the other side' could not be trusted to behave reciprocally or would behave deceitfully, and this could have the gravest consequences. All saw aid as having political and economic, as well as humanitarian, significance.[10] The result was that everybody negotiated everything, save their most sacred shibboleths (which rarely coincided with the terms of any Geneva Convention).

VOLUNTARY COMPLIANCE WITH HUMANITARIAN STANDARDS?

What were the alternatives? That the UN would fight its way through, or summon Jove's righteous thunderbolts to sear a humanitarian path? And then back again? And the next day? And the day after that, when the whole countryside would be ablaze, and the UN be overwhelmed in some humiliating and terminal encounter? The other alternative was, that having met blank refusal when the UN insisted, as of right, to pass through road-blocks and deliver sustenance to the enemy (as the other party saw it), the humanitarian effort could have been called off. Some agencies, certainly, considered this possibility. But they concluded that, once present, it was politically impossible to withdraw. Had they done so, the war would have continued. Perhaps, after one or two appalling, genocidal clashes, it might have been abbreviated, though this, in the circumstances of Balkan history, must also be dubious. After a Tito-enforced period of stability among peoples, many of whom have long been uneasy with one another, each has determined to hack out its Lebensraum. Their time for humanitarian solidarity, pluralism, reconstruction and reconciliation, will be later.

It would be gratifying if belligerent parties knew and respected the Geneva Conventions and the other aspects of international humanitarian law. But the ICRC has a monumental educational task in inducing governments to make effective the solemn instruments which they have signed and by which they are legally bound. Former Yugoslavia has not been unique in its recent savagery. It has brought home, once again, how wide is the gulf between what parties promise and what they do; especially in the field of international law, where enforcement is rare and sketchy. Perhaps vigorous and well-focused political pressure by one or more of the humanitarian NGOs could begin to have some positive effects, if the ICRC feels that it would be inappropriate for it, as 'guardian' of international humanitarian law, itself to undertake this politically-charged follow-up work.

There is no permanent court to oversee the application of international humanitarian law. The international community has been no more enthusiastic about creating one during the last 50 years than it has been ready to take enforcement action against the parties in former Yugoslavia. (UNHCR appears not to believe in enforcement action to secure the delivery of humanitarian aid.[11]) But if the parties remain adamant in their disregard of international standards, and force and withdrawal are ruled out, the alternative can only be negotiation.

The Balkan conflict has again brought home to Europe some harsh lessons and realities, 50 years after the Second World War and the Nuremberg judgements. Some aid organisations are newcomers to some of these circumstances, and to the peacekeeping environment, in which slender forces seek to prevent conflict, or to minimise its barbarity without, save in exceptional circumstances, much in the way of coercive power or sanctions. This also reflects the general character of international relations and its regrettably weak law. It almost always means negotiation and compromise in the pursuit of standards, because they are unsupported by the kind of community enforcement that takes place within nations.

This often means not endorsing, but living with, the fact that worthy ends might have to be achieved by indirect means, not all of which will in themselves be wholly pure and defensible when evaluated in isolation. The decision-maker will also be aware, however, that this might instead result in worthy ends being corrupted by compromising methods. In actuality, the real issue is how to achieve humanitarian goals and standards *despite* having to use methods that may at times be less than perfect. *This* is the habitual problem of those who often risk their lives to bring some humanitarian aid to the victims of war and oppression.

Yet some feel that there may be even more painful dilemmas than those that have been explored here. If aid delivery prolongs a particular conflict, as some have come to think, should it be continued, notwithstanding that saving some lives could be at the cost of others, and some even greater evil? Who, the alternatives being open to them, will be so resolute as to decide that the ultimate common good requires that some siege not be lifted, vulnerable groups *not* be relieved? Some organisations are already edging towards such conclusions.

It is rare to find a morally perfect solution to the kind of dilemma habitually met in the actuality of humanitarian action, when warring parties give only a grudging and qualified consent. What, however, is sure is that gaining compliance with even minimal humanitarian standards is more complex, in both practical and moral terms, than is sometimes publicly propounded.

Notes

1. The views expressed in this chapter are entirely personal.
2. For the UN's official account of peacekeeping operations until 1990, see *The Blue Helmets* (1990).
3. UNHCR, *Handbook for the Military* (1995); UNHCR, *Working with the Military* (1995); ICRC, *Symposium on Humanitarian Action and Peace-Keeping Operations* (1994). See also, Col. Kenneth Allard, *Somalia Operations – Lessons Learned* (Washington, DC: National Defense University Press, 1995).
4. *Working with the Military*, p. 50.
5. *Handbook for the Military*, p. 30.
6. *Symposium*, pp. 29ff.
7. Secretary-General's spokesman's noon briefings (and 10 March 1995).
8. Despite repeated UNPROFOR follow-ups, no local authority action was taken.
9. *International Herald Tribune* (4 November 1994) carries a summary of the report by Dr H. Vuori, WHO Special Representative for former Yugoslavia.
10. Similar dilemmas are arising in other theatres. Médecins sans Frontières decided, in February 1995, to withdraw from all Rwandan refugee camps in Zaïre and Tanzania because, they had concluded, international aid had become the key to Hutu leaders' efforts to restart the Rwandan war. See Alain Destexhe, 'A Border without Doctors', *New York Times* (9 February 1995).
11. *Working with the Military*, pp. 20–1 and p. 51; see also statement by UNHCR representative to the Fourth Committee of the General Assembly, 17 November 1994. The ICRC's position seems somewhat more nuanced: see *Symposium*, pp. 29–34, 99–104.

Afterword: Humanitarian Aid – A Personal View

Larry Hollingworth

'After Somalia . . .', 'After Bosnia . . .', 'After Rwanda . . .'. When is 'after'? It is certainly not yet. None of these crises are solved. The UN has left Somalia. The UN is deeply embroiled in Bosnia. The UN is learning to cope with the Hutu and the Tutsi. Somalia, Bosnia and Rwanda are better places for the efforts of the UN; this is an indisputable statement. Many people are alive today because of the assistance given by the UN.

A stronger UN might have saved many more lives in Somalia. A stronger UN could have saved many more lives in Bosnia. A stronger UN would have saved many more lives in Rwanda.

My experience in emergency humanitarian missions is mainly as a 'front-line' worker. The advantage, privilege and pleasure of this is that I see the last link in the humanitarian aid chain, 'the customer' – the recipient of the aid. The disadvantage is that I am distanced from those who influence the policy which dictates my actions. To see what they are doing, I have to peer up the wrong end of the telescope.

My aid experience has been confined to working for the UN and, more specifically, for UNHCR. This means that when I am in the field, the telescope I am looking through is the same one held in the hands of the masters of the UN in New York. There may be a little distortion as the focus is tweaked in the UNHCR head office in Geneva, and the image seen in the SRSG's office in the crisis capital might be over-sharp. But I am vividly aware that whilst I peer up my telescope, my seniors are holding not one, but many, and are viewing a kaleidoscope of images.

I am not working independently, to satisfy my own aims. I am not working for an NGO headquarters in some provincial town. I am not double-hatted, working for the UN but on loan from a donor nation. I am not working for a neutral international organisation, steeped in tradition and principle but overwhelmed by practical financial reality. I work with all of these. Sometimes side-by-side, sometimes in competition, and sometimes in ignorance of the others' presence.

On the ground, the great advantage of being UN is that the label opens doors. Some dignitaries believe that they have to see you, some are flattered to see you, and some see you because you are the international local representative and they are the national local representative. All treat you as an equal.

The disadvantage is that you take responsibility for the perceived failings of the UN. You might be the eyes and the ears of the UN, but to the local people you *are* the UN. The hungry, the vulnerable, the displaced, the refugees, the local officials, and the local leaders see that we are there; some of them accept our presence, some object to our presence, some expect our presence – all question our presence.

Why are we there – for their benefit, or for our benefit? On whose side are we – theirs, the other, our own, no one's ? Are we there out of conscience, duty, justice, compassion?

What do we bring – what they want, what we want them to have, what someone else has a surplus of? Does what we bring change their diet, their habits, their customs?

How do we bring it – like a bandit in the night, like knights in shining armour? Can we bring what we want, when we want, how we want? Do we bring what we promise? Do we promise what we bring?

The UN staff member on the ground must be ready with answers to all of these questions. Our replies label us, and the organisation we represent. Are we 'Great and Good', 'Loud and Brash' or, worse, 'Weak and Ineffective'?

UN aid is not shiny beads to grateful natives, nor is it life-saving food to starving war victims. It is seen by the recipients as part of the front-line response of the greatest and most powerful international body in the world. Peace, cigarettes, aid, and in that order, is often the local demand. We bring little aid, fewer cigarettes – and rarely peace.

How does the UN, a politically, financially and morally accountable agency, compare with less fettered organisations? The role-expanding ICRC can claim historical exemption from some encumbrances and impositions, and is able to distance itself from resolutions and mandates. NGOs can bargain, and can wheel and deal; the most successful bring aid to where they choose, to which side they choose, pull out, expand, speak out, stay quiet. Funding is their single bogeyman. Host-nation local charities increasingly demand a greater role in the policy and distribution of aid. Some are government-backed, others government-hindered. Their knowledge of local resources, sources, nuances and affiliations make them the proverbial 'good friend and bad enemy'.

Should the UN response be military 'blue helmets' or civilian 'white helmets', or both? Who should respond first? Should there be a progression to match the aggression: UN civilian Agencies as Phase One, UN observers as Phase Two, and UN armed troops as Phase Three? Where is the warehouse of human resources to man these phases? Must every crisis demand an assessment mission, a Council vote, a tour of capitals with the begging bowl, and with the subsequent life-threatening delay? Must the response be ever less than needs?

Once the UN response is mounted, who leads – the military or the civilians? Is the military force adequately trained, equipped and funded? Is it cohesive; can part of it pull out unilaterally? Is the UN civilian response cohesive; who leads, who does what, who goes where, who overlaps whom?

Is there to be one appeal for funds, and one budget? Who coordinates? Who pays? Who pays late? Who never pays? Is a regional response the best response? If regional troops are best for regional crises, are regional civilians also best? Is it the task of the UN to save the world? Is this its Charter; its obligation? Is it to solve a crisis with the necessary resources, or is it to nibble at each crisis? Can it pick and choose where and when it operates? Can a group of wise men assess the likelihood of success or failure, and commit or deny a response? When is enough enough? When is it time to go home? How can the UN withdraw – physically, or morally? Who dictates UN policy? Is it bureaucrats, diplomats, politicians, presidents, the men with the guns, or the media? Is the UN a debating society, or an expensive club? Are the members happy with the committee, the subscriptions, the activities? Is it a luxury we can do without? Is there an alternative?

Too many tasks, too little resources, too great expectations, too few successes.

The present cry is for 'preventive action'. Can we teach the old dog new tricks? If funding, manpower and resources cannot be found for a disaster brought before our eyes – with shocking and obscene images of dying mothers, dead babies and mass graves – will enthusiasm and money be found to send observers, consultants, developers and helpers to potential trouble spots? Will the media switch its enthusiasm to following water engineers digging bore holes and agrarians planting seeds, or will it still chase the smoking coals, the fanning flames, the bleeding bodies – and demand an international response? Will the funders of prevention programmes find emergency money?

What about the ongoing 'failures' or, let us be gracious, the 'non-successes': the existing long-drawn out confrontations which have dented the reputations of roulements of generals, muted and emasculated peacemakers, exhausted legions of aid workers, and drained the coffers? Is it time for covert action to induce heart attacks in the obstinate leaders? Is it time to pension off the negotiators? To stir up the masses?

Time for the front-line infantryman, the 'hands-on' doctor, and the convoy leader to peer up the telescope and to pick up the megaphone; 'Is there anyone at the other end, is anyone watching, is anyone listening? Please give us a clear policy, sufficient resources and a rapid response. Hello . . . hello . . . hell'.

Index